Best wishes

F. Shwe
12.6.97

Fortunate Circumstances

FORTUNATE CIRCUMSTANCES

TREVOR McDONALD

'When I look back on my professional life, it occurs to me that so much of what I've done, has been due to fortunate circumstances'

ARTHUR ASHE

WEIDENFELD AND NICOLSON
LONDON

First published in Great Britain in 1993 by
Weidenfeld & Nicolson
The Orion Publishing Group Ltd
Orion House,
5 Upper Saint Martin's Lane,
London, WC2H 9EA

A catalogue reference is available from the British
Library

ISBN 0 297 81265 3

Filmset by Selwood Systems, Midsomer Norton
Printed in Great Britain by Butler & Tanner Ltd, Frome,
Somerset

For my children Tim, Jo and Jamie,
and above all for my parents Geraldine and Lawson
who gave me so much of their time and all their love

Contents

Illustrations

Between pages 108 and 109.
[Photographs are taken from the author's own collection. In some instances the only images available have had to be taken from film and video, hence the lack of definition.]

Foreword

In trying to assess the many influences which contributed to my writing this book, I come back time and again to that of my late father. Whenever we talked about my work as a television journalist, he contrasted his life with mine in one respect: he had barely travelled outside the West Indies and was fascinated by my journeys to such a variety of places around the globe. His world was much more compact, more circumscribed. Fate had assigned to him a job for life in the Caribbean, looking after his four children. In the marvellously perspicacious and selfless way of West Indian parents of his generation, my father, more than ably supported by my mother, knew what was needed if his children were to succeed in the awesome business of life and living. He dedicated his life to helping me achieve my ambitions, although he must have been aware that it would eventually result in my leaving the society which had nurtured me. In other words, he knew only too plainly that, if his lofty aims for me were realised, I would in all probability leave the West Indies. He accepted that with grace.

Almost as a compensation he enjoyed talking about all the things I had done. When he told friends about my career, he did so with swelling, joyful pride. He boasted, vastly exaggerating the interesting things I had done. He liked to suggest that my career had so far been an outstanding success and set out to make me feel that I had more than repaid the heroic exertions he had made on my behalf. He was wide of the mark there. No one, me least of all, could have possibly repaid the care and thought my father lavished on our upbringing. A genius of a man, he was the most devoted father, counsellor and friend, fallible, of course, but to me entirely wonderful. He firmly believed that our lives had been placed in his trust and that he was expected to explain and justify how he had exercised his stewardship. When I recounted to him places I had seen and events in which I had been involved as a reporter – in Pakistan, the Philippines, Nicaragua, the Lebanon or wherever – he listened in awe. He was fascinated by travel. Rightly, in my view, he saw it as an enriching experience and would certainly have agreed with Tennyson that

> ... all experience is an arch wherethro'
> Gleans that untravell'd world, whose margin fades
> For ever and for ever when I move.

My father insisted that I record my experiences and kept saying I should write a book.

I was in Moscow on an assignment when he died.

Before I hurried off to Trinidad, I went to the Kremlin to explain to one of Mr Gorbachev's assistants why I would not be keeping my appointment with him the following day. He had heard about my father's passing through the ITN office and asked whether there was anything he could do, kindly offering to help get me a priority seat on the next plane and arrange a visa for my replacement. I was very touched. Quietly he persuaded me to talk about my father's life, saying we should not pretend that we could carry on as though nothing had happened. I recount this only because I have never ceased to reflect how proud my father would have been to have heard his name spoken in hushed and respectful tones in the corridors of Soviet power. He would have smiled that wry smile of his and waved his hands in a mildly dismissive gesture, before being overcome by the incredulity of it all. In the curious symmetry of life it was my turn to be proud for him. I will always be.

For most of this book I am indebted to ITN, who gave me the

opportunity to travel around the world, first as a general reporter, then successively as sports correspondent, diplomatic correspondent, diplomatic editor and as *News At Ten* anchorman. I have enjoyed (and hope to continue to do so) the thrill of it all – danger and discomfort, the challenge of my assignments, the frequent ironies and the unforgettable moments of fun.

In the middle of the civil war in Lebanon we managed to get in a few games of tennis on a court which only a few weeks later was cratered by a massive bomb. One year in Moscow I took a party of friends to see the ballet at the Bolshoi and played bowls at midnight before being kicked out of the country by the Soviets the next day. I was asked to leave because I had reported that Brezhnev's speech to that year's Party Congress was long, rambling and self-serving, and that it would only ensure that he was remembered as the President who had destroyed détente by invading Afghanistan and failed to do anything to halt his country's economic decline. I had ignored his 'arms control' proposals as a political gesture – more confusing and tortuous than a genuine search for peace.

Many years later in Uganda, I was being marched off to jail by two unfriendly policemen when a passerby, seemingly unaware of my predicament, stopped his car to ask whether he could have my autograph. I was happy to oblige in exchange for a promise that my admirer would kindly call my producer back at the hotel and alert the British High Commission in Kampala that I would not be back for cocktails.

We travel to learn and I have learnt a great deal from the places I've been and from the people who were kind enough to lend me their time. In Bueno Aires in Argentina in 1978 I spoke to mothers – shrouded in sorrow – whose children and husbands had been taken away, never to return, by a ruthless, authoritarian regime. They had been forbidden from making any protests about this, but every week, on an appointed day, they would gather in the city square. At the stroke of mid-day they would begin a silent march and vigil. The brutish police invariably tried to break up these harmless expressions of hopeless resignation, though, on the day I was there, our presence acted as a deterrent. I can never forget the words of one of those brave women; I asked her to explain why she was marching. She said simply that she had to do something, anything to draw attention to the plight of women in her country. Then she delivered this hauntingly powerful line: 'Every mother has a basic right to know what has happened to her child.' These words are forever etched on my consciousness. Time and again they return to mock the equanimity with which we have come to regard the most grotesque injustices.

In a remote corner of Mozambique I saw people surviving on a daily diet of grass and roots gouged out of river beds burnt dry by the drought. There were painful, searing scenes of mothers unable to feed their children. The children tried to suckle, but found no nourishment, no sustenance. Yet in their darkest moments these same people managed to retain an enviable dignity and received us with kindness. The healthier ones among their fellows were keen to help us in our work and showed no resentment at our incursion. They are the real stars in any journalistic career – I wish I could list all their names.

I am deeply indebted to all the ITN camera crews who have undertaken assignments with me, who have laughed and suffered with me, and who have taught me so much. Their work is so consistently outstanding that it is easy at times to take it for granted. I have been reminded of that brilliance time and again, in scores of countries and in difficult circumstances. Once, on a visit to Beirut, I expressed frustration at the fact that, although fire fights raged across the city every night and were widely and comprehensively reported in the written press, we had no evidence of these events on camera. My plan was that I should go with a cameraman to a rooftop that night to try to record the flares and tracer which characterised these deadly nocturnal exchanges. The man looking after ITN's interests in Beirut heard me out in silence.

Then, saying not a word directly to me, he picked up the telephone and summoned a cameraman to his office. I was shocked by his appearance – the man was clearly ill: he had lost weight, was in obvious discomfort and his neck was swathed in bandages. Before I could enquire what had happened to him, it was explained to me that his condition was due to the fact that he had tried filming from a rooftop only a few nights before, had been spotted by a sniper and had almost had his head blown off. Fortunately he had moved his head just in time, but the bullet had smashed into his neck. I was deeply ashamed of my original suggestion.

I learnt a great deal and was given marvellous assistance in my travels by ITN producers and researchers. It is invidious to attempt to name them all, but to make no attempt to do so would be unforgivable. Numerous trips to America, reporting the Falklands from the United Nations in New York, East–West summits and American presidential conventions and campaigns were made with Alexandra Henderson. I could have done little without her expert eye, perception and advice. I have profited immeasurably ever since from Alexandra's numerous channels and contacts around the world. Graham Walker and Cliff Bestall taught me a great deal about South Africa. I am indebted to Angela Frier for so much work in so many countries in which we have toiled together. Her work in Baghdad, before, during and after the Gulf War, was a stunning success. Similarly, I owe great debts to my friends John Morrison, John Mahoney, Tony Millett, Richard Clemmow, Jamie Donald, Garron Baines, Sue Inglish, Helen Armitage, Chris Hulme, Jim Akhurst, Simon Bucks and to the organisational skill and drive of Mike Nolan. He helped me discover Australia and, more recently, was the master of logistics for a large ITN team on a swing through Southern Africa.

I reported and anchored parts of *News At Ten* in three different countries on three successive nights. After twenty years in television, it was unlike anything I had ever done. Our project energised engineers in Mozambique, Zimbabwe and South Africa, and bewildered aid agencies and charity workers. We were reporting the worst drought in the region for almost a century, which had crippled communities and threatened Southern Africa's abundant wildlife. One night, deep in southern Zimbabwe, the proprietor of the motel at which we stayed persuaded us to follow him into the grounds. Only a few yards from the motel reception, we saw compelling evidence of what the drought had done. The proprietor had placed bales of hay and troughs of water under a large tree. Around midnight half a dozen hippos had gathered in the motel grounds to feed, a most unusual event, but the drought had forced them out of the bush. They were not alone. Warthogs, wildebeeste and zebras were there too. From a distance of no more than a few yards we sat, drinks in hand, watching them; they were too tired and hungry to be worried about us. It was a strangely moving sight. I felt the drought had done the unimaginable: it had begun to affect the natural order. Animals which once proudly roamed the wild, carving out areas of bushland and forest as their own, had been forced to abandon their habitat and to rely for their survival on isolated acts of human charity. I felt there was a sense of the apocalyptic in what we saw that night.

Nigel Ryan, who employed me, David Nicholas, Don Horobin, Derek Mercer, Paul McKee, Stewart Purvis, David Mannion and Richard Tait were the editors who assigned me to report in various countries around the world. I am grateful for their faith, their counsel and their friendship.

There is no great mystery to television journalism and it confers no immense power on its participants. Although it plays an important part in the way we look at the world, its importance can be overestimated. We may change attitudes, but we err if we set out deliberately so to do. However attractive a prospect it might seem, our job is not to soothe the anxieties or to dim the horrors of the world. We report what happens in the world as it is – we can do nothing else. We cannot be social engineers, we cannot always succeed in making people feel good about themselves or about the world and I am not even sure that can be defined as part of our job. The job of a television journalist or any other journalist is to report fairly, accurately and in a balanced way what he sees and what he learns. That is not always easy, and ITN showed faith in my work, even when they were not sure I was getting it right. Reporting the diplomatic attempts at the United Nations to avert the Falklands War, we began most days with statements by Secretary General Javier Perez de Cuellar. Questions about how the talks were going, shouted through the scrum of international reporters, always elicited the same response. Morning after morning he would say, 'I am optimistic, I am hopeful that we will succeed. The talks are going well. There are difficulties, but I'm sure that with good will on all sides they can be overcome. I must be confident and optimistic.' And that optimistic view of events would be flashed around the world. The Secretary General was not being disingenuous; to a large degree optimism must be his stock in trade. What concerned me was that, from talking to British and American diplomats, I got a slightly different view of the unfolding drama. I learned that the talks were, in fact, getting nowhere, and were destined to go nowhere unless Argentina backed down and announced unilaterally that it was pulling out of the Falkland Islands without conditions. Even if they had done so, there was still, by then, the question of the British Task Force. The Task Force had set sail from Portsmouth with due ceremony and great emotion and was by then on the high seas, heading for the South Atlantic. One evening, in a hamburger bar in Washington, a senior British diplomat told me that avoiding a conflict was virtually impossible since, in his words, 'the task force has sailed'. So, for all those reasons, my reports to London every night began with the pictures and sound of the Secretary General, but were followed by on-camera pieces from me saying that, despite the Secretary General's stated optimism, a Falklands War was almost a certainty unless Argentine forces turned tail and went back home. ITN's Editor in London, now Sir David Nicholas, was quick to spot the contradiction between what Perez de Cuellar was saying and my distinctly more gloomy assessment. He was worried about which of us was correct. Perez de Cuellar was, after all, convening the talks – surely he would have a better sense of what was going on. I was on the outside. On what basis could I so strongly cast doubt on the Secretary General's sentiments? And yet, to his credit, Sir David never challenged me. When, much later, the negotiations foundered on the intransigence of the military regime in Buenos Aires and my gloom proved sadly well founded, the Editor confessed that he had been concerned about the way in which I had consistently gone against the Secretary General's mood of optimism. But he managed to keep his worry to himself. He showed faith when I needed it most. For the mercies of such editorial wisdom, restraint and belief, I shall always be grateful. Fiona Dodd, Daksha Patel and Glen Marshall helped me recall, through records of stories and pictures, the great body of my journeys for ITN. And I shall always treasure the warm-hearted support of the Editor of this book, Ion Trewin.

In the actual preparation of this manuscript, Mike Thompson was a pillar of strength. He tried to help me come to grips with sophisticated computers and, when he failed, or rather when I did, he was always willing to clear up the mess.

Fortunate Circumstances

1

Under Fire

I who am poisoned with the blood of both,
Where shall I turn, divided to the vein?

DEREK WALCOTT, '*A Far Cry from Africa*'

THE first shots must have been aimed at a target at least a
hundred yards away. From the position in which I had found
myself, lying flat on my stomach, in the claustrophobia of a run-
down Belfast housing estate, I could not be sure. They always
sounded so much nearer than they actually were. I understood the
reason for that: it was partly because of fear and partly because I
found the environment deeply unpleasant. The hostility which
enveloped the place was keen enough to be felt, cutting like a knife
drawn across the throat. It was no less than I had come to expect.

Bitterness and anger were the very ingredients of life here, and
they exercised an uncompromising hold on the people and the
place. Nothing had been done in these Northern Ireland communities to conceal the horror of people's lives. Hate and privation
had bruised their souls. Their existence had been distorted by an
all pervading sense of gloom and violence. At great cost to themselves and to their province, these areas had sought and won a
reputation as the seedbeds of urban war. I was not at home here;
in fact, the surroundings were entirely alien to me and I found it
easy to believe the worst.

To the best of my knowledge, the British Army had only ever
fired rubber bullets when trying to break up riots on these housing
estates, but on that afternoon in Belfast what I knew did not

reassure me. People had been killed by rubber bullets, if they were unfortunate enough to be hit in the head; countless others had been seriously wounded. My terror was fed by that, and by a nagging fear of violence of any kind. It was reinforced by cowardice and by a long history of detesting conflict. I hated the sound of anything being fired from the barrel of a gun. I hated the feeling of being trapped. I hated being there. Riots have never held any interest for me – they are too unpredictable, which renders totally meaningless any suggestion of safety. And yet it was all so mundane, so ordinary, part of an endless repetition of events.

This was, after all, just another assignment in Northern Ireland. It was another regulation Friday afternoon disturbance in Belfast and, as I had done on countless occasions, I was attempting, as a television reporter, to make some sense of both an incident and a process which seemed inherently senseless to me.

To our right, vaguely, were the targets of the British Army's fusillade, the Republican riot-makers. Theirs was an ancient cause, shaped by powerful hatreds and sustained by a continuing sense of betrayal, across many decades and countless generations. Every single quarrel and transgression of yesteryear, great or small, had been pursued with pride and passion, kept alive, refreshed and shaped into a focus for contemporary bitterness and discontent.

That afternoon, as usual, the rioters were using any weapon they could find. For several hours they had ripped up paving-stones along whole streets, it seemed, to attack a police station at the far end of the street. Its occupants – the enemy in this case, in Republican jargon 'the brutal forces of repression' – were under siege. Huge slabs of stone crashed on to the roof of the building every few seconds.

At the heart of this moving tide of fury, I found myself drawn to an elderly man. To my astonishment, he was explaining to a group of young boys, in an almost schoolmasterly way, how the paving-stones could be broken down, with their sharp edges preserved, to cause maximum damage to the police station. He was doing it soberly and chillingly, without rancour. He could just as easily have been showing the boys the way home on a dark night. When our eyes met and it dawned on him that I fully understood what he had been doing, he paused briefly, shuffled about as a conspirator would, and I thought I detected a wisp of embarrassment in his weak smile. The young stone-throwers were not as composed. They showed a purposeful greed for conflict, their much younger, more eager eyes blazing with an anger I found difficult to understand except through the refractions of history.

We had, by this time, moved a long way up the street, almost to the point where we were in danger of being hit by missiles falling short of their target. The Army's response – the point in the confrontation we had all been expecting – nevertheless came without warning. The Royal Green Jackets appeared from our left in a wave of fearsome noise to disperse the rioters and we were caught in the middle. It was a classic error of judgement. Stay with one side, I had been told, never get caught in no-man's-land. My fury at forgetting such a basic rule was more than overtaken by terror. I tried to run, aimlessly, out of trouble. A colleague pulled me back and together we flattened ourselves against the wall of a house, hands over our heads, as the soldiers rattled past. They looked at us impassively, with no hostility, but with no obvious warmth either. To them we were irrelevant. They meant us no harm, but neither were they particularly concerned about our safety.

Sent to Northern Ireland not to do battle but to act as peace-keepers and to prevent rival factions from killing each other, British soldiers find themselves at the explosive epicentre of an unremitting war. It is a conflict of unconscionable brutality, which respects few boundaries and only the most obscure rules. And the Army has never taken kindly to people who get in their way, no matter who they are. Never very far from my mind was the suggestion, sometimes explicitly made, that journalists and cameras con-stituted an incitement to the rioters. Considering the combatants in Northern Ireland had been at each other's throats for many centuries before we dawned on the scene with our cameras and lights, I had always been slightly bemused by the contention, but this was neither the time nor the place for civilised debate. The Army claimed some anecdotal evidence in support of its case. One fragment of local folklore held that the stone-throwers always stopped in time to get home to see themselves in action on the early evening news. No one ever discovered how true that was, but in general the Army seemed happy to accept that interpretation of the effect of our presence in the ghettos of Belfast.

Another company of soldiers charged down the street towards the rioters. Until then the houses in the street had seemed inert, silent witnesses to civil disorder, backdrops for another violent scene in a long-running drama, but suddenly there was a sign of life. A door opened and someone furtively beckoned us. I did not need a second invitation – I literally fell in, exuding relief from every pore. Inside, strangely, the atmosphere was one of near normality. Two young children were falling about their toys. Tea was brought to a table in the living-room. In a distant room a telephone rang. From somewhere in the kitchen one voice rose above the others. It was one I recognised instantly: it was not Irish.

When its owner appeared, she offered me tea and cakes, and safety until the clamour outside subsided. Even before I could murmur my thanks, my stomach slowly returning to its ana-tomically designated place, she explained what I suspected, that she had been born in Trinidad. She said she knew I had been born there too and felt the riot still going on outside was much too un-West Indian for me. She did not use those words, but she didn't need to and she was absolutely right. She had married an Irishman and, in the course of two years in Northern Ireland, had become quite accustomed to the afternoon riots.

I found it difficult to rid myself of the feeling of how extremely strange it was that, in the depths of a Belfast housing estate, I should be reminded of the Caribbean. I felt as if, in some extra-ordinary way, my past had caught up with me. And not for the first time. As a journalist for a well-known, well-respected British television company, I have worked in countries and cities thousands of miles from where I was born. Many of them have been places which, in my youth, I had known only as romantic shapes on a fading atlas. Since then, I have been to scores of those locations, in stressful and in pleasant times. I have observed rebellions grow and wars begin, and seen countless examples of the wretched face of humanity. I have watched children die and reported the work of the saintly and the good. I have witnessed the genesis of great movements and have been caught in the swirl and noise of revolutions. In the course of it all, I have found myself in the company of peasants and kings, in tents and palaces, and in locales where the culture and manners are vastly different from the ones I knew as a young reporter in the West Indies. On so many of these journeys, however, as on that particular afternoon in Northern Ireland, something has happened, frequently an incident of little apparent significance, which has dragged me back in time to the West Indies of my youth. Indeed, so profound has been the effect of these incidents that, at times, it is almost as if I had gone round in immense circles and covered enormous distances only to arrive once again at the point where I began.

These incidents have occurred in circumstances varying from the extraordinary to the bizarre, but they have always engendered a strange nostalgia. They have encouraged reflection, when memories which lie partly submerged, like footprints brushed over by a gentle wind, resurface in sharp relief. They curb, for a while, that restless urge which is so essential to success, but which can also be so distracting to the demands of the daily grind. They help recall the pain of struggle, the desperate battle simply to survive, and they help to anchor the soul. Most important of all, they remind you of who you are. T. S. Eliot argued that the use of memory is for liberation; for me it has been all of that and more.

Shortly before the leftist Sandinistas were swept from power in Nicaragua in Central America, I went there to make a series of television reports on the deep political divisions within the country. They were brutally dramatised by the war between the Government of President Daniel Ortega and the American-backed Contra guerrillas. We had travelled from Managua, a capital broken by old neglect and by more contemporary poverty, to the hills and forests of the border country with Honduras. In civilised encounters with Sandinista generals in offices around the capital, I had some difficulty in persuading the Nicaraguan army to allow me and a camera team to approach what passed for the front line. The Sandinistas were suspicious of all journalists who were not overtly committed to their cause. If only on that account, they had no reason to warm to me. Their campaign had won them a stirring chorus of international support from a spectrum diverse enough to encompass artists, high court judges and political activists, but I had never become involved. I had never been a fan.

One senior military aide had listened coldly to my pleading. Then, taking careful note of my new French-designed shirt, gold watch and squeaky clean trainers, had talked straight past me to address to my interpreter the pointed question, 'Has *he* ever been in a war before?' The question was laced with sarcasm. I made a spirited defence of my record as a 'war correspondent' and listed a number of close calls in the field – in Northern Ireland, in the Middle East and in parts of Africa. It was of no use. I failed to convince my interlocutors that I would be anything but a nuisance or a liability.

Words and persuasion are the indispensable tools of a journalist's trade. When they fail, a fearful panic sets in, fed by a sickening sense of inadequacy. That is when all self-respecting hacks fall back on the time-honoured device of trying unashamedly to buy their way into the hearts and minds of those with influence. The method is simple. Commonly known as 'hospitality' or 'entertainment', it has given rise to the not entirely spurious belief that

6

journalism is the rock upon which the success of many of the finest bars and restaurants in the world has been built. And had I cause to fall back on this ancient ploy one evening, though in a singularly ordinary bar at the edge of the central range of hills about a hundred miles from Managua. My target was a commander of the Sandinista army. He had claimed a number of contacts with the Contra guerrillas, and I wanted him to agree to take me on his next mission into the bush.

He was a stocky man with big hands and stubby fingers. He had large piercing eyes, which were reddened by fatigue, I thought, and by lack of sleep, but they had lost none of their intensity. Although we sat in one corner of a rambling, dimly lit room, his presence overwhelmed the place. I remember so well that, as he talked in short, angry bursts, making his points by slicing his palms through the air, the rain beat down noisily on the bar's galvanised iron roof. It was getting on for late evening, but it was still warm and humid. I loosened my shirt collar. The Commander did nothing to put me at my ease. He wore a perpetual scowl. He did not smile; just when I thought he had and prepared to respond, his dark features would crease into a sour grimace, mocking my every feeble attempt at common civility. People threw us awkward glances; no one wanted to be caught looking. The Commander radiated fear.

We began by drinking beer. I was an attentive host. I thought I was doing quite well in my campaign to be taken to the front and did not protest when the Commander suggested that we change to whisky. He became more animated after the first three or four and asked me questions about my antecedents and my early life in Trinidad. He then launched into his version of the history of that part of the Americas, explaining, as he warmed to his theme, how all Third World countries with colonial backgrounds should band together to fight contemporary oppressors. It was clear that one 'contemporary oppressor' prominent in the Commander's mind was the United States.

Historically, Nicaragua had been done few real favours by the Americans: Washington courted and encouraged the most ruthless dictators because the country had been a vital pillar of US regional control since Roosevelt's time. The legacy of this was a form of cultural imperialism impossible to escape and unbearably painful to experience. It was obvious even to the Americans themselves. In 1956 the American economist Otto J. Scott, arguing that investors would find Managua congenial, observed: 'An American would hear many of the old familiar US songs on the radio in English. A trip to Managua ... will disclose the ubiquitous McDonald's, billboards extolling the new Visa Bank cards and Diners Club ... and American movies. He can fill his tank at a Texaco, Chevron or Esso station for $1 a gallon.'

Times had changed since then. Nicaragua had rid itself of its corrupt dictators and had staged a political revolution of sorts, of which the Americans did not approve. So now, working through an ideologically disparate band of Central Americans in Miami, the Reagan administration had sanctioned the activities of a battalion of bag men and political misfits to fund the Contra rebels to wage war against the ruling Sandinistas. Mr Reagan had given his assent to this covert operation, although he had been explicitly denied Congressional approval. The Reagan-funded war had done what wars are supposed to do: it had convulsed the country and had sent it spinning into a spiral of painful decline. But, although the Contras had been embraced by their friends in the Reagan White House as the modern equivalent of the founding fathers, they still lacked the ability or the will to win the war on the ground. Many preferred the good life in Miami to the discomfort in the jungle.

From my conversations with some of their leaders in Miami, Florida, their rhetoric was as confused as their disorganisation in Nicaragua. What they were good at was ransacking Nicaraguan country villages, laying siege to them and terrorising the inhabitants. That became their hallmark. In productive areas of the country, they destroyed crops and killed or frightened off the peasants. The idea was that the general discontent sown by such a policy would, in time, destabilise the Sandinista regime and eventually run it out of town.

Mr Reagan saw the Sandinistas as dangerous Communists. From his days in Hollywood, fighting make-believe battles in tinsel town, he had become famous for his primitive obsession with Communism. Communists had created what Mr Reagan defined first in his mind and later in his political pronouncements as the 'evil empire'. Reagan's America, that shining city on the hill, that Emersonian 'land of tomorrow', where it was forever morning, was to have no truck with such infidels. That, coupled with a Manichaean need to divide the world into villains and heroes, had led the President to conclude that Daniel Ortega and his ally, the Cuban dictator Fidel Castro, were between them hellbent on spreading Marxist revolution throughout Central America. Such conduct in America's backyard was anathema and could on no account be tolerated.

The President felt one way of curbing it was to bleed Nicaragua's economy dry by the imposition of American sanctions. These had worked with a vengeance – decay now touched everything. Managua was a shell of a capital, its heart ripped out. Were it not for its twentieth-century facade, Managua could easily have been passed off as the relic of a civilisation which had long since died. The core of what was once a city, destroyed in an earthquake two decades before, had been left unrestored and untended. American aid money had been squandered. Now empty buildings, blackened by neglect and disuse, and peopled by miserable specimens of the uncared for, evoked a sadness it was impossible to describe. The lower floors of what were once high-rise office blocks, where people and enterprises had prospered, had been overrun by giant weeds and rampant creeping plants. Managuans had become accustomed to telling visitors with mock pride that there was only one functioning elevator in the entire city. Sanctions, age-old corruption and the economic ineptitude of the Sandinistas had made it impossible to import the machinery or the parts to undertake repairs. Everything else was in short supply.

I found it incredible that, when I went there in 1987, it was possible to buy decent Nicaraguan cigars – but impossible to get matches anywhere. I was not impressed by a revolution which could not produce matches. The innocent act of lighting up a cigar in the lobby of the single functioning hotel attracted a small procession of people hurtling towards you in search of a light; after a while it became difficult to believe that people came to this hotel lobby for any other reason. As an occasional smoker of cigars and armed always with half a dozen boxes of matches somewhere in my bag or on my person, I quickly became one of the most sought-after tourists in the capital. Watching with progressive incredulity night after night the hunt for the trivial box of matches, I began to form the fanciful view that a modern day Prometheus, far from 'straining in vain with ruthless destiny', as he prepared again to steal fire in the less worthy cause of the Nicaraguan smoker, would be performing a service so clearly valuable that he might, in the name of ordinary human pity, escape the capricious wrath of the gods.

Much more serious than the scarcity of matches was the fact that the city could no longer afford to feed itself or pump water regularly to its population. Food was scarce and the water which did reach the taps at odd times was disconcertingly brown. Having a bath in water so discoloured was to feel that I'd been forced to share a private moment with the nastiest bugs in the world. The taste of the water, even when it was enhanced with a liberal helping of whisky, was indescribable. Drinking it, without Scotch, was possible only with a feeling of utter recklessness.

Nicaragua's currency mirrored the state of the economy. It had become so worthless that converting even a modest amount of sterling or American dollars meant taking an escort in the interests of safety. The city's beggars, very often children of no more than five or six, had become expert at singling out those visitors who had just changed money. It was not difficult: anyone approaching a hotel with a large bag or with tell-tale bulging pockets was quickly engulfed in a sea of tiny, desperate, seeking hands. When the children were not begging outside the only working hotel in Managua, they were scavenging for scraps of food in evil-smelling dumps on the outskirts of town. For all practical purposes, their city had died and with its demise had disappeared their simplest claims to a decent existence.

The Commander did not tell me how his country, battling with day-to-day survival, would conquer the American oppressor. I felt it would be infelicitous to ask. However, he swiftly went on to suggest that Nicaragua and my native Trinidad might join forces to fight racist South Africa. I was not entirely prepared for such a proposition, but was reluctant to betray surprise. Even so, I could sense our conversation drifting from the course I had intended and into the untaxing realms of improbability. Nevertheless, he refused to let the matter drop.

Refining his point with a flourish, he suggested that we people from the developing world should never lose our identity and that, no matter where in the world we found ourselves, we should always remember the concerns of our compatriots. Nor did he stop there. During my stay in Nicaragua, he suggested that I should talk to President Daniel Ortega, who I was due to see, and to the President's brother, Humberto Ortega, who ran the Defence Ministry, about the formation of a joint Sandinista/Trinidadian brigade. The Sandinistas, he said, would be happy to train such a brigade, which would then go to Southern Africa to join the armed struggle for liberation being waged by the African National Congress. I feigned interest. It was, of course, pure madness, certainly as far as I was concerned. Joining armies of liberation was not a part of my job, nor did I have any personal inclination to do so, but, lurking somewhere in the distant recesses of this Nicaraguan's mind, was a point of view interesting enough to cause me to reflect on why he had said what he did.

I had gone to the Commander with a request as a British television correspondent with British interests in mind; I had been sent to report the war from a British perspective. In the nicest possible way, he cut through all my metropolitan pretensions. He saw me as West Indian, fixed me firmly in the developing Third World and was urging me to identify more closely with those causes.

Only a few years later Colonel Gaddafi of Libya took a similar line once I managed to get near him.

The Colonel was the icon of international terrorism during the 1980s. I was sent to Tripoli to interview him not long after American missiles, dispatched to kill him, missed their target, wrecked one of his houses and killed the Colonel's adopted daughter Hanna. The raid had been planned as punishment for Libya's alleged involvement in the bombing of a discotheque in Berlin sometime before.

Gaddafi proved as elusive an interviewee as he did as a target for American missiles. The difficulty for any journalist visiting Libya, even one who has been assured of a meeting with the Colonel, is that Gaddafi appears to have no regard for appointments or for other people's time. Even those appointments made with his agreement, one suspects, are treated with capricious disdain. His ministers and his aides can apparently do nothing to change that. If they can make the Colonel more receptive, they chose not to do so in my case; certainly none of the people I met appeared to have the courage or the inclination. Not even for other heads of state would his underlings commit the Libyan leader to a meeting at a specific time.

On one celebrated occasion the head of the Palestine Liberation Organisation, Yasser Arafat, turned up at Tripoli airport at short notice for urgent talks at Gaddafi's request. But the talks were evidently not sufficiently urgent to merit the Colonel's presence. Arafat was told that Gaddafi had gone into the desert to communicate with God. Apparently, he did a lot of divine communing.

Arafat was a political ally, always grateful for facilities the PLO had been given on Libyan soil, and Arafat's championing of the Palestinian cause was dear to Libya's heart, but none of those factors was sufficient to guarantee how the Colonel might choose to spend his time.

I was not an ally and had never been to Libya before, so for two days and nights I followed Gaddafi around the country. I was – loosely – part of his entourage, but permitted no contact with the man himself. The frustration was intense, testing my patience and resolve to the utmost, firstly because there was little else to do and secondly because Libya as seen on an assignment like mine is stultifyingly dull. It lacks even the spice of common incident: there is no buzz, no great rush of traffic, no surge of people or of life. Conspicuously absent is any sign of the revolutionary fervour for which the country is so feared in the West. The sole exception is when patriots are mobilised to march noisily in support of government policies or to attack foreign embassies for some perceived slight on Libya's honour. On such occasions the city briefly comes to life to make a point to visiting cameras and to the world. But, for the most part, Tripoli dozes on with nothing of the visual cacophony that is a necessary part of the spirit of any capital. The place seems condemned to survive on inaction. In consequence, the visitor becomes infused with the feeling that something is being hidden, that the city has been kept on a very tight emotional rein and that something much more suspicious than the external calm must be lurking just below the surface.

Even so, my travels around the country were not entirely without interest. I was able to observe the Colonel at work and to form an impression of the public face of his politics. Gaddafi seized power in a bloodless coup in 1969. He has ruled with an iron fist and does nothing with subtlety. Whenever there has been a call for symbolism in his politics, it is heavy and inescapable. In the aftermath of the American bombing of Tripoli, for example, he was attempting to inspire his people to a passionate display of anti-Americanism and of support for his leadership. This meant that, whenever he left Tripoli on journeys to other parts of the country, he was always met by 'spontaneous' demonstrations of affection. One afternoon I joined his motorcade heading for a customs post on the Libyan/Tunisian border. It is a trip of some two hours, but, with several stops to greet the faithful at selected villages along the way it ended up three times as long. Wherever the leader's convoy paused along the route, hundreds of people crowded on to the streets. They beat drums, danced around the Colonel and shouted pro government slogans. All other village life seemed to come to a halt.

If Gaddafi enjoyed this adulation, he did not show it. At times he appeared quite unnerved by the clamour, which his advance team had in all probability orchestrated. With a dull, sometimes vacant look, his eyes scanned the throng. They were not charismatic eyes. And, if he has a talent for stirring his followers into frenzies of adoration, he kept it well in check on that afternoon's journey. He looked out from his heavily guarded Landrover with well-worn diffidence. His occasional attempts to wave his arms in time to the shouts of the people lacked conviction. He never once caught the rhythm of their chanting. He looked for all the world like a musician thrust unhappily into conducting a score he had never seen before and failing in the basic task of keeping the orchestra playing together. He appeared distant, distracted and aloof. Street hawkers in Tripoli seemed more at one with the passions of their countrymen.

Only after many hours, when we reached the border with Tunisia, did Gaddafi noticeably warm to his task. In the fast fading light of a desert afternoon slipping rapidly to dusk, he climbed on to a bulldozer, aimed it at the customs post and charged. For the next forty minutes, with more vigour than skill – there was an ear-splitting crunching of gears – he launched an assault on the tiny building. Every time a great slab of concrete fell to the ground to loud acclaim, the Colonel sent the machine into reverse and prepared to attack the customs post again. It had been well built, but it was not strong enough to withstand the zeal of a determined attack. On and on Gaddafi went until nothing was left but a spreading cloud of dust and a mass of twisted metal rods sticking out of a pile of rubble.

The final charge had been accompanied by great cheering. For the first time that afternoon a look of pleasure appeared on the face of the Libyan leader. He wore the quiet satisfaction of a man who had made his point. Seasoned diplomats would have found subtler ways of demonstrating a change of policy towards a neighbouring country, but this was quintessential Gaddafi. He wanted to impress on Tunisians the fact that Libya was putting relations with their country on a different footing and he chose to do it with a masterpiece of political theatre. No Libyan or Tunisian peasant looking on could have failed to grasp the point; the barriers between the countries had literally been torn down.

I had quite expected to be summoned to my interview with the Colonel right there and then, immediately after his memorable lesson in political symbolism. Indeed, in my more cynical moments as the demolition went on, I'd wondered whether the whole affair had been organised partly for the benefit of our cameras. I was wrong in trying to read what the Colonel would do. I was the only one who had seemed that interested. Everyone else in his entourage had been content simply to tag along.

In that tortuous way of authoritarian regimes, where facts are elusive and where it is nearly always impossible to discover how decisions are arrived at, I was told that Gaddafi had decided to spend the night in the desert. We were to accompany him. The matter was not open for discussion. Invitations had begun to acquire the sound of Presidential orders, and I was beginning to tire of being part of the baggage on the Colonel's cross-country odyssey. However, retaining the option of driving myself back to Tripoli that night in the convoy or on my own, I agreed to sit for a short time at least on the fringe of Gaddafi's desert retreat.

The Colonel makes much of his Bedouin culture. He was born in a nomad tent somewhere between Tripoli and Benghazi, and his forays into the desert are said to energise him and are meant to show that he has never lost touch with his roots. After an hour's drive, our motorcade swung into a sprawling military compound. In my naiveté, I had imagined a small forest of Bedouin tents dotted around in the desert, romantically illuminated by the light of the rising moon. All I could see in the semi-darkness were half a dozen huts. The roofs were galvanised iron and some of them seemed in desperate need of repair. Behind us, as we drove in, huge iron gates clanged shut. I did not see the Colonel again that night; he went off in one direction and we were ushered with friendly firmness in another. We had been taken into the compound only for food and drink. Just before midnight and after I had insisted on going back to Tripoli, word came that the Colonel had been exhausted by his evening's work with the bulldozer and had retired for the night. He would see me in the morning.

We returned from Tripoli bright and early next day only to find the Gaddafi convoy in the desert about to set off again. There would be no interview here, I thought. No one would say where it was heading; in fact, no one would say anything of consequence at all. When the convoy came to rest again, we were told that the Libyan leader was visiting one of his many houses in the country. For a man with a country to run in an increasingly troubled world, he appeared to me to be simply passing the time in a singularly unfulfilling way. He was doing nothing useful that I could make out. Even so, there was to be no interview. By mid-afternoon we were back in the Libyan capital.

My natural impatience, anger and frustration were beginning to merge into a surly melancholy, when the phone in my hotel room rang. The Colonel would see me at once. This time the auguries were good, although I made a point of pretending to take my time and not be hurried when it suited the Colonel and his lieutenants. We were taken at last to the Aziziyah Barracks, where

Gaddafi has his Tripoli home. In the grounds of the barracks is the famous tent, where the Colonel meets his interlocutors. The tent is gaudily decorated, mainly for television I'm told, but sparingly furnished. There was one small table and three chairs.

Shown the general direction from which the Colonel would appear, we set up watch with our cameras. After what seemed another long wait, we detected some movement in the bushes behind us. It was emphatically not the side from which we had been told to expect our host. Turning round, I caught sight of three guards armed with sub-machine-guns, inching forward on their stomachs, commando style, through the undergrowth. Their guns were pointed our way, but only a few yards from actual physical contact they fanned out in three directions and disappeared somewhere behind the tent. They had succeeded in appearing to ignore us, although, in fact, we were the only people in the vicinity. In the circumstances their vigilance seemed a trifle over done, but I took it to mean that the Colonel could not be far away.

When Gaddafi did finally appear it was from behind a rose bush. As he edged unhurriedly into view, he paused for a moment to hold a flower in his hand. He examined it theatrically, caressed it, sniffed its fragrance and left it to vibrate on the stem before greeting us.

In a quarter of a century of journalism, I had witnessed no entrance quite like it. Over the years I have replayed that scene in my mind a hundred times and yet I have never quite been able to decide whether it can be explained by the Colonel's deep affinity to the natural world or by an overwhelming desire for political showmanship.

The Colonel was courteous, and he responded to all questions thoughtfully. When he talked passionately about great issues like pan-Arabism, relations with the United States and the Palestinian cause, his eyes wandered off into the middle distance, so much so that for long periods I was not quite sure whether I had fully engaged his attention. He seemed capable of being totally absorbed in the force of his own thoughts, and clearly enjoyed the process of framing and articulating them.

He had agreed to do the interview in English, at my pleading. He was unconvincing in his denials of assistance to international terrorist organisations. He gave the game away by saying that he preferred the term 'liberation movements'. He had frequently asserted Libya's unbreakable bond with peoples seeking liberation. He was equivocal about what assistance he had or had not given the IRA, but his short, passionate lecture on Britain's occupation of Northern Ireland showed his hand: Gaddafi was a friend and provider for the IRA and their campaigns. Confronted with the inescapable logic of his policies, he had neither the courage to defend them, nor the decency to admit that he might have been wrong. After nearly two decades of contact with political leaders, I was not entirely surprised. He insisted, though, that Libya wanted friendship with the world, including Britain. From the conditions adumbrated, he seemed to be saying that such friendly relations could only be successfully established on Libya's terms. It was a warmed up version of the old Gaddafi rhetoric, with policy pointers submerged in the customary subterfuge and inaccuracies. With charm and a pretence of openness, the Libyan leader had told me little that was new. I was left to ponder whether the major point of the whole enterprise was that I had finally got to the Libyan leader.

The formal interview over, Colonel Gaddafi looked at me intently. 'Where are you from?' he asked. In saying that I was from Trinidad in the West Indies, I enquired whether he had heard of it. One of the first lessons I had absorbed in talking to people on my travels in the Middle East, in Southern Africa or in South-East Asia was that the small islands of the Caribbean are not always in the forefront of world consciousness. Gaddafi had indeed heard of Trinidad, but his questioning moved on impatiently.

'But how did you end up in England?' he wanted to know.

I thought I would give the Colonel a brief history lesson of my own, so I began by explaining Britain's colonial relationship with the islands of the West Indies, about the way in which British-transported culture had become so much a part of everyday West Indian life that it was no surprise so many West Indians aspired to, and ended up, in London, once the hub of metropolitan colonial power. I had got no further than putting some dates to the era of European expansionism when he interrupted me.

'Oh, I know all about colonialism,' he said with a knowing smile. 'We in Libya know all about that. Are the islands free of Britain now?'

I responded by saying that the majority of them were now fully independent, although links with the former 'mother country' were still close.

My lesson had apparently caught the Colonel's interest because, just when I thought my audience was coming to an end, he re-ignited the discussion. 'How big are the islands? Why did they choose independence on their own and not some kind of larger grouping?'

I detected the pan-Arab glint in the Libyan leader's question, so I told about the attempt in the region in 1958 to form a West Indies Federation, describing how it broke up in failure and acrimony.

Gaddafi threw his head back and laughed. 'The colonialists divide their colonies too much for them ever to succeed in a federation.'

He paused. I had my own views about his thesis, but I felt we had taken the discussion as far as we could. I thanked the Colonel for his time and prepared to leave.

'Listen,' he said, 'you must go back to your country and work again for a federation. Work for your people. If not, you must come and work for me here in Libya.' I laughed and thanked him.

I did not treat his offer of working in Libya seriously and his suggestion about my returning to the West Indies to work for a new federation was certainly unrealistic, but it touched a chord. It brought back to mind the fact that I had cut my fledgling journalistic teeth on the story of the demise of the old Federation in 1960. It had been one of the most traumatic periods in the history of the region, and I had had a small part in reporting it.

For three million people trapped on tiny islands blessed with sun and fabulous beaches, but in the backwater of world politics, the Federation had offered hope of greater international stature. On its own, no single island had much clout; collectively it was hoped that they might acquire some measure of influence in world affairs. With the collapse of the Federation that hope had died. For a while the islands busied themselves with preparations for full independence from Britain, each on its own, every one a tiny country, unconnected to its neighbours except by unbreakable links of history and geography. There were week-long celebrations and universal expressions of joy as, one by one, each island hauled down the British flag and hoisted its own. And there were grandiloquent statements about the political significance of independence from Britain. Even so, the collapse of the Federation had left a legacy of bitterness and suspicion; it was a lost opportunity. The West Indies changed for ever and, with them, all our lives had changed too.

It was all coming back to me as the Colonel agreed to autograph for me a copy of his 'little green book', his manifesto for revolutionary rule, and as I prepared to leave his gaudy tent that afternoon in Tripoli.

2

A Trinidad Apprentice

There is, it seems to us,
At best only a limited value
In the knowledge derived from experience.
The knowledge imposes a pattern and falsifies.

T. S. ELIOT, 'East Coker'

WEST Indian children of my generation were, in the enduring description of the late Trinidadian author and philosopher C. L. R. James, pushed through school very much as prize horses are trained up for the Derby or the Oaks: the preparation for life was passionate, fierce and unrelenting.

The two most respectable professions were law and medicine, and we were all supposed to be British-educated lawyers or doctors. Even qualified engineers, who were of such obvious value in the Trinidad of the 1940s and 50s, were slightly looked down upon, especially if they were unfortunate enough to have a degree from an American college. This reflected a kind of colonial snobbery and ill-informed elitism which showed itself in much of Trinidad life and which was quite remarkable in a developing country. I flirted with the law, had only a childish interest in medicine and, much to the dismay of my parents, set my heart upon a career in journalism. I saw real possibilities in the business of communication and was fascinated by radio journalism with its scope, I believed, for the imaginative use of language and colour. For that I was indebted to the BBC. Its World Service was like a friend and mentor throughout my adolescence and for much of

my adult life in Trinidad. On warm Caribbean evenings, after
night had fallen like a stone and long before the advent of television
in Trinidad, the mellifluous cadences of John Arlott, the precision
of Richard Dimbleby, and the professional skill and polish of BBC
correspondents around the world were my inspiration. What I
liked most about the BBC's reporting was its authority and apparent fearlessness. Very early in my career my attempts to emulate
the latter were to get me into trouble.

The radio station which gave me my first job was owned by the
British media group, Rediffusion. To the group, which managed
sister stations in the other islands of the Caribbean with something
approaching monopoly status in the region, Radio Trinidad was
marked down as a sound investment. Our aim was to make sure
we did not disappoint. Our modest radio station tried to provide
a public service and was led in that aim by some of the finest
broadcasters I have ever encountered: Michael Laing, Val Douglas,
Ed Watson, Ken Gordon and June Gonsalves. However, everything
they did had to be shaped by the need to attract advertising revenue
in order to make money for its London owners and, while that in
itself was never a hindrance to good journalism, journalism was
not the priority: nothing was allowed to supersede the *raison
d'être*.

In my time at Radio Trinidad our indefatigable and inventive
Sales Manager duly obliged. Sam Ghany was unquestionably the
most powerful man in the lives of programme-makers and journalists. A salesman *par excellence*, no idea or project, however
abstruse, escaped his laserlike determination to sell radio time. He
was a big man and, seated behind a desk too small to conceal his
ample girth, was the fitting butt of all the fun poked at his methods
and clichés. It had been said of him by his friends that, even on
his bad days, Sam could convince Eskimos that they desperately
needed to buy deep freezers, such was the nature of his consummate skill as a salesman. Employing irrepressible bluster and
a few well-aimed threats, he once persuaded me to cover an entire

afternoon's play in a boringly unimportant cricket match. As I was about to leave the radio station that lunchtime like a reluctant schoolboy creeping unwillingly to my assignment, I was delighted to see rain pouring down. Surely there would be no cricket, I surmised with an inner glow of gratitude. Close on my heels was Sam.

Sensing that the heavy tropical downpour was the source of my mischievous look of satisfaction, and reading my thoughts with unfailing accuracy, he fixed me with a penetrating stare and said, 'Look, Daddy, I know why you're smiling. You think the rain'll wash out this afternoon's cricket. But I've sold it and there must be play. I'm off home now and, when I get there, I'll be switching on my radio. And, when I do, rain or no rain, I want to hear commentary.'

Suitably chastened and very fortunate in the fact that the rain did let up to allow some play, I was able to provide Sam with his commentary. Our sponsors were happy and my reputation survived in Sam's esteem for a while longer. And I have always remembered his words: 'Rain or no rain, I want to hear commentary.' I came to think of them many years later as a metaphor for the unflinching professionalism required of a television journalist or presenter. He or she is required to perform competently, if brilliance is not possible, no matter what the circumstances. Minor distractions such as civil war, revolutions, satellite failure or bad weather are never sufficiently good reasons for failing to do so. The front man, the anchor, must never betray to his audience or to the sponsors the fact that there may be problems, and he should always be ready to accept the responsibility and the blame.

One of Sam's more insane ideas was that I should attempt to broadcast a race meeting, although we had been denied permission by the racing authorities to enter the grounds. Radio Trinidad had broadcast racing for many years and I had been one of the commentators who 'called the horses', as they say in Australia. One season the racing authorities suddenly increased sevenfold the amount we paid for the broadcast rights. Sam Ghany was incandescent with rage, so much so that he resolved to stage a one-man assault on the racing establishment and sent us into battle as his forward troops.

On racing days, we positioned our outside broadcast van carefully beyond the precincts of the race course, but close enough to see what was going on with the help of powerful binoculars. Looking back at it now, across the passage of so many years, it was one of the more ridiculous episodes of my journalistic life. We could see the races begin, but we could never see them end as they crossed the finish line in front of the grandstand. Sam had a solution to that small problem, one unique in the coverage of sport. When we lost sight of the horses, we would go to a long commercial break. A runner, a very fit one, had been engaged to sprint across to the grandstand from our van to get the result and sprint it back to us. By the time the commercial interval ended, we were ready to give our listeners the result. It was totally absurd. I was immensely relieved when we struck an agreement with the racing authorities and were once more allowed to broadcast from the grandstand. Because Radio Trinidad's prime aim was making money, we accepted advertisements for everything from potions which encouraged regular bowel movements to milk powder for babies, not forgetting funeral parlours. The major question about any project was: 'Can we get it sponsored?' Anything and everything that could be sold was ... the news, cricket and racing commentaries, record request programmes, visits to the zoo, the opening of Parliament or the opening of a new shopping arcade. And, most important of all, for a handsome profit, we sold death announcements. Much more than anything else I have ever done, these loom prominently in my memory.

Although the face Trinidad presents to the world is of an island dedicated to carnival and endless parties, religion is very important and death is a serious business, requiring due public ceremony and regard. Announcements on Radio Trinidad were an essential part of that. To the fading and suitably doleful strains of music by Handel, the Radio Trinidad announcer would begin with the words, 'We've been asked to announce the death of...' and proceed to name the dead person, how she or he died, and then intone the names of almost every known surviving relative, whether in Trinidad or abroad. Since so many Trinidadians went to foreign parts in search of higher education or to broaden their professional horizons, it was a matter of considerable family pride if, among the names of relatives of the deceased, some lived in Toronto, New York or London. The announcement ended by giving details of the plans for interment and specified which religious rites would be observed.

People were charged by the number of names in the announcement and the time it took to read. Our perennial difficulty was getting all the names right. An enormous measure of communal, village pride was attached to these announcements. It was not only important that the neighbours knew about your bereavement, but it was important that they heard the formal death announcement as well. That was why families paid for them in the first place. But we were frequently confronted by impossibly difficult names and equally frequently got them wrong, which caused the most heated disputes between us and our customers. People angry at our broadcasts of these announcements would occasionally storm into the radio station to make their complaints in person, which was always highly unpleasant, and, since complaints endangered a slice of our radio station's earning power, our superiors were most displeased. While repeatedly mispronouncing the names of the deceased never came close to being a sacking offence, it did little to improve the chances of a junior radio announcer rising in the world. I survived the regime of having to read thrice daily death announcements more by good fortune than ability.

THE story of the West Indies Federation and its demise ran right through my career as a radio journalist. It spoke volumes about the effects of the history of the region and about the way the islands saw themselves in the modern world.

With the benefit of distance and hindsight, the auguries were never very good. By promoting an idea of federation in the West Indies, Britain was reversing the basis of every policy decision it had applied to the islands. Hitherto these 'hewers of wood and drawers of water', as they seemed in the eyes of their European colonial masters, had been wrenched from their regional moorings and had been dedicatedly kept apart.

It was not surprising, therefore, that from the earliest stirrings of the idea of a federal Caribbean there was distrust, suspicion and petty individualism. In reality the islands, spanning an area of no more than 1,000 square miles, knew very little about each other. There would be no encouragement to change that. None of this was ideal preparation for attempts at unity. The battles among the islands' politicians for federal preferment were legion – I reported many of them. When Trinidad won the hotly contested race to be the federal capital, Jamaica and other islands sulked. As Trinidadians gloated, others planned their revenge. The federal experiment lasted barely three years and was almost consumed by acrimonious debate. One steamy afternoon in the Jamaican Parliament, the Prime Minister made the fatal error of offering the Opposition a referendum on the West Indies Federation. Jamaicans voted against it and the whole edifice swiftly collapsed.

The first and only Prime Minister of the Federation, Sir Grantley Adams, shot off to London to seek Britain's help in picking up the pieces. He failed. Britain said it was powerless to help.

I was the only reporter at the airport – it was way past midnight – when he returned to Trinidad. It was a sad assignment. Sir Grantley looked a broken man. Bad news had travelled fast. He had clearly already lost his entourage of private secretaries and minders. There were few people to meet him; the scruffy VIP room was deserted.

A lone information officer tried to prevent me talking to the Federal Prime Minister, suggesting he might be too tired after his unhappy flight from London.

Sir Grantley pushed the man aside and, putting his arms around me, said, 'Mc, take a seat. I'll tell you everything.' And for the next half hour he poured out his soul. He recited the litany of mistakes made during the early days of the Federation and was bitter about the role of some of his senior political colleagues in the region who had always seemed so anxious to talk the Federation down. Looking disconsolate and tired, he asked, 'What's to become of us now?'

He was already thinking about salvaging what remained of the federal ethic in the Caribbean, keeping intact institutions such as the University of the West Indies. He talked, too, about the folly of losing all that the Caribbean had achieved in embarking on the federal experiment and, just before we parted on that cheerless night, he said, 'How tragic it would be, for example, if the West Indies cricket team disintegrated and didn't ever play again as one team.'

The Federation was dead. Nothing could be done about that. And one by one the constituent elements of the attempt at Caribbean unity began to form a queue leading to Marlborough House in London to be given full political independence of Britain. To borrow the sentiments of Benjamin Franklin, they had decided against hanging together and in favour of hanging separately.

The disaster of the Federation became an unexpected professional bonus for me. To my delight, and to the consternation of my more senior colleagues, in 1962 I was sent to London to report on Trinidad and Tobago's Independence Conference. I arrived in one of the coldest summers on record; indeed it was still close to freezing the first morning I turned up at Marlborough House in the Mall.

All international conferences are theatrical, designed to play to a particular audience or constituency, and they all contain elements of high farce. On occasions it is their sole point of distinction. Trinidad and Tobago's was no exception: Government opponents, with no seats in Parliament and hence with no *a priori* right to attend the conference, decided to turn up at Marlborough House anyway in the hope of making some sort of impact. They failed. Their aim had been to delay or prevent the move to independence, but they had misread one simple fact: once the Trinidad Government had been invited to London, independence was a foregone conclusion. Those campaigning against it were not even allowed into the grounds of Queen Mary's former house. They looked a dejected bunch, standing day after day in the cold, waving and shouting ineffectually as official delegates swept by in their British Government official cars.

I was marginally more fortunate: allowed brief exchanges with the delegates as they went in or as they prepared to leave, I could spend the major part of the day in the warmth of the Conference Press Office. The only problem was I learnt nothing of consequence concerning what went on inside the meeting. That situation did not improve with the release of the daily communiqué, which merely said something to the effect that the Trinidad and Tobago Conference met in full session at Marlborough House today under the chairmanship of the Secretary of State for the Colonies and discussed, among other things, the framing of new constitutional arrangements for Trinidad and Tobago; after the morning session the Conference split into two working parties and would meet again in full session tomorrow at ten.

To say that I became anxious about the self-effacing brevity of the communiqués is to understate the case. Radio Trinidad, which never knowingly undersold any event, had persuaded a paint manufacturing company to sponsor my reports as fifteen-minute programmes. Even allowing for copious descriptions of the unseasonal cold, the colourful window boxes in Piccadilly and frequent references to the history of Marlborough House, I was still desperately short of genuine conference material. My visit to the

Epsom Derby that year did not help me beyond a single broadcast on Derby day. One interpretation of the chaos theory of mathematics is that the concept of straight lines finds little real application in the general chaos of real life. 'Life,' says the chaos theory mathematician in Michael Critchon's *Jurassic Park*, 'is actually a series of encounters in which one event may change those that follow in a wholly unpredictable way.' So it was that my encounter with Learie Constantine at the Trinidad and Tobago Independence Conference had an extraordinary effect on my career.

Learie was one of the noblest men my country has ever produced: a giant among his peers and the quintessential West Indian hero. His reputation was so great, his fame so international, that we much lesser mortals were able to find shade and succour under his wide acclaim. He was one of the greatest cricketers of his age – a swashbuckling batsman, a demon bowler, an explosive fielder. Don Bradman, no less, described Learie's career in the Lancashire League, which opened the way for countless other West Indian players, as unsurpassed. He had also been a fighter in the cause of good race relations, a raconteur, a superb broadcaster, a lawyer, a diplomat and the most consummate ambassador Trinidad has ever had. His gentle appearance and the genuine warmth of his lilting voice described a man of immense human kindness. And it was to him I turned in my hour of need.

Constantine was a Government delegate at the Conference. I arranged to see him every afternoon at his hotel, hours before my reports were due, in the hope of prising scraps of information out of him. I aimed to do this in the artless guise of watching India's cricketers struggle against England on the television. Learie knew what I was up to, but he had clearly decided to help a struggling compatriot, and so we developed a regular afternoon routine. I would ask a general question and he would respond. I would then try to be more specific, and he would become slightly more cautious. If he ever felt he had told me too much, he would suddenly take fright and insist that he could say nothing further unless my question was more precise. Because I knew so little of what had actually gone on at the Conference, some of my inquiries were vague, if not totally irrelevant. When I pleaded for an overview of what was being discussed in the gilded chambers of Marlborough House, Learie would counsel, 'Ask me a specific question, Trevor.'

The result of this pleasant, but tortuous process was that I did surprisingly well in a journalistic sense – or, to be more accurate, Learie Constantine and I did well. No other reporter discovered as many scraps of information as I, and my reports won rave reviews at home. The five-hour time difference between London and Trinidad, and the significant difference in deadlines between me and my newspaper colleagues, operated in my favour, so I managed a few scoops. The sponsors were ecstatic, while Radio Trinidad was delighted that it had made an impact on one of the more important episodes in the country's history – its independence from Britain. At a party at the Mayfair Hotel at the end of the Conference, the Prime Minister Designate of Trinidad and Tobago, Dr Eric Williams, greeted me with the words, 'Whatever have you been broadcasting in your conference reports? I hear the whole country has been tuned in to you every night.' I feigned surprise, but it was confirmation of the debt I owed Learie.

My visit to England was a success in another way, too. Covering the Marlborough House meeting, I encountered correspondents and producers from the Caribbean Service of the BBC based at Bush House, who were well informed and helpful. Their output impressed me just as much as if I had been listening to them back in the West Indies and I liked the atmosphere in which they worked. A combination of events made me decide to do something about it.

Eric Williams, even in the first flush of power as Prime Minister of independent Trinidad and Tobago, became increasingly remote as a leader, his chosen method of communication being his weekly press conferences. Holding court before a small, carefully vetted group of journalists, he always began with an opening statement which ran for about an hour. These monologues, informing the population on what its government had been up to in the last seven days and his *tour d'horizon* of world affairs, were delivered in flat, nasal, soporific tones. There was a sense of the oracular about any thoughts the Prime Minister chose to share. Questions were tolerated with varying degrees of irascibility. Williams was brilliant, immodest and appallingly arrogant; he felt no one his intellectual equal. Above all, he detested challenge ... on anything. And, since it was impossible to avoid it altogether in Parliament, he had acquired the habit of using reporters' questions to demonstrate the futility of doubting his wisdom on any subject. That got me into serious trouble. I should have been warned.

On my visit to London, Lord Buckhurst, the Chairman of Rediffusion, as owners of my radio station, had insisted on my making an appointment to see him. When we eventually met, he came to the point very quickly, telling me that, as far as they at Rediffusion were concerned, Eric Williams was 'a fairly decent sort of chap and has our support'. I read the code instantly: it was that I should do or say nothing to offend 'London's man'. My employers had obviously come to the view that, if they managed to keep in Williams's good books, he would in all likelihood leave them alone to make their money.

I must confess that Lord Buckhurst's message was not at the forefront of my mind when, many months later, as a substitute for one of my editors, I went to my first Williams press conference. It was to be my last.

The point on which I clashed with the Prime Minister was trivial in the extreme. In responding to a rather tame question, he appeared to alter an earlier statement of Government policy. Politicians do it all the time. When I suggested that this was the case, Williams first became annoyed and, when I refused to give ground, grew incandescent with rage. With an enthusiasm born more of youthful inexperience than principle, I refused to back down. Williams was not amused. He reminded me at that moment of Trollope's character Louis Trevelyan, whose doctor makes the sad diagnosis: 'One thing is clear. He should be contradicted in nothing. If he chose to say that the moon was made of green cheese – let it be conceded that the moon was made of green cheese.'

Later that day members of the board of Radio Trinidad rushed to our offices to hear the tape of my exchange with the Prime Minister. They left muttering gravely to each other. Nothing was ever said to me, but I was never again asked to cover an Eric Williams press conference.

Nobody threatened to have me sacked and no one stood in the way of my progress. On the contrary I prospered in a variety of other fields, broadcasting on racing, tennis, cricket, soccer and water polo, and in the company of the kindest and most helpful people I had ever met. My immediate superiors and my colleagues guided me through a succession of broadcasting minefields with enormous patience and good grace.

My job as a roving journalist also enabled me to travel fairly widely in the region and to meet the memorable political characters of the time. At the cost to a reporter of only a large Scotch, St Lucian Dr Carl de la Corbinere, one time Deputy Prime Minister of the Federation, was a constant source of indiscreet information about his ministerial colleagues. He had the enviable political gift of being adept at his work, but knowing that politics should never be boring or taken too seriously. Dr Phyllis Alfrey from Dominica, who once held a Health and Social Affairs portfolio during the Federation, was always wonderful company and, as she later showed in her writing, possessed a brilliant mind. (Her books were much later dramatised on British television.) And I never failed to enjoy my encounters with Eric Gairy, the politically skilful, but decidedly eccentric, Prime Minister of Grenada. Gairy had a repu-tation for unpredictability. He was suspicious of reporters, and with good reason: he apparently had a lot to hide. At one stage in his career, while Grenada was still a colony, the Foreign Office in

London had summarily removed him from office for allegedly appropriating money intended for his island's development.

My News Editor felt the best way to charm Gairy was to pander to his passion for tennis. I was delighted to undertake the assignment of playing against him, though I never quite reconciled myself to the News Editor's advice that I should allow the Prime Minister to win. In the end discretion overcame pride and I did as I was told, and our matches succeeded in putting Gairy in the most splendid frame of mind. Flushed with the elation of winning, the problem of interviews evaporated as if by magic.

Even during his time as Prime Minister, Gairy appeared to have a controlling interest in a popular night-club in the Grenadian capital, St Georges. No secret had been made of this, but many journalists were surprised to find him at the door, closely involved in the evening's takings. Many years later, when Eric Gairy was guiding the political fortunes of an independent Grenada, having been in and out of power like a political Houdini, I happened to be at the United Nations in New York to hear his solemn warnings to delegates about the importance of UFOs (unidentified flying objects). He seemed puzzled and hurt when the contribution of newly independent Grenada to an august world body like the United Nations was not taken seriously.

Despite the undeniable pleasures of working as a journalist in the Caribbean, I became increasingly disenchanted by a climate in which challenge, criticism or anything which might be called dissent was frowned upon. Journalists were, by and large, expected to toe the official line. Investigative journalism, even of the very basic kind of which we were capable, was allowed only if it did not embarrass the Government or anybody else of importance, and my employers at Radio Trinidad were keen to make sure this convention was respected at all times. It should be said, in all fairness, that no one ever insisted a certain line should be followed; it was simply that everyone seemed to know what should and should not be done.

Television, a much later addition to the Trinidad media, had chosen to play by the same rules. I was once asked to be moderator and editor of a weekly television discussion programme called *Dialogue*. I accepted the job on condition that I could select the guests who appeared on the show. I felt the time had come to broaden our field of choice to include, for example, university professors who had become active in the continuing debate on national issues. Some of the people I had in mind were controversial figures because of their political views and I argued strenuously for their inclusion on the ground that what they espoused needed to be tested by tough questioning on national television. After much discussion and obvious reluctance, Trinidad and Tobago Television agreed. There was, however, one condition: I was asked to submit the names of the guests and the subjects to be discussed for each edition of *Dialogue*, not to the programme's Producer, but to the General Manager himself. He owed his job to the fact that he was a good businessman, but the appointment had to be approved by the Government too.

My meetings with him were always the same. He would express his horror at my choice of guests and would remind me how unpopular and or controversial each one had become. Then he would seek an assurance from me that I would not let them 'say too much' or 'go too far'. I was happy to give that assurance and to stress that all unpopular and controversial views would be well tested by searching questions. Finding it difficult to take his objections any further, the General Manager would then remind me, only partly in jest, that, if the programme failed, his job would be on the line. For more than a year and a half I was reminded of that every Friday afternoon.

Our society had become infected by a real fear of debate. To Trinidad and Tobago Television's credit, the programme was kept on and proved to be a great success, but I never ceased to worry about the poor General Manager's job. I found this inhibiting. It was not the kind of journalism I wanted to devote my life to. My ideas, even though they were hardly well developed, were on a grander scale. Even then I had formed the view that our leaders and our Government needed to be challenged, and they needed to be confronted on television by views opposed to their own. I had come to feel that press conferences should not be for the benefit of ministers, but occasions when they should be made to explain the reasons for their policies. I thought journalism had a role to play in popularising unorthodox views. Journalists, I felt, had to be seen to be acting on behalf of the people, questioning actions taken in their name and making politicians accountable. Such continual questioning was a crucial element of our democratic process.

I had grown fond of the 'publish and be damned' school. Radio Trinidad's foreign owners, keen to protect their investment, however, could ill afford that luxury of principle. The problem was not confined to Radio Trinidad or to Trinidad and Tobago Television: there was a more general feeling across several layers of Trinidad society that criticism or too much debate or dissent disturbed the equanimity of sedate West Indian life. You did not need too much of that, the argument seemed to suggest, in the land of cheap rum, steel bands and calypso, and the greatest carnival on earth, where the sun always shone, where the myth had taken root that all races and creeds got on with little or no friction, and where the slightest thought of a problem – in domestic or national life – could be wiped away by the certainty of the next party. I had come to see Trinidad as an improbable lotus land. We had reached an impasse.

Quietly, but sedulously, through a succession of other jobs, I hatched a secret plan to work abroad. It was helped by a remarkable stroke of luck and by the generosity and thoughtfulness of friends. The assistant head of the Overseas Service of the BBC, Christopher Bell, remembered my interest in working for the Corporation and, one day, when a vacancy arose, he telephoned me from London to offer me the job. I accepted the terms and conditions of the subsequent contract without demur, and left Trinidad for London in August 1969.

3

Inside Bush House

'The sublime and ridiculous are so often related, that it is difficult to class them separately. One step above the sublime makes the ridiculous and one step above the ridiculous makes the sublime again.'

THOMAS PAINE, *Common Sense*

IT is impossible to describe the joy and anticipation with which I began work as a Producer with the BBC Overseas Service at Bush House in the Aldwych. There are times when one senses in one's life the possibility of a new beginning. Bush House was all that for me and more. I was assigned first to the Caribbean Section, before being moved to the World Service itself. For a long time I had been fascinated with the history of the place, its prominence in world broadcasting, its role in the Second World War, its contact with major figures of the period like Winston Churchill and Charles de Gaulle, and its unrelenting battle for editorial independence – and all this despite the fact that its operation was funded by money from the British Foreign Office. It was a concept totally alien to the world outside. Stories about this assertion of independence were legion. The most memorable I thought was the BBC's stand during the Suez Crisis. Not very long into the confrontation with Egypt's President Nasser in 1956, it became clear that the British were not united behind the policies and perceptions of Prime Minister Anthony Eden. This unease went beyond well-advertised Government resignations. The problem for the World Service was a fundamental one: with Britain at war

37

with a foreign country, how far should the BBC World Service reflect support for the Establishment position and how far should it go in publicising internal dissent to the enemy? The question was obviously being raised in high places and considerable pressure was put on Bush House to stick to the Government line. When the Corporation would not agree, a Foreign Office appointee was actually installed on the premises. He was given enormous quantities of tea and sympathy, but little else. I'm told that after a while he left of his own accord, having encountered no personal hostility or wilful intransigence, but a carefully reasoned view about the need for the BBC World Service to maintain its editorial integrity. Close to four decades later it remains a shining example of what editorial integrity should mean.

Early on I discovered the degree to which that quality had come to be respected. I remember taking a call one day on a bad line from Accra, in Ghana. The caller, in the Ministry of Industry, requested a transcript of a programme I had produced on Ghana's economy. Believing that somebody wanted to protest at some point we had made in the programme, I was slightly defensive. The caller put my fears to rest by saying that the minister had missed the broadcast because he had been kept longer than usual at a Cabinet meeting and was terribly keen to hear our views on his country's economic performance; he was a fan and never missed an edition of our programme. A copy of the transcript was duly sent to the Minister in Ghana.

Bush House had become a magnet to the great and the good, the influential and the powerful. Political leaders and their senior ministers from all over the world beat a path to our studios. Almost without trying, we attracted poets and novelists, philosophers and entertainers, statesmen, sportsmen and the most impressive army of commentators on international politics to take part in the World Service's output. The difficulty on some occasions was keeping people away.

Of particular pleasure to me was the fact that I saw so many

West Indian writers, poets and personalities. Andrew Salkey, the Jamaican born author, was a regular contributor to programmes at Bush House. I saw Sam Selvon, V. S. Naipaul, and Wilson Harris. Whenever he was in London resting from his travels abroad, the splendid C. L. R. James grew into a regular visitor. In addition I became aware that West Indian politicians, who were never accessible to the organs of information in their own countries, invariably found the time to be interviewed by Bush House programmes. I began to enjoy myself hugely. Although overawed by the unwieldy bureaucracy of the BBC and from time to time critical of the pace at which things were done, I never ceased to be impressed by the wide range of talents to which one was exposed.

For the greater part of my time at Bush House I worked for George Steedman, head of the Overseas Service, one of the most brilliant broadcasting minds I had ever encountered. I was having a ball.

Soon after joining Bush House, I became involved in reporting a story which traumatised the sporting world. It acquired a higher international profile than ordinary sporting stories because of its political implications and, since it was also about cricket, it was close to West Indian hearts. In the year before I arrived in England the coloured South African cricketer Basil d'Oliveira, who had been forced by the inhumanity of apartheid to play professional cricket in England, was selected to be a member of the England squad to tour South Africa. Rather extraordinarily, d'Oliveira was not part of the team when it was first announced. A brilliant century – he scored 158 – on the eve of the selectors' meeting apparently did him no favours at all. Many commentators felt the decision to leave him out was inexplicable, and in the country at large it was widely felt that the MCC were playing fast and loose with principle and morality, conniving with South Africa's racist policies. A thunder roar of protests greeted his omission. Then, when a member of the selected touring party dropped out, d'Oliveira became the automatic choice.

Now it was the South Africans' turn to be outraged. Firstly, they appeared convinced that a clumsy plot had been hatched to embarrass them politically. D'Oliveira had, after all, been a last minute addition to the team; surely his selection had been fixed. In fairness to them, the South Africans had been on the look out for precisely that kind of development. Long before the touring party was selected, the South African Prime Minister had warned that, while racially mixed teams might be allowed from countries with which South Africa had traditional sporting ties, it was important to ensure that 'no political capital is made out of the situation'. Mr Voster's crafty political statement apart, there was a second, powerful reason, one that went right to the heart of the way minority White South Africans had chosen to run their country. If they were seen to accord a Coloured or Black player equal status to that given to Whites, they felt they might be agreeing to a critical assault on their most cherished belief: the inequality of the races. In practical terms that philosophy inspired the need for them to be seen at all times to be *separate*. Separate development, separate schools and facilities, separate lives were the bedrock principles of apartheid, and on no account could they be transgressed. D'Oliveira was, therefore, unacceptable to the authorities in the country in which he was born – because of the colour of his skin.

To me the issue was clear cut and its resolution beyond doubt. At the very least South Africa had sought to tell England selectors which members of a visiting team were acceptable and which were not, and this represented an unwarranted interference in the team selection of another country. In addition to which, there was a much broader issue: South Africa was insisting on displaying the most blatant and disgraceful racism. It was an affront to common human decency. England should, therefore, call off the tour and break off relations with South African cricket and sport in general at least until their system of government emerged into the light of the twentieth century. The

MCC Committee in London agreed up to a point: the tour could not possibly go ahead and there was a formal proclamation announcing its cancellation.

Incredibly, the MCC were still determined to maintain normal sporting links with South Africa. That fact emerged at a bitter Special General Meeting at Church House in London. A motion had been tabled by the Rev. David Sheppard, former England batsman and member of the MCC's Cricket Committee, regretting the 'mishandling of affairs leading up to the selection' of the party to tour South Africa. It was roundly defeated, along with two other motions which sought to link any future visits to South Africa with the country's progress towards non-racial sport. In the memorable words of one committee member, it would be a sorry day if 'avowedly sincere fanatics are allowed to dominate the scene by asking the government of every country ... to alter their policy' before the start of every MCC visit.

By the time I began to find my feet at Bush House the entire country had been caught in the swirl of debate concerning sporting links with South Africa. A young South African student, Peter Hain, organised a series of spectacularly successful demonstrations against the South African Rugby tourists, and became the motivator in the setting up of an anti-apartheid movement in Britain. I saw a great deal of Peter Hain and interviewed him on a number of occasions for the BBC, in the course of which he convinced me that the only way to force change in South Africa was to isolate it from international sport.

The MCC were not of that view, however, and announced their intention to invite the South African cricket team to England, less than two years after the d'Oliveira affair. By then the issue of sporting contact with apartheid had begun to be discussed around the world. Mindful of the reception the South African visitors could expect from Hain and his growing army of supporters, the England Test and County Cricket Board offered to insure the life of every England cricketer for £15,000. The money was the easy part. Force of public opinion was quite another. It had grown rapidly against the South African tour.

My work gave me the opportunity to meet the leading lights of the campaign to keep South Africa in international sport, cricket writers and commentators, cricketers and politicians. They deployed a wide variety of arguments in support of their case. In the process, I was learning much about life in England and about the freedom to debate in public, to say openly what you believe regardless of the controversy it causes. It was a far cry from Trinidad. The controversy in Britain was stimulating. At Bush House we mounted endless heated debates and, as is frequently said about the most contentious debates in the House of Commons, representatives of both sides of the argument ended up having a drink in the bar.

Despite my own opposing view, I accepted the propositions of the pro tour lobby with equanimity; many of their beliefs were genuinely held. The one exception to all this I found were those cricketers and administrators who insisted that they wanted to maintain sporting contacts with South Africa in order to force the pace of change. Another phrase used was about 'the need to build bridges'. Rhetoric of the same sort was later voiced by those players of all nationalities, West Indians included, who averred that their trips to Pretoria, Cape Town and Johannesburg were meant to encourage and help Black South Africans, rather than in pursuit of their chosen profession and for a great deal of money. That argument continued to be used by participants in 'rebel tours', even when their every move in South Africa was dogged by Black protests. My insides boiled whenever I was confronted by such transparent hypocrisy. Its much later equivalent, just as venal, was the assertion by senior politicians that the policy of opposing economic sanctions against South Africa was somehow meant to ensure that Black people were not harmed. Few assertions in contemporary political life have been more patronising or dishonest. Dr Johnson said that inscriptions on tombstones were never meant to be models of honesty. Many of South Africa's friends were ensuring, by their deceit, that for a long time South Africa's sporting contacts would languish in the graveyard of international isolation.

Far more difficult to judge was how many people really did believe it was possible to 'keep politics out of sport'. I first encountered the view as a young reporter in the West Indies and found it quite unsustainable then. Nor did it make any practical sense where South Africa was concerned, since it was that country's policies which ensured that politics of the most hated and divisive kind intruded in every facet of the lives of its people. Black people, living under a regime in which oppression was systematic and brutal, were deprived of the luxury of any thought of sporting prowess. Many years later, when I had a chance to see conditions in South Africa for myself, I found nothing in the squalor of township life conducive to producing great batsmen or tennis champions. I found no Black South Africans consumed by the desire to walk out to bat at Lord's or Trent Bridge. What I did find instead were people desperate for decent housing, good schools for their children and the means to make something of their lives in a fair and equitable society. Denied access to those basic human rights, Black people had an agenda for personal enhancement in which cricket was never prominent. As the reformed South African Cricket Board itself admitted in 1977, when it began trying to ease its country into non-racial sport, there can be no 'normal cricket in an abnormal society'. Politicians and dictators have always used sport when it suited their Machiavellian ends. In 1936 in Berlin Adolf Hitler paraded his political philosophy about racial superiority at the most time-honoured sporting festival – the Olympic Games. In South Africa politics and sport were one and the same thing.

This was not how the MCC or, to be more precise, the Test and County Cricket Board viewed South Africa, or the world. At their meeting which decided that the 1970 South African tour should

43

go ahead, they cited the threat of disorder by demonstrations as one reason for their decision. No group, they said, should be allowed by their actions to alter plans made by cricket's governing body; the very fabric of society would be endangered. So, suddenly, what had been an issue about racial discrimination in sport in South Africa became a British 'law and order' problem. The Test and County Cricket Board stated that its members were 'unanimous in their resolve to uphold the rights of individuals in this country to take part in lawful pursuits, particularly when those pursuits have the support of the majority'. The *Observer* put the matter more succinctly, writing of the TCCB's decision: 'This was their opportunity to apply all their dislike and loathing of permissiveness, demonstrators and long hair. Staging matches is their chance to make a stand on these things.'

The TCCB annoyed many of its own supporters in the middle of all the controversy about the tour by saying it would go ahead, but would be cut drastically from twenty-eight games to twelve. Despite the aim of the pro tour campaigners to prove that politics had nothing at all to do with South African sport, by late winter 1970 it became difficult to separate sport from politics in Britain. We interviewed the Conservative Shadow Attorney General, Sir Peter Rawlinson, at Bush House. In his view, injunctions should be taken out against the stop-the-tour organisers, because their public statements 'constituted a direct threat to illegal action'. Sir Peter also criticised the Home Secretary, James Callaghan, for remaining 'neutral' and 'acknowledging the licence to riot'. After that the question of whether or not the South Africans should be allowed to play in England never left the political arena.

I was in the process of producing a programme on the controversy for the Caribbean Service of the BBC on the day of the most significant political development: Prime Minister Harold Wilson opposed the tour. In our programme we suggested that this was probably the end of the affair. How naive we were. The MCC continued to receive offers from volunteers to help them protect grounds and matches from 'hippies' threatening to disrupt the fixtures. And to anyone who expressed the slightest doubt, they continued to say that the tour would go on. Cricketers in increasing numbers began to come out against the tour. Prominent among them was Mike Brearley, later to captain England, but others like Peter Lever of Essex and the Trinidadian born, Glamorgan batsman Byran Davis did so too. While a number of their colleagues sat on the fence, some anti-tour views made news headlines. George Best, the Manchester United star, wrote in the *Sun*: 'I think it is an absolute disgrace that we are allowing the South African cricketers to tour this summer ... We have been playing them for years, but they have done nothing about their scandalous apartheid policies. Put them in isolation until they see sense.'

By April matters began to move apace. Only a few weeks before the tourists were due to arrive Harold Wilson dropped another bombshell. He specifically attacked disruptive protests, but said people 'should feel free to demonstrate against the tour'. John Arlott, on the other hand, announced that he had decided not to broadcast on any tour match. It seemed almost time for the MCC to call off their guard dogs and roll up the barbed wire which had already been ordered to be placed around grounds and pitches. But not quite. The Conservative leader, Edward Heath, said he felt the tour should go ahead, while the MCC announced it had written to all club members inviting them to become honorary stewards to help the police. From Lord's as late as 12 May came the announcement: 'Plans for the tour are unchanged.' Some time before that a statement by Jack Bailey, Assistant Secretary to the TCCB, had shown that the cricket authorities were well up on the art of buck-passing: 'If for political or other reasons the Government decides that the tour should not take place, let them come out in the open and say so.' The time had arrived for English cricket to be saved from its own dangerous myopia and for the Government to save Britain's sporting reputation from total disgrace.

It fell to Home Secretary James Callaghan to settle the question. I was outside the Home Office, BBC tape recorder in hand, on the day he asked the MCC to withdraw their invitation. Given the chance finally to escape from the hole into which they had dug themselves, they took it. In fact, they had scant choice. The tour was called off, but the manner in which this eventually came about enabled cricket administrators to shelter behind Government skirts. It signalled the beginning of South Africa's isolation from international sport and, in the minds of many people, it set in train a series of complex events which were to lead eventually to dramatic political changes in South Africa and its re-entry into the civilised world.

The extraordinary events of 1970 came back to me many years later, when in conversation with a senior cricket official, the name Mike Brearley came up. I said how much I liked him and what a wonderful inspiration he had been to the England team. The official agreed only grudgingly, and said there was a serious down-side to Brearley. I wondered what it was. He replied that Brearley had never got on well with the cricket authorities, because 'he's a bit of a Communist, you know'. I have been on tours with Mike Brearley and so expressed surprise. The official immediately cited Brearley's support for the 1970 Stop the Tour Campaign as evidence of his attempt to subdue the MCC by the force of Communist thought. Of course I knew this to be ridiculous.

The work of a journalist, especially one who travels widely, can appear at times to be a rambling, disjointed excursion touching places and subjects which are never likely to be visited again. Occasionally, though, one is more fortunate. Places, subjects and events long discarded by the active mind resurface to help shape the context of current work. My brush with the Basil d'Oliveira *cause célèbre* gave me certain invaluable reference points for my later work in South Africa. I learnt a great deal from d'Oliveira himself, who managed to keep himself with stoic majesty above the noise of battle. What an admirable sporting ambassador he would have made for his country had his colour not got in the way. In addition I learnt much about the MCC and the administration of English cricket. I found that useful some time later, when a pugnacious Australian named Kerry Packer took on the full might of the international cricket establishment.

That year, 1970, I reported the Commonwealth Games in Edinburgh for the Caribbean Service of the BBC and had the pleasure of working with two world-famous athletic sprinters, E. McDonald Bailey, a fellow Trinidadian and a wonderful teacher of the art, which made him a household name in Britain, and Harold Abrahams, whose exploits were later to be so brilliantly portrayed in the film *Chariots of Fire*.

Abrahams, then an old man, had been engaged by the BBC to do the none too taxing job of commenting on performers' times. Although memory can be notoriously unreliable, I still have locked firmly in my mind this image of Abrahams: bespectacled and with only the suspicion of a stoop, he wore his many years of international acclaim with modest ease; his eyes twinkled with determined mischief as he listened patiently to lesser mortals, although no one doubted that he was the acknowledged expert. I heard it suggested, even at those Commonwealth Games, that Abrahams was arrogant, overbearing and tended towards crusty irritableness. I saw none of that. The great man was charm personified and wonderfully kind to people like me who knew so little about athletics. I have golden memories of that summer in Edinburgh, watching the predatory style of the Kenyan middle distance runner Kip Keino, a young Ghanaian runner Charles Asati, the Jamaican sprinter Marilyn Neufville, and the Australian with the golden hair, Raylene Boyle, or sitting at the feet of Abrahams and walking along Princes Street in the company of McDonald Bailey as he was constantly accosted by fans. They remembered his feats on the running track many years before and were anxious to shake him by the hand. I was fortunate to be part of it all.

It was said that the fourteenth-century philosopher Erasmus was such a genius that people became famous simply on the basis of claiming they had once received a communication from the great man. I felt gloriously privileged to have been at the same event as some of the brightest stars in the history of sport. Somebody once suggested that the best we lesser mortals can ever hope to do in life is to be given the chance to touch the hem of the garments of the truly great. I somehow felt I had done that in 1970 and experienced something approaching the joy of a young child given the keys to an Aladdin's cave. Of course it was too good to last. One cannot, as Herman Wouk suggested, survive for too long on a diet of cream puffs. From the Greek philosophers we know that the real glories of life are its hazards and one is judged on how its difficulties are faced. From that time on there would be precious few occasions when I could spend my time reporting what was essentially one sporting event. By the time I joined ITN in 1973, I was determined to pursue my original aim when I first came to Britain: to report international politics and the big domestic stories. And prominent among those domestic stories in 1973 was Northern Ireland.

4

Religious Vices

Our religion is made so as to wipe out our vices;
It covers them up, nourishes them and incites them.
MICHEL DE MONTAIGNE, *Essais II, xii*

IT has been said that there is a pattern to trying to unravel the complexities of Northern Ireland. On arriving there for the first time, it is impossible to make sense of the place or its politics at all. After a few months and after being introduced to the issues, and with suitable indoctrination (given with alacrity to any newcomer to the province), that changes. A Damascene clarity emerges, or so one thinks. Those knotty issues which at first seemed so resistant to logic begin to appear clearer and, to anyone who will listen, one begins to feel sufficiently confident to suggest fairly simple, rational political solutions. In a relatively short time the beginner, no longer worried about ever coming to grips with his subject, becomes something of an expert. Fortunately that belief in one's own solutions does not survive for long. By the time your assignment is over and you leave Northern Ireland, you are seized again by crippling doubt and incomprehension. The reaction then to any questions about possible solutions is spluttering bewilderment.

In five years, off and on in reporting Northern Ireland, I never ceased to be baffled by the discursive nature of the violence. I struggled for a long time to try to understand why people take their disagreements to such extremes. I never did. Every time I reported a violent incident, it was the same: I was always shocked by the fact that human life could be treated with such disdain. Gunmen would open fire with semi-automatic weapons in bars crowded with people, while other terrorists would plant bombs in busy shopping areas, and they would do so in the knowledge that the death of scores of innocent people is a real possibility.

Part of my time in Northern Ireland was spent attempting to follow the uneasy course of a variety of political solutions inspired by Whitehall. I had gone there after the brutal Protestant response to the civil rights marches and the biggest political experiment after that was a power-sharing administration, involving Unionists and Nationalists. The Northern Ireland Assembly came into being in 1973. Two years later it was gone. I watched the birth pangs of that power-sharing attempt, was moved by hopes of its success and I saw it die. The Northern Ireland Assembly was followed by the Northern Ireland Constitutional Convention. The life of that was even shorter. There were a variety of other political developments, but etched too painfully in the memory are the incidents of violence. Sadly, they, more than anything else, provided a framework for the way in which Northern Ireland came to be seen: it is one of the most beautiful places in which I have worked. I was shown hospitality and graciousness easily surpassing anything I have known, but, as a journalist, I could never free myself from thoughts of the violence in Northern Ireland. I can list examples by the score.

One afternoon we were tipped off about a murder on the outskirts of Belfast. Somewhat reluctantly I decided to go because even then there was scant journalistic mileage to be had by reporting murders. They had become much too commonplace and the constant repetition of gory details had helped to dull the senses. These, after all, were the years when the terrorists seemed bent on flattening the city centre: huge car bombs had been going off everywhere. A certain bravado accompanied their planting. We were very often given so much advance warning that it was easy to position our cameras to capture the explosion on film. The hotel where most journalists stayed, the Europa, was a prime target. On more than one occasion members of our ITN team watched the bombers arrive. They were allowed into the hotel to plant their bombs by the same security guards who only an hour before had ransacked the suitcases of arriving guests. In reality, no one ever confronted the bombers, and the hotel's security was something of a mirage. The security guards had become part of the fiction that the Europa Hotel was safe, at least until the bombers arrived with their familiar threats and their guns.

That afternoon I travelled with an ITN crew to a house just outside Belfast. My interest in the story grew once I went inside. A gunman, for little reason apparent then, had come down the long drive leading to the house, had knocked and gained admission through a kitchen door. Realising much too late what they had done, the occupants of the house sought shelter in another part of the house. The gunman followed. He caught up with his two victims near the living-room and opened fire as they attempted to hide. Cowering in terror, they had fallen and died without dignity in a corner of their own home. I was horrified. I felt the incident would make a riveting television news story and we began to film a reconstruction of the double murder. The gunman's trail was easy to follow, marked as it was by ugly splotches of blood. It was everywhere – on the kitchen sink, on the grey walls of the house, on door handles and on the living-room carpet in a hideously stomach-churning pool. I felt sick. The cameraman dutifully tracked the tragic course of the couple's dying moments with the help of a relative who had watched the whole episode and who for some unknown reason had been spared by the killer.

Once or twice as this woman was explaining the path along which the killer had remorselessly tracked his victims, a young child, a girl of eight or nine years old, appeared to correct our older witness. Overcome by the horror of the killings, I had attached no significance to her intervention at the time and we carried on filming. Much later, as we neared the end of preparing our report, something the witness said clicked and I became conscious of something I had overlooked. Looking across the garden at two children playing on a swing, the woman said that her main problem would be to try to repair the lives of the two girls who had seen their parents brutally murdered before their eyes. Only then did the truth hit me with the force of a thunderbolt. The two girls had seen their parents hunted and killed like two wild animals. They remembered the gunman's pursuit to the point of correcting others who reported it inaccurately. Although I had failed to acknowledge it at the time, they had memorised in great detail precisely what had happened.

I have seen little in my career as a television journalist to compare with the shock of seeing children exposed to such violence. In my darker moments in reporting Northern Ireland I formed the view, perhaps an exaggerated one, that there could be no hope, no secure peaceful future for any society which traumatises its children and its people by such violence. Either they become inured to it, in which case their personalities are warped by its horror, or they copy it and become perpetrators, thereby hastening their own destruction and any hope their society might have of a normal existence.

Many months after this incident I spent a lugubrious evening listening to a psychiatric report about children whose lives had been traumatised by violence. My guest, a doctor at a local hospital, described to me the symptoms of children he had been treating. One child who on his way to school saw a man shot and killed could no longer to be coaxed into going out. He spent his days behind closed doors, frequently breaking down, crying for no apparent reason and inconsolable. The father of one young patient, a girl of nine, had been gunned down in his home in the presence of his family. What she remembered of the incident was the slamming of a car door outside the house which announced the arrival of the killers. Ever since that night the noise of any car door closing sent her into an epileptic fit.

When I first went to Northern Ireland, it had become fashionable to dismiss or to make light of the religious dimension to the problems of the province. One was always told that to see the Unionist/Nationalist conflict in such a way was to be much too simplistic. It certainly is. Expert writers on Ireland such as Liam de Paor have argued the point with great conviction. In de Paor's view, to describe Northern Ireland Catholics as Blacks who happen to have white skins is a much better analogy than the over-simplification which sees the struggle and conflict in terms of religion. After all Catholics and Protestants, he says, are not quarrelling with one another (most of them) because of matters of theology and faith; there is no burning urge on either side to convert the other to the one true faith. De Paor maintains that the Northern Ireland problem is a colonial one and the 'racial' distinction (which he argues is actually imagined as 'racial') between the colonialists and the natives is expressed in terms of religion.

It would be unforgivable to fail to grasp the colonial dimension of the Northern Ireland problem and yet, in my years there, I saw the degree to which Protestants and Catholics were prepared to use their religions as the main point of emphasis of their respective places in the community. On my very first visit to the province I went to see William Craig, a leading Protestant politician. We spent some time discussing the security situation. It was 1972 and things were bad. When our conversation turned to the controversy about the make up of the security forces, I asked Mr Craig why there were not more Catholic policemen. He went into a long spiel about Catholic families being much larger and the boys not always coming up to the physical requirements necessary for joining the force. I reminded Mr Craig it was not terribly convincing to put such an argument to a black West Indian to whom explanations of discriminatory behaviour were not persuasive, but I was aston-ished at his perception of how religion had operated against a section of the community.

Religion may not have been the original or even the most significant point of departure between the two communities, but that was the distinction which asserted itself in every sphere of their daily life. Religion, in my experience, got in the way of attempts to forge a wider relationship within the community. It kept people apart and, because it did so in a volatile society, it acquired a profile which was probably out of proportion to its true significance. It can surely be argued that the colonisers saw substantial advantage for them in keeping Ulster divided, and in religion they found a more than useful tool. Notwithstanding the political history of the province, I became convinced that religion was in contemporary terms the main, the deepest and the most obvious dividing line between the peoples of Northern Ireland. I saw it everywhere. There were Protestant and Catholic areas and streets; streets are described by the religious affiliation of the inhabitants. Over many years certain jobs acquired an unofficial religious classification. If you were told what a person did, you could in all probability be reasonably sure what church that person went to. In the years since I was a regular reporter in Northern Ireland, it would appear that little has changed. As recently as April 1993 I was drawn to some news copy about compensation paid to individuals because they had successfully contested in the courts charges of religious discrimination. Religion even showed itself in sport. In general Protestants played rugby, soccer and cricket; Catholics almost never did – Gaelic football was more likely. To this day it seems to me extraordinary that it is possible to tell a man's religion by his choice of sport. It appears a clear example of religion collaborating with history in keeping people apart.

To people born in Northern Ireland religion appears at the cradle, shapes their lives and defines their places in the society. It stays with them till they die. In many parts of the world I know the term 'mixed marriages' is usually applied to the bonding of two people of different races or different colours; in Northern

Ireland it is used to describe people who marry across the religious divide. On numerous occasions I tried to encourage my Northern Ireland colleagues to write pieces, do television reports or even simply to discuss in a smaller forum the question of mixed schools. It was never difficult to reach agreement: that, in theory, they would make a major contribution to the creation of a more cohesive society. Almost everyone agreed though that, in practice, a policy of mixed schools would be difficult to promote. I have never ceased to be amazed at how many children of different religions spend their entire school lives without having contact with, never playing against, or never even having met or talked to a child of another religious persuasion.

I once covered a story about a group of Northern Ireland children, some Catholic and some Protestant, who, with the help of a perspicacious benefactor, had been given the opportunity to spend a week together in England. Ostensibly, the idea was to give the children a break from the terrible cycle of violence which was so much a part of their daily lives. When we interviewed them some time later, the most common response had to do with religion. The majority of them commented how well they had got on with others who had different religious beliefs. More poignantly and more sadly, so many of them said that they had never before been given the chance to meet or to talk with their contemporaries from other religious backgrounds. I felt that the experiment made a persuasive case.

Nor was the problem, as I saw it, very different in the mid-1970s in the Irish Republic. I have never forgotten being sent to Dublin late one afternoon after a number of massive explosions shook the city centre. Among the casualties – many of whom had been killed – were children. On the day of the mass funerals I stood in one of the city's cathedrals, trying not entirely successfully to control my emotions as the caskets were brought in slow procession past the packed congregation. From the manner in which they were carried, I could see that some of them contained very little. The terrorists' victims had been blown to pieces. I lost my composure when a colleague's whispered conversation confirmed my suspicion that some of the tiny coffins had been weighted with stones for sake of appearances and the dignity of the occasion.

Later on that day, reaching the cemetery some time before the funeral processions, I had the chance to talk to the Roman Catholic priest who was to conduct the final obsequies. We talked about the unmitigated sadness of the event and about the futility of violence. We were as one in believing that violence of this sort would never succeed in shaping political solutions. Emboldened by the similarity of our views, I felt sufficiently confident to state my views about the strict religious lines along which education was organised in northern and southern Ireland. I said I felt the current religious lines along which schools and colleges were run, the overwhelming emphasis on Catholic schools for Catholics, Protestant schools for Protestants, and the almost total absence of any mixed schools gave no assistance to the coming generations to close the yawning gaps of ignorance and incomprehension in the societies. As the first of the processions to reach the cemetery that afternoon snaked solemnly towards the open grave over which we stood, the priest replied. He felt my suggestion had gone much too far. He said he thought nothing was more important for the young than their thorough indoctrination in the religious values of their fathers and their grandfathers; the idea of mixed schools was far outside any possible agenda for bringing peace to the country.

I had been given the doctrinal line. I am afraid it hardened my views about the negative role of religion in any possible political reconciliation in Ireland.

The object of most of the violence in Northern Ireland was the British Army. It had been sent to protect the mainly Roman Catholic Nationalists, but very quickly it had earned their bitter hatred. British soldiers came to be seen as an unwelcome army of occupation, a modern-day extension of the unsympathetic colonialism which had scarred Ireland's history. The Nationalists now campaigned for the Army to be withdrawn and, to make sure their point was not missed, the Irish Republican Army, the IRA, which saw itself as the military arm of Nationalist thinking, pursued the British Army with dedicated ruthlessness and with the bullet and the bomb. Our reporting of stories of attacks on the British Army was a major element of my work in Northern Ireland. The point has never been lost on the IRA, for these are the stories which get Northern Ireland noticed outside the province and they provided what former Prime Minister Margaret Thatcher came to regard as the 'oxygen of publicity' for the IRA. After a while I became heartily sick of reporting the deaths of soldiers. A point is reached, very quickly in my case, when one is overwhelmed by a sense of the futility of squandered lives.

We were called out very early one morning to Belleek, a small village near the border with the Republic. A landmine, set off by remote control, had exploded under an Army truck, killing six soldiers. The incident had occurred the night before, but the Army, fearing another ambush, had decided to wait until it was daylight to go in. We went to the scene with them. It was barely light; dawn was breaking weakly through a haze of mist and fine, persistent rain. What we saw there I remember to this day. The Army vehicle had been travelling along a road bordered by open country, there were no houses to be seen for miles. To one side the undulating fields rose to a prominent hill, a few hundred yards from the road. To the other the land stretched out much more evenly and was heavy with gorse. What looked like the undercarriage of the Army truck had been blown off the road and hurled by the force of the blast a clear fifty yards into the gorse field. Other, barely recognisable bits had come to rest in a ditch between the roadway and the field. A massive crater had made the road impassable. The explosion which claimed the lives of those poor men, must have made a terrifying noise. Now all was uncomfortably silent. About twenty of the men's colleagues, armed with white plastic bags, began the search for what was left of the bodies of those who died.

Standing there, watching this dreadful process, I felt for a time that I was part of a bizarre, surreal scene. Either because they were overcome by their loss or by the shock of their sombre task, no restrictions were put on what we could film. Usually the Army followed the practice of 'cleaning up' before television news cameras arrived. They had not done so that morning in Belleek. We were left alone to follow, as quietly as we could, the men with the plastic bags.

I had never before, nor have I since, been in any place so overrun by a feeling of wasteful death. Dismembered parts of bodies were everywhere – limbs that once must have felt so powerful, fed by hearts so hopeful, now dangled helplessly from flowering trees and bushes. Hands and feet, wrenched from their limbs, were the parts we could easily recognise. Much more had been so badly mangled and so cruelly distorted that it bore no relation to anything in anatomical textbooks. I was desperate to find some parallel experience on which I could call. Denied that relief, I felt only despair – deep, black despair. I vaguely recalled some character Dante described as having been 'torn from the scabbard of his limbs'. I could not be sure whether it was appropriate, although the brutality of the metaphor most certainly was. With little reflective thought you could almost hear the sound of the explosion which had abruptly ended so many lives. I had heard them many times before in Belfast. We had all grown to recognise what sounded like huge doors being slammed shut in the mighty caverns of some dark, mysterious underworld: the gates of mercy closing on mankind. If you were close enough to the blast, you felt its sensation more in the lower abdomen than in the head. It churned your insides. No matter how many times I heard large bombs go off, I was never able to stand my ground. I always set off at a frantic pace in the opposite direction, running aimlessly and with the utmost futility. The squaddies who died would have been offered no such chance. I could not resolve in my own mind whether they would have heard anything. Who can say if one hears the noise that smashes your life into the next world?

The explosion in Belleek had transformed the gentle, rolling countryside into a grotesque killing field. Allowed unprecedented access, we moved about, watching the operation. No words were spoken by members of our team. Glances were exchanged at every new piece of horror. As quietly as we had gone about our work, we left for the drive north to our base.

I prepared a report for the mid-day news in which I attempted to show what really lies behind the carefully sanitised words and timeless euphemisms we employ to describe the catastrophic passing of human life. I suppose it was my intention to shock as I had been shocked. In deciding to do so, however, my report crossed the boundary between what is acceptable on lunchtime television and what is not. I was made, quite correctly in my later view, to tone down visually my reports for later bulletins. Interestingly, the British Army press office in Belfast felt that the 'shock tactic' approach in my earlier report was fully justified. Perhaps by that time in their tour of duty in Northern Ireland they had become inured to all the indignities which go with the loss of life. They confessed to me they had come to believe that only by shocking television viewers could they fully convey to the wider British public the impossible position in which the Army had been placed in Northern Ireland.

It was probably just as well that we reporters were never frequently threatened ourselves. Only once did a threat make me cold with fear. I was at a rally in Londonderry held to mark the appalling events of Bloody Sunday in 1972, when the Army had opened fire, killing thirteen civilians, who were said to have been unarmed, a claim now accepted as fact. The people of Londonderry and some leading political figures have for years sought a formal apology from the British Government. We were standing around waiting for the fiery speeches to wind up, when I noticed a very striking young woman making her way towards me. I kept looking around, trying to discover the object of her attention, as she continued to pick her way with resourceful determination through the crowd of about 10,000. I had spotted her from a long way off and, although she kept heading my way, I suspected she was looking for someone else, a feeling arising partly from instinctive self-denial as I thought her terribly attractive. By the time she was only a few feet from where I stood, I had prepared myself to be embarrassed: I felt certain she would address me as an acquaintance, although I was sure I had never seen her before. I would definitely have remembered her. She was in her twenties and was reasonably well dressed. Her large intense eyes never seemed to lose their focus. She came right up close and, as I anxiously scanned her face for some friendly sign of recognition, I felt she might smile. She didn't. In fact her expression had not changed from the moment I had first spotted her walking towards me. Now, near enough to touch me, she spoke. I have never forgotten what she said.

'I want to say something to you. We don't like the way you report the troubles here. We don't like your sort. And if you ever come back to Derry, you'll never leave this place alive.'

Having delivered her message, she sought no acknowledgement. She turned and headed back in the direction from which she had come. In next to no time she had been swallowed up by the crowd, leaving me to wonder whether I had dreamt the whole thing. No one had ever before made so direct a threat on my life, not to my face anyway.

I stood frozen to the spot, looking round to see if anyone else had heard the warning. I was desperate for confirmation and to share what I regarded as the gravity of the threat. To my immense relief, Peter Wilkinson, the ITN cameraman, who had been standing fairly close to me and who, also having an eye for a pretty face, had watched the woman approach, turned from the camera and said to me with a wry smile, 'I heard that.'

By that stage, I had seen a fair amount of bombings and gun battles, and had managed to cope with their implicit threats with varying degrees of equanimity, but hardly had they ever been so personalised. In the black humour of war, I felt I had seen the bullet on which my name had been inscribed.

Peter soothed my anxieties. At my insistence, though, we finished our work in Derry very promptly that afternoon, and for a long while after I gave the city a wide berth. Throughout my time in Northern Ireland colleagues such as Peter Wilkinson were the real ITN heroes: they braved the shooting and the rioting, while I escaped ostensibly to make telephone calls to the office in London. They took the pictures from the front line, while I usually hid some safe distance behind. None of which stopped me from encouraging them to do better, to take more pictures, to be even more brave. I discovered, though, how easy it was to be insensitive to their fears for their own safety.

One afternoon I was pushing a reluctant colleague to take more pictures of a riot just outside the city centre. I became rather testy when he appeared to resent my entreaties. Some time later that afternoon, in conversation with a local politician, I was made aware of the reason for my colleague's discomfort in our surroundings. He had been saved by that same politician from a merciless beating by a group of thugs some months before and that afternoon we had returned to the very place. I later heard the story. He had been surrounded and hit about the head with pieces of wood in which nails had been embedded for good effect. He had been taken to hospital by our political friend and promptly shipped back to London. I apologised profusely to the cameramen and felt thoroughly ashamed I had been pushing him to relive the horror of his earlier experience.

The incident taught me a great deal: I would never again make the same mistake and I would always attempt to put in proper perspective the dangerous business of getting television pictures. I have seen few stories worth the risk of one's life. Much later in

Beirut and other cities, I always did as the young men with large guns suggested. The role of the reporter is to survive to report, a task not enhanced by getting hurt.

If violence has distorted life in Northern Ireland, it has never succeeded in totally corrupting its people. In the province's darkest hours while I was there people showed resilience and fortitude, and were capable of genuine acts of kindness and of love. Throughout my years reporting there I was always astonished at the number of men and women who not only managed normal lives but who were also prepared to risk all they had to take highly principled positions on the most controversial issues of their time. Against the odds and at times when it seemed pointless to do so, they spoke up courageously for what they felt was right, for community reconciliation and against divisions and bitterness. They came from every strand of life, high and low, from the Church, academia, from the commercial sector, politics, and from the ranks of ordinary people. Their spirits soared above the poverty of life around them and challenged that of others to do the same. They were the bright and shining stars to whom we journalists turned every time we tried to extract points of light from the prevailing gloom.

Sometimes, as journalists, we fell into the trap of attaching too much significance to the work of the conciliators. We were desperate to believe that a solution was possible to Ulster's troubles. In a curious way our profession, which devotes so many of its resources to reporting disasters, thrives on hope. Even when it seems a distant mirage, we reach out for it. We did in 1976. In that year the Northern Ireland Peace People Movement was launched on the wave of outrage and emotion. Mairead Corrigan and Betty Williams brought thousands of people on to the streets to call for peace after a tragic car accident in which three children died. The three children, two baby sons and a daughter, had belonged to Corrigan's sister, Anne Maguire.

The accident had occurred in a Belfast street. Mrs Maguire had been out with her family, when a car driven at high speed by an

IRA gunman ploughed into them. Mrs Maguire herself was badly injured. One child survived. There was another twist to the story: the gunman had been shot by a British Army patrol and was dead at the wheel by the time his car killed the children. The political dimension of the incident was thus inescapable.

Although people's sensitivities had taken a sustained battering in Northern Ireland by years of bloodshed and ghastly killings, the death of the Maguire children moved the province to tears. The needless death of children can drive even mighty nations to despair. In Northern Ireland it mobilised people unlike any previous incident. Armed with no other philosophy or policy than the slogan that 'something must be done to stop this', the Peace Movement sprang spontaneously to life. With Corrigan and Williams at its head, it organised rallies and marches, and galvanised many of the rival Protestant and Catholic communities into a soul-searching appraisal of their tolerance of violence. Its effect was immediately dramatic. More than 10,000 people attended the Peace Movement's first rally. It was a memorable day for us, a story of hope. For once television pictures emanating from Ulster carried a different message. Thousands of Catholic women from the Falls Road district crossed the religious divide to the Shankill Road area, where thousands of Protestant residents embraced them as sisters. Before that, people in Northern Ireland had been bracing themselves for the possibility of civil war. Some had been hoarding food. Suddenly, it had all changed and on a fine August afternoon, we were witnessing what looked like the green shoots of peace. The occasion was redolent of the emotions of people power. Where the politicians had failed, perhaps people power could succeed. Speeches made by the peace campaigners used history itself to bury the most profound historical and tribal distrust between Protestants and Catholics. Someone said that what the people of Northern Ireland have in common goes back 9,000 years; what they fight about is only a few hundred years old. It was heady stuff. We had heard nothing like that in public before. Other rallies and marches quickly followed. Their influence began to engulf a troubled land, and soon the Peace Movement had even the cynics in its seductive embrace.

It was not the first peace campaign in Ulster's history, but it was the one which caught the imagination of the world. Reporters and television cameras descended on Belfast from as far away as South America and Australia. Seminars about peace in Northern Ireland were organised in Germany and Denmark. Williams and Corrigan began to travel extensively to promote their cause. Although it sought to address a Northern Ireland problem, somehow it was felt that, if the problem were internationalised, a greater degree of world pressure could be brought to bear on the political decision-makers. The stature of the Peace Movement grew. More international acclaim was to follow.

Less than two years after its inception, I followed Williams and Corrigan to Oslo to report their acceptance of the Nobel Peace Prize. They were ecstatic that the King of Norway himself especially asked to see them before the grand ceremony. We spent a riotous evening in our hotel in Oslo, toasting, almost till dawn the following day, a new beginning for Northern Ireland. But that was the last high point in the Peace Movement's short and promising life. Splits appeared in its ranks. It lost its fervour, its revolutionary, reforming zeal faded, and it began to slip sullenly to its death. As is *de rigueur* when organisations die, the recriminations were not far behind. Spasms of activity were cited to support the belief that it had not died and that it had simply taken a break, to reappear and be prominent again. But *rigor mortis* had set in, and Northern Ireland went back to politics as usual and its immense tragedies.

Four years later Anne Maguire was found dead in her house in Belfast. She had slit her wrists and her throat. On the day her body was discovered by her only surviving child she had been due to appear in court to seek compensation for 'grave psychological damage' caused by the death of her children.

It was a deeply painful end to a story which had begun with so much hope. The unforgiving bleak landscape of hostility and attrition had reclaimed the province.

There has been endless speculation about why the Peace Movement failed, why hope died so soon. Some have suggested that the seeds of its failure began to germinate while the movement was at the height of its popularity. This thesis goes on to say that the award of the Nobel Peace Prize was probably the one single event which ensured the movement's eventual collapse because it lost sight of its goal and became diverted from what it set out to do. Others believe, of course, that the two women who influenced the birth of the movement were too inexperienced and too easily diverted by baubles such as the Nobel Peace Prize and international acclaim to lead it to any long-term success. They were not strong enough, nor had it ever been clear where they thought the movement should go. No thought had been given, says this line of reasoning, to how they would eventually graft the movement on to a proper political instrument. Organisationally, too, the movement was always something of a mess, always amateurish, never properly professional. All these explanations may be true and the peace people themselves would almost certainly agree.

It is, though, as far as I am concerned, far from being the whole story. Having had the chance to follow the life of the movement in Northern Ireland and having accompanied its leaders on a number of journeys outside Ulster, I am convinced that something more fundamental was responsible for its failure, and I believe it to be this: the desire for true, long-lasting peace was never sufficiently deep seated to push people into making really big compromises. There was never, in my years in Northern Ireland, any shortage of talk about peace. Everybody talked. Talk was cheap, and abundant. But that was as far as most of it got. Bombings and killings have always had the ability to shock and to evoke cross-community sympathy, which is why at the Peace Movement's glorious birth Catholic and Protestant mothers reached out across

65

the barricades to embrace each other. When the time came, however, to build on that experience of shared sorrow and to lay the foundation for a more lasting relationship, the participants baulked. The truth is they always have. There was, it seemed to them, still a great deal of mileage left in separateness. In as far as that may be true, it can also be said that the fate of the Peace Movement was similar in many ways to the high hopes for moderate, cross-party politics in Ulster. Everyone professed a desire for it, but somehow the moderates never managed to tilt the political balance decisively in their favour. Meaningful moderation was, it turned out, one compromise too far. Without wishing to pronounce or be too prescriptive, it remains Ulster's political problem to this day. Talk about new peace movements and new political solutions abound. The people of Ireland suffer greatly and they wear their emotions on their sleeves. Horrible, sickening crimes frequently drive them into deliriums of private hurt and public outrage. From the abyss of deep despair they lift their eyes heavenward and dream dreams of better days, of a time when tears will be wiped away from every eye and when, at long last, the killing and the bombing and the dying will cease. These are honest and sincerely held views – and yet they remain essentially superficial. The public outrage is froth. It never penetrates, or sinks far enough into, the complicated subterranean layers of Irish society; it never addresses the deep-seated, fundamental differences between Irish Nationalism and Unionism. The occasional peace movements which arise somehow contrive to convey the impression that the bombings and the shootings can be swept away on a wave of public disgust and by a few spirited renditions of 'We shall overcome', but, when the singing stops and the echoes of rousing speeches fade into the night, people retreat to their ghettos, entrenched and separate, deeply divided and never fully a part of the whole.

5

Nothing to Say

I'd stand at the back of the train and, as it pulled out of the station, I shouted: 'I just want you to think of this – I have absolutely nothing to say.'
ROBERT REDFORD, *promoting his film* The Candidate *on a*
whistle-stop tour

IN 1971 Robert Redford made *The Candidate*. It provided a cynical view of how a man sells out all his principles and his lofty ideals for a seat in the US Senate. To promote the movie it was decided that Redford should emulate the great American tradition of the political whistle-stop tour on a cross-country train. The idea was that the actor should follow that year's Democratic candidates into Miami. As Redford told the critic Iain Johnstone many years later, he managed to draw larger crowds than the real candidates, Lindsay, McGovern, Jackson and Muskie. His standard speech, which was a deliberate attempt to focus people's attention on the sterility of so much of American presidential campaigning, was that he had nothing to say. The crowds turned out none the less to see the famous actor and to cheer the message. Perhaps they felt it was not so very different from a number of other speeches they had heard that year.

I found reporting the 1980 Reagan presidential campaign not dissimilar to the Redford experience. Tracking a presidential candidate across the vast and awesome beauty of the United States allows the journalist an unrivalled opportunity to take the pulse of the nation. It was also the most tremendous fun. Many years afterwards it is still possible to recapture the exhilaration of waking up, after a late arrival the night before, to dawn in Galveston, Texas, or Savannah, Georgia, racing to a campaign stop in some obscure town in Illinois or Pennsylvania, or travelling through New England in the fall, when the colours on the trees range from brown to burnished gold. Exhausting cross-country trips were sustained for me by a sense of discovery. American presidential politics are lyrical compositions of the endlessly fascinating and the totally absurd. Reagan's campaigns were no exception.

By common consent, when Ronald Reagan won the guber-natorial election for the first time in California, he had entered real politics with the fresh, uncomplicated eye of a total beginner. Put another way, he knew nothing about it. He was later to claim that his role in the Actors' Guild or trade union afforded him a valuable insight into politics, unions and people. That assertion had more to do with his penchant for a good story than his devotion to fact. We have it on the authority of one of his closest aides in the California days that Reagan arrived in big state politics with minimal knowledge of what he was getting into and with no philosophy of what he wanted to do. He had 'no political background, no political cronies and no political machine. He hadn't even run his own campaign.' These may have been fine qualifications for running California, but the problem posed in the presidential campaign, when he ran against the Democrat's Jimmy Carter, seemed much more serious. Reagan had accumulated no vast knowledge of public affairs in an American sense and his understanding of international politics was circumscribed less by the little he knew than by his life-long prejudices. He had the ability, though, to express his prejudices as positive statements of policy. With little or no intellectual content, his speeches were constructed around so-called 'Reagan ideas'. These were home spun, stubborn and compulsive. He had a strong belief in indi-vidual freedom, although his definition of what that meant could be tryingly narrow. He believed in conventional morality and in patriotism, and he had a passionate hatred of Communism. At many points in his career he would pin the Communist label on any left of centre government which was perceived to be acting against American interests.

This uncomplicated view of life, with no real knowledge of the world at large, was reinforced by continual references to the glories of the past. As one of the oldest candidates to run for the office of President, Reagan saw himself as a reassuring link with the values of old America. To him this was a mythical land of successful people who inhabited an imaginary realm of small towns, where problems were always solved and where there were always happy endings. 'Happy endings' was a persistent Reagan theme, used to obscure the fact that there were aspects of the present which needed to be changed. It was tailor-made for American television coverage of a presidential race.

During the campaign Americans became immersed in the psychologically bruising process of watching their citizens subjected to humiliation and terror in Iran. Fellow citizens had been taken hostage in a foreign land; the American flag had been defiled. The American embassy in Teheran was under siege. Reagan had no answer to any of this, as he himself admitted: 'People say there are too many things I don't understand. And they are right. I don't understand why American hostages are being held in Iran. I don't understand why Americans are being held by tyrants in a foreign land.' He would then go on to preach of hopeful future days when on his 'watch' such national disgraces would never occur. Reagan began by preaching to a nation yearning for hope. It studied the national television news for signs. Thus it was that in the first Reagan race for the White House, presidential politics and television arrived at a most propitious confluence. Reagan the B movie actor revelled in the power of the medium. He had been given what every actor dreams of: the leading role. He looked good, delivered his lines well, was amiable and sincere, he said simple things simply, and he was happy to be told what to do and what to say. Difficult or troublesome issues were ignored – he believed in simple solutions. His campaign was unfailingly optimistic in tone, expressed faith in individual enterprise and in the certainty that American values were best. His speeches would frequently describe America as 'the last best hope of mankind'.

Though it was easy to write of it disparagingly, Reagan's optimism was America's optimism. It struck a responsive chord with voters. American optimism is rooted in the continent's abundance and in the supposedly inalienable right of all Americans to share in that abundance. This is not always understood in Europe, say, where people's expectations have been circumscribed by a culture and a history of struggle and scarcity. Reagan's optimistic political rhetoric was *the* essential American message; it was also a part of the man. Long after he had become President, I met his one time Budget Director, David Stockman, who had come to London to promote his book. Stockman enjoyed telling a story which showed how far Reagan took his optimistic view of life. It was about a young child whose father had promised him a bicycle for Christmas. Came Christmas morning and all the child could see, right in the centre of the living-room, was a huge pile of horse manure. The child's optimism was so strong that he plunged into the smelly mess, knowing that somewhere in the manure, there must be a bicycle. In Reaganland treasures lived in unexpected places and even the darkest night foretold the glories of a bright and hopeful dawn.

Occasionally, the candidate would stumble on to dangerous ground. Reagan had no head for facts, he had a life long allergy to detail and he garbled the truth even when he recognised it. As Kafka said of one of his characters, 'No matter what he says, something is missing.' On one memorable occasion Reagan felt he should make a contribution to the debate about the environment. Since this was an issue which had come to popular attention at a time when Reagan was long past middle age, he could summon nothing from the past to help him. He was lost. Forced to address the question of pollution in the 1980 campaign, he offered the view that some pollution was natural because the giant redwood trees let off as much carbon-dioxide as anything. Trees that caused pollution – vintage Reagan. He had, of course, mixed up the gases. His aides did a splendid job of clearing up the embarrassment, making light hearted fun of it in such a way that no criticism ever clung to their 'Teflon man' – to whom nothing stuck. One evening, as the campaign plane headed across California, one of Reagan's people pointed to the trees and gestured to the accompanying press: 'Look down there,' he said, 'them's killer trees!' On other occasions the boss launched into strangely apocalyptic meanderings about a coming 'Biblical Armageddon' and even suggested that South Africa under P. W. Botha, that dinosaur of the apartheid era, was a fair model for democracy. It is chastening to ponder whether America's later policy of 'constructive engagement' with Pretoria may have been based all along on a perverse misapprehension.

Ignorance about matters high on the public agenda was not this candidate's only fault. Reagan had an unpleasant record of ignoring facts which were unpalatable and of making up others when they suited his purpose, even if they were shown to be demonstrably false. While he was Governor of California, Reagan bluntly refused to acknowledge that members of his staff had been dismissed for homosexual activities. Although he knew precisely what had been discovered and was aghast at the discovery, he closed his mind to the unpleasant truth. In a brilliant book about Reagan, Robert Dallek gives a fascinating account of Reagan's philosophy and the way in which he was able, when it suited him, to cut himself free from all thoughts of reality. He writes about Reagan's second term gubernatorial campaign:

> Although he had made no significant headway in reducing the size and the cost of government, that did not deter him from once more making it his campaign theme. Even though he had

been Governor for four years, he campaigned as if he were going to Sacramento to clean up the mess someone else had left behind. The tone was set in a confidential cabinet memo in which Reagan called for an 'all out war on the tax-taker. If we fail, no one ever again will be able to try. We must succeed.' The focus of the attack was to be welfare, which he described during the election as 'the greatest domestic problem facing the nation today and the reason for the high cost of government'. Also playing on the resentment of the middle class toward anti-Vietnam war activists attacking the American system, Reagan declared his faith in the decency, generosity and fairness of the nation's treatment of disadvantaged peoples at home and abroad. 'It is time we ended our obsession with what is wrong and realise what is right.'

That was Reagan on the campaign trail, short on hard facts about the record of his administration and unable to face up to the degree to which he had failed to deliver what he had earlier promised. Many years later, as President, the tendency toward make believe would become more pronounced. Reagan would proclaim celluloid movie heroes as real life people, confuse battles fought in Hollywood studios sets with real life engagements in World War Two, and make up stories, while pretending they were real, to demolish an opponent's argument. The conservative columnist William Safire coined the word 'anecdotage' to categorise a kind of Reagan statement, such as the one in which he saw 'battalions of welfare queens, students investing loans monies in money market funds, and rich children getting free school lunches'. He had the extraordinary ability to live in the fantasy land of his own creation.

Running a presidential candidate of such obvious limitations, his public relations handlers devised a brilliant strategy: it was to play to his strengths, and to hide his many weaknesses. Roughly translated, that meant giving the candidate the appropriate stage, discouraging him from attempting to articulate views about complex issues and, above all, it meant keeping the press at arm's length. It worked to perfection. Reagan had few friends among the working press and never felt the need to share any thoughts with them. On his campaign plane he never left his forward cabin to talk to those reporting his tours; waving to them was about as far as he ever got. One *Washington Post* reporter quipped that 'covering Reagan means having to say you never saw him'.

Reporters could observe the candidate in action only at campaign stops, when he delivered his set speeches. I watched numerous such performances. Reagan would talk about getting government off the backs of people. After a while this acquired the status of a mantra, the solution to all the problems known to man. He would talk about keeping America strong, curbing the rise of Communism and making America respected abroad, without ever committing American lives in battle. He talked hardly at all about his country's social problems; instead he preached the value of individual initiative and of the free enterprise system. Issues such as civil rights found no place on the Reagan agenda. The respected civil rights activist and Supreme Court Judge Thurgood Marshall said Ronald Reagan had the worst record on civil rights of any American President since the war.

Since reporters were kept away if the candidate failed to raise an issue, there was no way the press could raise it with him. That was the essence of his campaign strategy, and by and large the press had little option but to follow meekly. There are many examples of the way in which this distorted the campaign. Throughout the 1980 race for the White House Reagan travelled the length and breadth of America saying that it was possible to 'increase defence spending, cut taxes and balance the budget'. A leader of a political party in Britain would have been crucified in the newspapers and on television had he or she been unable to produce the arithmetic to show how this unrealistic proposition was likely to work. Reagan got away with it. George Bush's comment before he joined the ticket that Reagan's plans were 'voodoo economics' was repeated only as a terrific line from a man who was usually incapable of them. One night in a Dallas hotel I had a long conversation with one of Ronald Reagan's principal press operatives, Lynn Nofziger. Acknowledging that no political system anywhere had all the answers to an open political process, I said I was astonished at how 'closed' to the press the candidate had become. As a British journalist in an election where we were quite properly regarded as second-class citizens with no ability to influence American voters, I had never been under any illusions about getting close to the candidate myself, but, as I pointed out to Mr Nofziger, neither had our American counterparts. I was particularly struck by the fact that, throughout the campaign, I had seen no proper in-depth interview with Reagan about domestic and foreign policy. No one, I said, had really put him to the test on his tax cuts and balanced budgets plan. Then, unfortunately, I destroyed my chance of putting Nofziger on the spot by suggesting that under the press scrutiny of a British General Election campaign, in which a candidate was expected to answer close and continual enquiries about his beliefs and his policies, Reagan might not find it such an easy ride.

Lynn Nofziger listened carefully to my comparative study of political campaigns on either side of the Atlantic. Shaking the ice in his glass, he replied with a shrug, 'We don't allow long television interviews because we want our candidate to survive.'

That night in Dallas we had all just returned to the hotel from a typical Reagan rally, where the bands had played inspirational American favourites, drum majorettes had paraded up and down the main body of the hall with tremendous precision and style and Roy Rodgers had appeared (or was it Dale Evans?) with a horse, only to be superseded by the leading American football player. The 4,000 people in the hall had been in ecstasy. Such had been the hype and the atmosphere that the candidate was required to say little in order to receive a standing ovation after every line. I do not remember much about the speech apart from Reagan being wildly applauded for saying about something or the other, 'You ain't seen nothing yet.' And he had told marvellous anecdotes about optimism, bravery and about what he called 'the American spirit'. The audience hung on his every word.

Some years ago a British psychiatrist described how it was possible to whip people into a frenzy of emotion and susceptibility in advance of the main event at a political rally, an evangelical revival or a pop concert. The psychiatrist argued that, to some extent, the tactic had been used at Beatles concerts – witness, he said, the uncontrollably hysterical teenagers – and at Hitler rallies in Nuremburg. I felt something similar about that evening in Dallas. If the gist of the speech was not memorable, the atmosphere was unforgettable. Outside the huge stadium as we left, I saw the effect this had on the faithful: there were a handful of demonstrators campaigning against Reagan's stand on abortion – they were attacked and almost ripped limb from limb by the Republican Party faithful, fired up by their candidate's words and the hysteria of the evening. In one blinding flash, centuries of democratic tradition and free speech seemed about to be replaced by mob rule and anarchy.

There was one interesting footnote to my presence at that Dallas election rally. At one point in the proceedings, a man tapped me on the shoulder: it was Harvey Thomas, who was then at the Conservative Party Central Office. I enquired, rather naively as it turned out, what had brought him to Texas for this event. He was disarmingly honest; he said he had come to learn and he invited me to remember what I had seen that night when the next big Margaret Thatcher election rally was held at Wembley. When, later, I did attend that rally, I came to the conclusion that Mr Thomas's ticket had been worth the money.

Meanwhile, however, the Reagan bandwagon rolled on from Texas to the Carolinas, on to glorious New Orleans, then up through the Mid-West and back to the open spaces of California.

The speeches were always the same – home-spun remedies and clichés, optimistic rhetoric about 'morning in America' and about making America 'a shining city on the hill' – and no questions from anyone. The pictures which reached the living-rooms of millions of Americans every night were of staged events with all the spontaneity of May Day parades in Moscow.

The media had scant choice but to play the Reagan game. In a campaign singularly bereft of issues, we all became obsessed by how the opinion polls rated the candidates. That gave Mr Reagan's handlers minimal trouble. His was unquestionably the triumph of the 'sound bite' and Reagan's mastery of that put him almost beyond all reasonable challenge.

It was thought by some that the presidential debates would redress the balance. The Reagan/Carter debates did not. I reported the final one in Cincinnati, Ohio. Nobody was allowed to pursue any promising line of questioning and the participants were never required to give specific answers. It looked less like a presidential debate than a political beauty contest. Reagan, the Hollywood man, was destined to do well. When Carter tried ineptly to steer the debate to world affairs, Reagan said with his genial, lopsided grin that he believed in world peace and that force would only be used as a last resort. When Carter, back on domestic policy, accused his opponent of once having opposed Medicare, Reagan, still grinning, said, 'There you go again,' and stole the show. The one-liner had been crowned king.

Reagan won the debate and went on to win the election by a landslide. Carter, overwhelmed by the issue of American hostages in Iran and beset by a sea of economic troubles, lost badly. Cynics were quick to spot Carter's other major problem: attempting to deal with the issues with clumsy seriousness, he had been slain by the deadly sound bite. The other losers were the American voters, who might have hoped for a more vibrant discussion of national problems and priorities. Instead they were given news about the campaign, which was treated as a commodity and sold as soap powder. Fundamental questions about where America was heading never had a chance.

It must also be said that photogenic Mr Reagan, master of the well-honed speech, demonstrated throughout the campaign an unbeatable asset: to a degree unmatched by almost any other politician in contemporary history he had the common, likeable touch. I once asked the conservative columnist George Will, at one time very close to the Reagans, to help me explain Reagan's appeal to a British television audience. Will thought for a moment and said, 'Look, it's partly the fact that he appears such a nice guy. You feel you can invite him to dinner and he wouldn't steal the spoons.' If Reagan was uncomfortable with facts, he found his true métier in stagecraft and before friendly crowds. As more than one commentator has noted, he shared a strange kind of alchemy with the American public; the great communicator would happily perform with and for them. It was Hollywood all over again. I saw it clearly at a campaign stop in Raleigh, North Carolina, one sparkling summer evening. After Reagan had given his set speech, he was invited by a number of basketball fans to have a go at throwing the ball into the basket. I know several politicians who would have politely declined the chance to make a fool of themselves in the presence of a sell-out crowd and with the cameras recording every move for the other millions at home. Reagan, however, accepted both the ball and the challenge with a good-natured grin, before stepping a respectable distance from the basket to have a go. When the first two shots missed, men not made of sterner stuff might have recoiled from the challenge and given up. And Reagan was in friendly country here and giving up after two attempts would have been no disgrace. But that is not the actor's way. If part of a scene does not work, the actor tries and tries again. That evening Reagan did. His third throw rose into the air and, urged on by the hopes of thousands looking on, spun right down the middle of the basket. The acclamation almost blew the roof off the hall. It was a tremendous performance, and what a picture for the television news stories that evening. The former Democratic Congressional Speaker, Thomas P. 'Tip' O'Neill said of Reagan: 'There's something about the guy that people like. They want him to be a success. They're rooting for him.' They rooted for him that evening in North Carolina, and he succeeded.

The incident demonstrated another cardinal rule about the politics of the Reagan years: as with Hollywood, the image, the picture was king – almost nothing else mattered. It was true of the presidential campaigns as it was true of the Reagan presidency. One White House correspondent tells the story of having done a critical report about the Reagan presidency on the main evening news on television. To make her points, she had used footage of staged Reagan events. The commentary, though, was fairly hostile. Because the administration tended to take umbrage at any criticism, she was rather worried about the reception she would find the following morning at the White House. She felt her concern was justified when no one mentioned her broadcast the night before. She had been frozen out. Unable to bear the suspense of not being spoken to, she asked several White House staffers whether they had seen her story. They all said they had, but made no further comment. By then bursting with the need to be told something, even to be openly criticised about what she done, she pressed her enquiry. She confronted an administration official: 'What did you think of my report?' Back came the reply: 'Great.' The correspondent was puzzled. 'Which bits did you like?' she persisted. 'All of it,' was the response. Only after the conversation had gone further did she discover the truth: the White House had watched the news story with the sound turned down and had loved the pictures of the President at various events. Marshall McLuhan could never have predicted the medium would so completely become the message. To the framers of that message, the directors of the Reagan campaign, the candidate had ceded control.

Jane Mayer and Doyle McManus, writing in the book *Landslide* concluded:

> This detachment from daily decision-making suited Reagan's temperament. Unlike most of his predecessors – men like Lyndon Johnson and Richard Nixon, who were obsessed with controlling all the facets of power – Reagan was aloof, even disengaged. His lack of vanity or curiosity enabled him to stay serenely removed from most of the machinations around him. Although they took care to portray him publicly as forceful and vigorous, his campaign advisers saw the other side. One conceded: 'The President was never really involved in any of the planning or strategy of the campaign. He'd make some small talk some of the time ... but there was never any real inquisitive effort to get to the nitty gritty. I don't think he ever focused on it. The truth of the matter is that Ronald Reagan is a perfect candidate. He does whatever you want him to do. And he does it superbly.'

Any one of Robert Redford's film directors would be hard pressed to pay an actor a higher compliment.

The Reagan campaign showed beyond question the way the race for the presidency can be stage managed – as are most campaigns at this high level. Reagan's reached the apotheosis of the art, however. I covered only a small amount of American domestic politics during Reagan's first term, but I was back in Washington to see the President's conversion to the belief in arms control agreements. The fascination of this stemmed partly from the fact that Reagan's hatred of Communism and the Soviet Union was legendary. He had once denounced the Soviets as liars and cheats who could never be trusted to observe the spirit of any bilateral treaty. To anyone not quite sure where the President stood on the question of the old Soviet Union, he said of them in another speech: 'Let us be aware that, while they preach the supremacy of the state, declare its omnipotence over individual man, and predict its eventual domination of all the peoples of the earth – they are the focus of evil in the modern world.'

By his second term Reagan was looking for something new to do. He had succeeded in scaring the hell out of the Soviets with his plans to bury them in the arms race. At great cost to America, his administration had made decisions on costly MX missiles. Now the President had conceived an even costlier idea: the science fiction solution of a space shield which would protect civilians in the event of a nuclear holocaust.

According to White House aides, Nancy Reagan had become concerned about her husband's image, anxious that he should concentrate on his place in history. She herself had come to see the presidency essentially as a performance requiring a 'big finish'. A number of other people close to her husband had viewed presidential politics in exactly that way. Stuart Spencer, once an influential Reagan aide, confirmed it. He said, 'Politics is just like show business. You have to have a hell of an opening, coast for a while, and then have a hell of a close.' An arms control agreement with the Soviets would be a 'hell of a close'.

It was greatly assisted by Mikhail Gorbachev, whose flirtations with reforming his country convinced him that he could do very little unless he first managed to curb Moscow's economically crippling expenditure on armaments. To do that he needed American help. Thus the stage was set. Although Reagan did not succeed in Iceland, he persuaded Gorbachev to agree to go to Washington and sign a treaty limiting intermediate-range nuclear weapons. It was an important agreement and a theatrically perfect occasion. The President learnt a Russian proverb for the summit and used it whenever Gorbachev loomed into view. He never once sensed that his guest was becoming terribly bored by its repetition. A senior official in the White House explained to me one afternoon, shortly after we had broadcast the signing of the agreement live on ITN, why the President was so pleased by Gorbachev's visit. Reagan's belief in his country was so unshakeable that he felt, if a Russian leader could be shown the wonders of America, he would in all probability abandon Communist ideology and beg for political asylum. That was why Reagan had wanted to take the Soviet leader on a tour of America. Unfortunately Gorbachev had declined. The momentum for more bilateral agreements did not slacken, though, and in due course the Reagans were invited to Moscow. I tried to imagine Reagan's thoughts as he set foot on Russian soil for the first time to a welcome ceremony of goose-stepping soldiers. Having no real work to do, since the agreements had been secured beforehand, Reagan drank in the atmosphere. All that was required of him was to turn up for the ceremonial signing.

Everything went like clockwork. Late one evening I had a grandstand view from our office in the Russiya Hotel as the Gorbachevs took the Reagans for an after-dinner stroll around St Basil's Cathedral. It was a wonderful scene. St Basil's, floodlit, looked a picture. The crowds, surprised to see them, acclaimed the Reagans. Cameramen jostled to record the event for posterity. Here was the leader of the free world, a hero, in the camp of the enemy. What a script. In a wonderful transformation, Ronald Reagan had sealed a relationship with the man whose empire he had once denounced as evil, corrupt and inherently dishonest. The two crusty antagonists in the old Western film had reached across the crowded bar and shaken hands just before walking out into the sunset as the credits rolled. No film producer could have wished for more. 'Reagan conquers the Evil Empire', the billboard might have said, or 'The Reagans and the Gorbachevs – a thrilling climax to the story of worldly folk'.

In one breathtaking sweep the B movie actor had achieved the starring role of his life. With a panorama of stirring images and against a backdrop of the Kremlin's golden domes, the Reagan presidency was passing into legend. It was the kind of happy ending the old man sought all his life. He had finally starred in Russia. His own, real life version of Hollywood had gone to Moscow and triumphed.

The legacy of Reaganism in the USA was much less glamorous. In his determination to make Americans feel good about themselves and their country, Reagan avoided difficult issues and unpleasant truths. He led the country by pandering to its prejudices and by encouraging the belief that Americans had a right to consume without thought and to spend as much as they wanted. As the budget deficit continued to rise to unprecedented levels, the President talked about a costly Star Wars programme to protect America from the danger of intercontinental ballistic missiles, refusing to face up to the economic, scientific or diplomatic ramifications of such an idea. All of this might have encouraged Americans to grow smug, insensitive to some of their own problems and those of more fallible peoples. More than any other President, Reagan and his managers became obsessed by how their policies played rather than the effects they had. Perhaps that is why Nancy Reagan, according to some White House aides, turned to astrology to help determine when the President should take certain initiatives. The position of the heavenly bodies was probably as good a guide as any in the circumstances. The American political commentator and columnist Sidney Blumenthal put it well: 'The Reagan presidency may be best remembered as a succession of *tableaux vivants* staged by the directors and producers of his White House.' Blumenthal quotes Michael Deaver, Reagan's chief press impresario, as openly acknowledging the way in which the press were manipulated to give an appearance of considered presidential policy. Deaver saw the press as indispensable bit part players, performing the functions of key grip, camera operator, sound recordist, gaffer and best boy. He said with commendable frankness: 'I never thought of going round the Washington press corps. We planned several weeks in advance what our story was going to be every day. The media were like starlings on a line.'

6

Reading Their Lips

I generally favour the goals as outlined in the Great Society –
a better life for all, elimination of poverty and disease, fair
play in civil rights. You know, I took some of the far Right
positions to get elected. I hope I never do it again. I regret it.
Read my lips: no new taxes.

GEORGE BUSH

I SPENT more time reporting the 1988 American Presidential
Campaign than any other, watching the Republicans and the
Democrats slug it out in the early primaries, and following Senator
Robert Dole through the Deep South before at last catching up
with Jack Kemp and George Bush in the Carolinas by Super
Tuesday. I reported Michael Dukakis's campaign swing through
the Rust Belt and down across the frontier states. We caught up
with Jessie Jackson in Mississippi and stayed to hear him preach
in one of the cradles of the Civil Rights Movement, the Ebenezer
Baptist Church in Atlanta. Ebenezer is a small white-painted building with brilliant red carpets and hard, shiny mahogany benches.
The building's structure is too modest for the size of its reputation.
In the tradition from which it draws its inspiration, it is both a
church and school. It is the place where Martin Luther King
preached, shaking the nation out of its sullen apathy about the
dispossession of Black Americans. To both those who had known
King and those who had not, listening to Jackson recall his words
was an emotionally stirring experience.

Unfettered by any reasonable expectation that he would be

elected President or even that he would win his Party's nomination, Jackson, unlike his fellow candidates, could speak his mind on the many social ills facing America. He could afford the luxury of political honesty. It was frequently alleged that his politics were naive, that his statement of problems and his approach to their solution was much too simplistic. That was probably true; but his arguments compelled thought and his persistent hammering away at basic themes eventually demanded attention. For example, Jackson could never understand why it was possible to spend so many millions of dollars on new sophisticated weapons of mass destruction and yet found it so difficult to devise a system to help poorer Americans. Talking about the issue of education during the 1988 presidential race, Jackson told me:

> It is not unusual in urban America to have a 40–50 per cent drop out rate from the first grade to the twelfth grade, so you have a growing number of young people who are functionally illiterate. In the long run, ignorance costs more than education. A state university in America costs less than $40,000 over four years. It costs $160,000 to keep a person in jail for four years. In Washington this year about 3,000 seniors graduated from high school, but there are about 12,000 people from Washington in jail. Yet the President is calling for more jails, not more schools.

On the controversial issue of abortion, Jackson could be very direct: 'The essence of freedom is choice.' He found it impossible to understand Washington's failure to speak out more often and more openly about the evils of apartheid. He felt and said explicitly that the Reagan administration's position on sanctions was one of utter hypocrisy. Although sometimes with too little thought, Jackson encouraged the White House to demonstrate a more even handed approach to Arabs and Israelis in pursuing the goal of peace in the Middle East, and he continually reminded America of its honourable pledge to care for 'huddled masses and all those yearning to be free'. Singlehandedly he encouraged more Black

Americans to register to vote than his party had ever been able to do before. Seeing this as the unbeatable weapon in the fight for change, he reminded Black Americans in speeches across the country that 'the hands that once picked cotton can now pick a President'. It was a call to arms more powerful than any other in modern politics. Encouraging people to show pride in themselves and in what they did, Jackson would chant and demand that his audiences said after him, 'I am somebody, I am somebody.' One of his many biographers has written that 'his somebody battlecry is reinforced by similar slogans to motivate, to inspire, to reverse the prevalent feeling of "nobodyness"'. He proclaimed his constituency 'a rainbow collection' and sanctified it with the slogan: 'Black, brown, yellow and white, we're all precious in God's sight.' Where Reagan preached the optimism of those who lived in his shining city on the hill, Jackson knew the darkness and turbulence of the human condition, yet counselled against despair. He identified with the downtrodden, the forgotten and the left out, urging them to 'Keep hope alive'. He was also fond of saying, 'Tears flow, blood flows, but hold on, the morning comes.'

Wherever we found him on the trail, Jackson gave the presidential election a powerful charge, he created its excitement. The force of his message and his charisma transformed mundane meetings into memorable ones. Throughout the campaign he proved to be the most inspirational speaker on the political scene. In one particularly rousing finale to a convention speech he encapsulated his beliefs about the power of the vote, the position of women and their importance to society and the country. To sustained shouts of acclamation and in ever rising cadences, he said: 'When Black people vote in great numbers, women and children benefit; when women and children benefit, society benefits; when society benefits, we all benefit. We must all come up together. We must come up together.' Jackson talked about children a great deal. He understood the pain of the children of the poor, but he always saw, even in their suffering, the hope of a better future. That is why they

85

could not be written off and their talents left to rot in the wasteland of urban American slums. His political message seemed to echo the words of William Blake that 'Grace' is underwritten by speechless suffering and by the future of children. I watched him tell a young audience in Harlem, 'You may be in the slum, but the slum doesn't have to be in you. Freedom ain't free. It must be earned. It's not the *altitude* that determines how high you fly – it's your *attitude.*'

Jackson's failings as a politician are much debated. He is frequently guilty of overstating his case – hyperbole a close companion to his sermonising. When his hot gospel rhetoric is in full flow, he can make unpardonable errors, although his fulsome apologies have been known to move audiences to tears. Jackson can be arrogant, tetchy, disorganised and can display an ego not always matched by his ability. I once asked an American television colleague what he felt Jackson would do next. Not naturally unsympathetic to the preacher politician, after pondering for a while, he told me: 'Oh, I think Jesse Jackson will continue to be what he's always been – a great big pain in the ass.' Such a comment may be a trifle unfair, but Jackson has always aroused strong passions, a factor he would probably count as one of the major assets of his campaigns.

The most serious charge against him is that he appears to relish the role of guerrilla fighter, never wanting the responsibility of governance. He lacks direction and, for example, has shown no inclination to run for Congress. Although he wants the glamour of a high profile, to be a star on the presidential hustings, he refuses to pursue the art of patient power-building. Jackson wants to be the maverick, forever sniping from the outside; indeed, he has been at times a very divisive force, even in his main constituency.

In 1988, however, he made his party and his country listen. By putting the voice and the concerns of Black Americans prominently on the agenda, he made himself and his message difficult to ignore. In the 1988 campaign the candidate who ran closest to the eventual Democratic Party nominee was the Reverend Jesse Jackson. In the complex grammar of American politics, it was never seriously believed that Dukakis and the Democratic Party brahmins would choose Jackson as his vice presidential running mate, but that was more a reflection of the party and American politics than it was about Jackson's ability to do the job.

In the end, Jackson's failings were America's failings. He preached the politics of hope, which in itself was a failing since the enthusiasm generated by his campaign created the belief, the misplaced faith, that a radical departure in American politics was possible. It was not, and Jackson must have known that. He lacked the power, the will and the means to make it happen; in fact, many of his ideas had more sound than substance. His 'rainbow coalition', far from being practical, was an almost surreal idea in a country which yearns to think of itself as a 'melting pot', but where divisions of class, sex, religion, race and colour are as profound now as they were before John Kennedy pioneered changes in civil rights and before Lyndon Johnson launched his Great Society.

At the 1988 Democratic Convention in Atlanta, Jackson nevertheless rallied the party to his 'rainbow coalition' call. I watched his speech from the excitement of the convention floor. When it ended, people were moved to tears by the high emotional charge. A strange joy swept the hall: people of all colours and races joined hands and held them aloft, singing and dancing and swaying to the inspirational music of the convention band. Jackson had long before lost his party's nomination, but had done the decent thing in exhorting it to victory. The occasion was a celebration and a requiem for the idea of a 'rainbow coalition' across the broad spectrum of American politics. Jackson's call had been a failure.

Yet his personality carried him to unexpected heights. I cherish, above all, one abiding memory of how Jesse Jackson made himself a player on the Washington political scene, despite the seeming irrelevance of his political message. Eclipsing efforts by the Reagan administration, Jackson went to Syria and returned to Washington with Lieutenant Goodman, a Black pilot who had been captured by the Syrians. President Reagan could do no less than graciously consent to receive Goodman, Jackson and their entourage in the White House Rose Garden. There is a marvellous picture of the members of the Reagan cabinet – I remember George Shultz in particular – straining to catch a glimpse of and take in the extraordinary sight of Jackson savouring his moment of triumph. The expressions on the faces of several members of the Reagan team ranged from shock to total incomprehension; as a group they were looking at Jesse Jackson with the studied care and wariness of a man who has seen a suspicious package and has heard it ticking.

Not for the first time, Jackson surprised his opponents. The man with no recognisable power base, but with a compelling message for modern America, forced the Government to salute what he'd singlehandedly done.

If Jesse Jackson failed to convince his party he would be a bankable electoral asset in 1988, George Bush, having won the Republican nomination, experienced some difficulty in convincing his party he could emulate Reagan and win. The real problem for anyone seeking the job of Reagan's successor was that the Reagan presidency was an impossible act to follow. No one else would have been able to survive in the White House for so long by imitating the Reagan administration's blend of passion and detachment, indolence and commitment. For George Herbert Walker Bush the problem of succeeding Reagan was even more acute because he had been thoroughly compromised by the Reagan presidency – he had been made to swallow the undigestible and he had been forced by the loyalty demanded of his position to keep his counsel. It might have been assumed that this had been easy for Bush. Throughout his life, he had acquired the propensity of taking on, mainly for the sake of convenience, the political colouration of his surroundings. This tactic had, on occasions, worked to his advantage, although it had also sometimes been a

puzzle even to those who knew him well, but his political contortions were not natural assets to a man seeking to represent the
passions of his people at home and the interests of his country
abroad. Indeed it was a substantial drawback that nobody could
put a finger on who George Bush was or what he believed in, and
the fact that he had spent a lifetime in some of the highest political
offices in the land did not noticeably help. Bush had represented
his country at the United Nations, had been American Ambassador
in China, had been head of the CIA and Vice President, and yet
any definition of what Bush stood for remained opaque.

If he had a clear political philosophy in 1988, he kept it a closely
guarded secret. The point was, though, that George Bush had
never been forced by any circumstance to parade, confess or make
a boast about his politics. The Bushes, Yankee aristocrats who
traced their ancestry back to the Pilgrim Fathers, felt solid enough
in the ambience of wealthy America not to have to make too big
a point about who they were or where they came from. Bush
grew up in an atmosphere of corporate executives, landowners,
investors and country club members, where money was the
common denominator and stated political positions had never
been important. Bush's American is patrician, unassuming and
understated. The political commentator Kevin Phillips wrote: 'The
America Bush truly represented was that of old multigenerational
wealth – of trust funds, third generation summer cottages on
Fisher's Island and grandfathers with the Wall Street bankers
Dillon Read or Brown Brothers, Harriman – which accepted the
economic policy of the Reagan era despite its distaste for its
arriviste values.'

When Bush began his campaign to follow Ronald Reagan into
the White House, what people remembered above all was that he
had compromised. They felt that whatever views he held when he
ran against Reagan in 1980 had been buried by Reaganism and
by the Reagan presidency. In the 1980 campaign Bush was the
bright spark who had predicted that Reagan would fail in his

promise to cut taxes, increase defence spending and balance the budget – and he had been proved absolutely right. Once in the administration, however, he had been forced to admit he was sorry he had ever said such a thing and once almost begged reporters to stop reminding him of his differences with the Reagan philosophy. That was the essence of the George Bush problem: he had been compelled to disavow his views even when he knew they made sense. Diluting what he genuinely believed, political boxing and coxing were the arts Bush had been forced to learn in his job as Reagan's Veep – he had been the faithful lieutenant – but the reputation of being a political contortionist stuck and was frequently painful.

His dilemma was neatly encapsulated in the 1988 campaign in a telling political commercial masterminded by the Democratic Party, which we made good use of on British television as we tried to show why Bush was finding it so difficult to get on terms with his Democratic opponent. The commercial opened with a brilliant winter scene and with the camera focused on two feet crunching uncertainly across a snow-covered field. The commentary went something like this: 'For more than twenty years George Bush has held some of the highest offices in the land, yet we have no idea what he's done. He has no record. He's left no footprints.' To match the voice-over the commercial showed two feet plunging into the snow and disappearing without the trace of a footprint. It was a stinging attack and set the agenda for Bush's 1988 campaign strategy.

The first priority was to try to spell out the candidate's vision of America and its future. In not untypical Bush-speak, he later came to refer to is as 'the vision thing'. It was a serious political problem. Unlike many of his contemporaries who had entered politics to 'change the world', George Bush had no such ambition, no great need to be President; he had merely followed the direction in which a privileged life had taken him. He wanted to be President because he had been Vice President. The presidency was desirable because it was the next stop on the line. Bush wanted to 'serve'. 'Service' was an important concept in his make-up, and he wanted to go to the White House simply, in his own words, to fulfil 'the honour of it all'.

Such aims were not easy to define during the campaign; in any event Bush has never been brilliant at putting together words which formed coherent sentences or thoughts which conveyed much common sense. His language has never been that of the Yale man he was. His knowledge of his country and of the world, as one observer put it, never seemed to go beyond the country club set, where people talked of honour and playing by the rules, and where a man was judged by the way he looked you in the eye and by the firmness of his grasp. Although he has given countless political speeches in his very public life, he has never overcome the tendency to mangle his syntax and to inflict on the language a most terrible mauling. Even today his utterances on diplomacy or domestic issues are strangulated and ungrammatical.

Very frequently, attempting what seemed the simplest of constructions, he would succeed only in leaving his audiences in a daze of incomprehension. Defending his choice of Dan Quayle as his vice presidential running mate, he once said, with a kind of bizarre intensity, 'My running mate took the lead, was the author of the Job Training Partnership Act. Now, because of a lot of smoke and frenzying of bluefish out there, going after a drop of blood in the water, nobody knows that.' Long after Bush became President the words kept tumbling out in meaningless torrents. In New Hampshire he quoted lyrics from a group called the Nitty Gritty Dirt Band. Bush renamed them 'Nitty Ditty Nitty Great Bird'. And in one celebrated attempt to sound totally contemptuous of Saddam Hussein he intoned, 'When I need a little free advice from Saddam Hussein, I turn to country music.'

This total lack of rhetorical competence alarmed his campaign staff. One of his aides confessed to me on a flight taking us to a campaign stop in the industrial North-West that 'the candidate could blow the whole thing sky high' if he were left to his own devices. So, in addition to their task of trying to get the candidate to define where he stood on the major issues, Bush's aides had the additional problem of keeping him on a tight leash. He would never be allowed to stray too far from prepared remarks.

The Bush campaign also adopted the Reagan campaign creed: at all costs keep the candidate away from the press. Unlike Reagan, Bush would occasionally come to the back of the plane to chat, but never seriously to discuss issues. In the full flow of his presidential run, he was never too discriminating about whose hands he shook, but no questions, please, by order of the campaign team. We could talk to campaign manager James Baker for hours, but not to the candidate. The Baker team managed to take this to embarrassing extremes by rigging the structure of presidential debates so that there was never a hope of pressing Bush to explain his position on any single issue. The format for the debates had been devised simply to allow the candidates to make well rehearsed statements no matter what the question and this proved so exasperating to everyone that even the American League of Women voters, who had traditionally sponsored the debates, announced in a huff that they wished to distance themselves from the charade. That did not worry Baker and his team one little bit; they stuck to their plan with iron-clad firmness. The big American television networks were given some access, but only when it suited James Baker's plans. For the rest of time, they huffed and they puffed, but they could not shake the essential fundaments of Baker's campaign strategy. Once again an American presidential candidate had carefully rationed access by the media.

None of this, though, took care of the other Bush problem: who he was and what he believed in. Years of trimming his beliefs to suit the political mood of the time had left its mark. At the beginning of his campaign for the presidency one Reagan aide commented, 'Grappling with Bush is like beating up on air. He likes to think of himself as a pragmatist, but pragmatists know where they're going. I don't know where George Bush is going or where he's taking us. I don't think that he does either.'

To follow the early days of the Bush campaign was to be convinced that the candidate had no real message. Equally serious was the fact that it became increasingly difficult to determine where the candidate stood on the major talking points of the campaign. Where did Bush really stand on welfare, on civil rights, on law and order? In 1970, for example, he had nailed his colours to the mast on abortion, an issue of persistent controversy in contemporary American politics, when he had said: 'I personally feel that women should have the freedom to choose or not choose an abortion.' By the 1980s, when he had begun to try to impress the new political crowd in Washington, he had changed his mind. Not that he was prepared even then to make too many unequivocal pronouncements on the issue. And what plans did he have for correcting the awesome imbalances in the economy with its bur-geoning budget deficit? Bush's answer appeared to change, depend-ing on where he happened to find himself on the campaign trail. In downtown Los Angeles he talked about help for the dis-possessed; later that same day, to an altogether more wealthy audience, he hammered away at law and order and on his oppo-sition to gun control.

In attempting to articulate his views on some of these issues, Bush could not afford to be seen to be venturing too far from what had been done by the Reagan White House. Running in his own right, he none the less found himself imprisoned by the tenets of the outgoing administration. One of his aides admitted the problem quite openly: 'It was awkward for Bush to follow Reagan and claim he might do things differently. It wasn't easy for him to mark out new policy lines on major issues, especially if they appeared to be different from what the old man had done. And we couldn't say we intended to clean up the Reagan mess. We'd have to contemplate it, but without ever talking about it.'

Loyalty was not the sole consideration here. Bush, without a natural constituency of his own, desperately needed the support of the Reagan voters. He needed to sound much more conservative than he actually was, which got him into terrible trouble, of course, but he had no choice.

If George Bush wanted to keep the Reagan supporters with him, he had to turn a blind eye to the dangerously escalating budget deficit, and he had to lie. Throughout his run for the White House, whenever the question of the economy came up, Bush found himself in difficulty. Voters remembered his 'voodoo economics' comment about Reagan's plans, a phrase which had become ever more appropriate as Reagan's term in office drew to a close. Sensing that people really wanted to know about taxes, Bush or Baker coined the slogan 'Read my lips – no new taxes'. That was never going to be sustainable, however, and Bush knew it; he had said it under pressure from Bob Dole during the heat of primary election contests. On the other hand, it had several virtues. From a man who usually finds it difficult to express himself it seemed an almost clever response, it made a perfect 'sound bite' for the television evening news, and it contained a hint of the optimism which played so well for his predecessor. America could get by, it seemed to say, without facing the really difficult options. Budget deficits are the richer side of American abundance. Enjoy and have a nice day. The down side was not only that this declaration stood in the way of any reasoned discussion about how the budget deficit could be reduced. It killed debate stone dead.

In an effort to keep the Reagan conservatives on board, George Bush was forced into one of the biggest compromises of his life. On this occasion, according to those who claim to know, Bush overrode even the advice of his chief campaign strategist and friend, James Baker: he chose Dan Quayle as his vice presidential running mate. I will never forget dashing round in the heat of a New Orleans afternoon trying to find pundits who might be able to explain to a British television audience who the hell Dan Quayle was and why Bush had reached so far into the realm of political obscurity to find a running mate. Quayle, relatively unknown, with no conspicuously successful record in Congress and with the stigma of having somehow contrived to avoid going to Vietnam, brought with his unexpected elevation one great asset: he would be the keeper of the conservative flame in a Bush administration. Bush knew how much his candidacy needed that. As Barbara Bush once remarked in a moment of unusual honesty, George was not one of those political figures blessed with a 'natural constituency' sufficiently large or influential to win him office; he had been given many top jobs in the past, but he had never been elected to anything.

Thus did the Republicans begin the coronation of their candidate in the wonderful city of New Orleans. It was high summer, there were oysters to be eaten by the plateful in the late afternoons, there were scintillating evenings on Bourbon Street, with jazz and indecipherable cocktails in enormous glasses, and there were endless discussions with Senator John Tower about how the party would shape its platform to help the Republican cause. With a conservative on the ticket and with Ronald Reagan's carefully orchestrated visit to the convention to receive the acclaim of the faithful and then depart into history, the time had arrived for Bush to make Reagan's party his own.

For years he had been the fall guy of the Reagan White House. When it suited his purposes, he claimed to have been 'out of the loop' on scandalous matters such as the Iran Contra affair, in which money from the illegal sale of arms to Iran was secretly channelled into illegally supporting rebel forces in Nicaragua. Now he was on his own.

Although Bush had earlier beaten Robert Dole to the Republican nomination with his 'no new taxes' pledge, this was not playing too well in the country at large. Meanwhile, the democratic challenger, Michael Dukakis, had opened up a lead of seventeen points on the Republican candidate.

Dukakis was in truth the Democratic Party's second choice. A full year before the first primary Senator Gary Hart had infused life into the campaign with his election programme of 'new ideas'. I had followed his early progress across the country. His campaign had a rare freshness about it, generating real excitement, staffed in the main by young people whose hope for change shone brightly in their eyes. Young and dashing, Hart stirred warm memories of John Kennedy and Camelot, when the torch had passed to a new generation of Americans. Hart seemed to be on an unbeatable roll. In the words of American commentator David Remnick, 'At the start of the 1988 presidential campaign, he had been headed, as if on the greased chute of destiny, for the White House.' Then, in a moment of monumental arrogance, he tried to take on the press and make fools of them. Suspected of carrying on extramarital liaisons, he invited the press to follow him around. He told the *New York Times*, 'I don't care. I'm serious. If anybody wants to put a tail on me, go ahead. They'd be very bored.' The press had the last laugh, although the climax of the episode was almost too painful to be made fun of. Hart was caught in sufficiently compromising circumstances on a weekend trip in the Bahamas, frolicking on the good ship *Monkey Business*. The fortunes of the man who would be king fell like a stone. Gary Hart went from potential presidential front runner to nobody in less time than it took to recall the sad story of his demise. Within days he became an also ran, a living punchline, a discarded footnote in the rich library of presidential politics. Distraught at his stupidity and desolate at the thought of what might have been, he spent his days reflecting on the brutality of his fall from grace, and receiving commiserating notes from the disgraced Richard Nixon about the ethics of the popular press.

So Michael Dukakis was now the Democrats' man. He was Bush's opponent and Bush aimed his attacks at Dukakis. In the New Orleans Superdome, Bush went to the podium with his core message: 'The Congress will push me to raise taxes, and I'll say no, and they'll push and I will say no, and they'll push again. And all I can say is, "read my lips – no new taxes".' For months before the New Orleans convention, he had been trying to dismiss complaints that he was a wimp with no backbone. What the speech was saying was that he would stand up to the tax high-rollers in Congress. In New Orleans he had a vision for America, too. Lowering his voice, he said, 'For we are a nation of communities ... a brilliant diversity spread like stars, like a thousand points of light in a broad and peaceful sky ... I want a kinder, gentler nation.'

By this time, though, the Bush campaign team had decided to fight the election with anything but kindness and gentleness. The race was about to enter its decisive phase. Campaign head Lee Attwater ordered his top opposition research aide to find social and cultural issues which could be used to clobber Dukakis. The latter had come to be known as 'that Massachusetts Liberal', the nastiest thing the Republicans could find to say and a phrase which Bush had begun to spit out with greater and greater contempt. But Attwater's aide, Jim Pinkerton, provided more material. He discovered that the Democratic candidate had vetoed a bill which would have made the Pledge of Allegiance mandatory in all Massachusetts schools; he was a member of the American Civil Liberties Union; he had delayed efforts to clean up Boston Harbour; he favoured gun control; and he had allowed a Black convicted murderer named Willie Horton to take a weekend furlough from prison. During that weekend Horton had raped a white woman. On hearing this last bit of information, Attwater is reported to have said of Dukakis, 'We'll strip the bark off the little bastard.' What is undoubtedly true is that the campaign decided to publicise the Willie Horton rape to such effect that voters would come to believe Horton was Michael Dukakis's running mate. So began what is to my mind one of the most discreditable episodes in modern American presidential politics.

Seized of the information about Willie Horton, the Republican National Campaign rushed to make a new and devastating television commercial. Just as the pugnacious Lee Attwater and the Republicans intended, it came be seen as defining the choice between George Bush and Michael Dukakis.

I had already been around in Washington for a few days before the night the commercial was first shown. Horton's face set in the context of his criminal record and used in conjunction with his latest appalling crime looked every inch the menace to society he was. The voice over the picture supplied the rest of the message: Michael Dukakis was indicted for pursuing a policy which resulted directly in women being raped. Equally powerful was the unspoken message of the commercial: Dukakis's policies were inimical to American life; if America did not want its White women to be raped by Black criminals, then it should make sure not to vote for the Massachusetts Governor.

There was uproar in some sections of the American press. It was suggested that the charge against Dukakis was singularly unfair since several American states allowed convicted criminals weekend furloughs. In some other quarters it was felt that the 'ad' was inflammatory, even racist.

Bush hardly ever needed to refer to Willie Horton by name – after all, he had emerged from his party's convention in New Orleans preaching a 'kinder and gentler' America – but he and his campaign team knew precisely the language required to play on the fear generated by the Willie Horton crime. The first time I saw Bush on the stump after the Horton commercial was on the West Coast. It was only two weeks after the 'ad' had first been aired, but already the Republicans had designed a whole new strategy to take advantage of the Horton factor. It involved painting Michael Dukakis as un-American in almost everything he had ever done. As regards his veto of the bill to make the Pledge of Allegiance mandatory, it was suggested that Dukakis's Greek origins might have had some bearing on his decision; Dukakis had advocated gun control, so he must be soft on crime, whereas people should be able to arm themselves against criminals like Horton; and he must be a dangerous libertarian – a reference to the fact that Dukakis had been a member of the American Civil Liberties Union.

I had never thought of the American Civil Liberties Union as a subversive organisation, but the manner in which George Bush enunciated the words on the campaign trail led me to think that perhaps I was wrong and that all the organisation's members should be rounded up, summarily imprisoned and given no weekend furloughs. To demonstrate the difference between him and Dukakis, Bush wrapped whole speeches in the pride of the Stars and Stripes. He would frequently end with the words: 'And always, always, pride in our great country, pride in these United States of America.' In Los Angeles, where crime had been a live day-to-day issue, Willie Horton or no, Bush had another trick. It was brilliant, because it never mentioned Dukakis or the Democrats. It did not need to. He praised the police and stressed their obvious contribution to law and order. The scarcely concealed subtheme seemed to be that Dukakis might, in some bizarre aberration, put the liberty of the individual above the imperative of effective inner city policing. During one appearance before the Los Angeles police department, Bush took a police badge out of his pocket and, in suitably emotional tones, with his voice quivering and tears in his eyes, told its story. A policeman had been shot on duty and before he died, asked that the badge be given to George Bush. The point needed no elaboration: a man who had paid the ultimate price in maintaining law and order had made it clear he thought George Bush was the candidate who would ensure that a policeman's life's work and death had not been in vain.

I watched Bush make the speech on a dozen campaign stops. On every occasion his voice went through the same contortions and his eyes grew moist. One evening, wearing a bulletproof vest, I went with the police on a tour of the front line dividing the two biggest gangs in LA. They had been killing each other with submachine-guns and the experience was a terrifying one. The new Bush strategy, with its emphasis on patriotism, law and order, and with all its unspoken themes and subthemes, seemed powerful and entirely relevant.

Dukakis's seventeen-point lead began to disappear, point by point, as election day drew nearer. At the final presidential debate he did not help his own cause. By that time rape, as Lee Attwater determined, had become the election issue. Everywhere Dukakis went he was hounded about his attitude to capital punishment. The subtext of all this was clear: the Democratic candidate had declared his position against the death penalty for rapists, but, with graphic evidence of the recidivism of criminals like Horton, should he not change his mind? On the night of the final debate in Los Angeles Bernard Shaw, CNN's popular anchorman moderating the televised encounter between Bush and Dukakis, was allowed to put the first question. Realising that the format made such debates almost totally useless for pursuing controversial policy issues with the candidates, Shaw had thought long and hard about his question. The toss had determined that Shaw would 'serve' and Dukakis would 'receive'.

The question referred to Dukakis's wife: 'Governor, if Kitty Dukakis were attacked and raped, would you favour the death penalty?'

An audible gasp came from the audience. The question had the virtue of being on the issue, but Dukakis was thrown by its personal nature. He was not the sort of man to deal with such personal matters in public and was slow to spot how it might be turned to his advantage. During the election he had sounded a bit like an automaton. Humour not being his strong point, he had mastered the facts and figures, and, in a manner which had been perceived as fairly bloodless and unemotional, he had worked out his positions. Now one issue had been personalised in a pointed question. Dukakis couldn't give the required personal human response. He fell back on his standard answer to questions about capital punishment and repeated his belief that the death penalty would be no deterrent.

I must confess that, as I listened to the debate and much later that evening as I compiled a half-hour programme about it, I failed to appreciate what a disservice the Democratic candidate had done himself. I thought his response to Shaw's question inadequate, demonstrating how difficult it is at times to pursue a moderate course on burning issues, but I made no deeper judgement about it. What I failed to realise was how his answer would be construed by the commentators who matter. It took next to no time for me to find out. The conclusion was that on a single question Dukakis had blown it. As an American television colleague put it to me, the Democrats could have won the election that night had their candidate assured Mr Shaw and the rest of America watching on television that, if anybody so much as brushed against Kitty Dukakis in an elevator, he would be wrestled to the floor and marched off to a public execution. The mild-mannered, mechanistic-thinking Governor of Massachusetts had failed to respond in the American way. His was not the response of a John Wayne or a Gary Cooper. A man who would not say publicly that he would defend his wife against the evil machinations of the criminal class could be no defender of a nation's honour. He is not *macho* enough, not man enough to be President of the United States. Perhaps, on reflection, it was much more serious than that: Dukakis allowed intellect and a commitment to principle to obscure basic human feeling. He had mastered all the statistics and the arguments to support his case, but he had showed a lack of instinctive passion.

Several months later Bernard Shaw told me about the hate mail he received from Democrats across America who felt that his single opening question to Dukakis torpedoed the party's chances in the election. Given the prominence of the rape issue in the campaign, some fanatic Democrats even suggested Shaw had been put up to it by the Bush camp. He has always deeply resented that suggestion, maintaining that his question should have been an easy one for a candidate with his wits about him. Sadly, it did not prove so for

Dukakis. His campaign never regained credibility. The Republicans surged ahead to win.

I spent little time in America during the Bush presidency; instead I was involved in reporting stories in Saudi Arabia and Iraq which flowed out of the President's decision to mobilise world opinion and the force of arms against Saddam Hussein. From afar I saw Mr Bush's popularity soar to unprecedented heights during the Gulf War and fall like a stone when disenchantment set in over his domestic record. Having absorbed the wisdom of those who know about American politics, I came to place an inordinate degree of faith in the ability of Secretary of State James Baker to 'orchestrate' diplomatic and electoral victories. From afar I watched Baker leave the State Department with lacrymose regret to try to rescue the fortunes of his friend, Mr Bush. Only Baker could have done it. Lee Attwater, having made a deathbed apology to the Democrats about his 'Willie Horton trick', had passed on.

George Bush lost the 1992 Election for the same reasons that kept him so far behind in the 1988 election for so long: he had no vision, no clear idea what to do in 1992 about an American economy stubbornly stuck in recession. He had beaten Saddam, which was good, but he had not run him out of town, which was unforgivable. Bereft of any real policy issues to dent Clinton's rise in the polls, Bush's party was forced to rely on old stratagems and spoilers – did Clinton have an extramarital affair, did he avoid the draft for Vietnam, did he smoke pot, did he or did he not inhale it, and, worst of all, did he speak ill of the United States while he was on a trip abroad? In charging Clinton with that last damning offence, George Bush reached again for the Stars and Stripes. He remembered how it had come to his assistance four years earlier, when he had been able to suggest that his presidential opponent was guilty of passing up a chance to show his patriotism. It was noticeable that very little memorable was said about the main issue worrying Americans – the economy, not by Bush anyway.

Americans took careful note and made their decision about a sitting President.

Bush lost the 1992 election because the man from nowhere had nothing to say and no clear direction for his country. And he lost it because there was no Willie Horton. For a time he tried to make Saddam his *cause célèbre*, but America never succeeded in putting Saddam behind bars. Had that happened, his picture would have been used on those Republican television commercials exactly as Horton's had been, but the Iraqi President, who had killed so many of his Iraqi enemies and raped Kuwait, had escaped. He remained on the loose and in power, perhaps to rape again, and not because of a Democrat opponent. This time it was George Bush who was letting rapists off the hook. He had been left without a cause, with no real issue, no true voice.

There is a poignant memory of Bush in his last presidential campaign. He was trailing badly in the polls by nine points, and on his last whistle-stop tour. As his train rolled by, his audiences were made up predominantly of curious children dressed for Halloween, their parents having long ago made up their minds about the election and having no need to listen to Bush any more. There's one searing image. The children are standing near the tracks as the Bush bandwagon chugs noisily into history. As it passes by them, they can barely see the candidate and only just hear his despairing words. Bush is shouting from a moving train, his voice sounding for all the world as though it is disconnected from his body or his brain: 'Victory ... character ... that's what it's all about' – the full force of his sentences lost in the wind. It was Bush's Via Dolorosa, the last tortured leg of a journey to political oblivion. It was in its a way a time-frame of the degree to which men will debase themselves to win the approbation of others, a glimpse of the joyless, undignified search for the poisoned chalice of high office.

There were few national tears for Bush. The tabloid New York *Daily News* described him across a banner headline as 'GEORGE

BUSH: A KINDER, GENTLER FAILURE'. The esteemed *Washington Post* was harsher, describing the departing President as 'an insufferable, pseudo-aristocratic snot'. By the time Bush was beginning the final political battle of his life, an incident occurred in Los Angeles, the scene of so many of his earlier 'law and order' speeches, which suggested that perhaps the issue had acquired a new dimension.

Rodney King, a Black motorist, was set upon by a group of White police officers and beaten to a pulp, apparently for having refused to obey a police order to stop. What brought the incident to life was the fact that it had been filmed by a man trying out a new video camera. It was dramatic and brutal. The forces of 'law and order' behaved like demented thugs from a dim and unenlightened age, and the horrifying video images were there for all the world to see. The roles of victim and attackers were clear beyond any shadow of doubt. On Bush's 'watch' the national focus shifted from the criminality of the criminals to the activities of the keepers of law and order. Rodney King was a significant departure from Willie Horton. His case was the American counterpoint.

Aristotle says, in effect, that men in public life suffer the history they have made. He could well have been writing about our time and our age. George Herbert Walker Bush suffered the history he made.

7

Opium and Arms

Invasions are part of the theme which runs through the history of my country. Alexander the Great came in 327 BC. Now we have been invaded by the Afghan refugees. And let's face it, their presence here has affected a lot of things in Pakistan. Not all of them for the better.

Senior civil servant in former Prime Minister
MOHAMMED KHAN JUNEGO'S OFFICE

I BEGAN making regular visits to Pakistan after the country had been thrown into turmoil by the Soviet invasion of Afghanistan. Pakistan was never less than exciting. As part of an immense continent in which ancient traditions and customs reach across the centuries to connect with the people who live there today, the romance begins with the geography of the country. To its north, long after the mighty river Indus tracks south to irrigate the rolling plains, are the mountains of the Himalayas. Beyond the mountains is the vast expanse of China. Seen from the mountainous terrain where Pakistan reaches its outer edges, it looks forbidding and glacially cold. A little further west is the sprawling landmass of what used to be the USSR (the Union of Soviet Socialist Republics). Even further west is Afghanistan.

The first thing which hits the visitor is the country's passion for hospitality. Tribal civilisations made the counterpoint to hospitality the determination to seek revenge if ever the honour of an individual or a people was impugned. Somehow there seemed, on balance, in the long term, less revenge and more hospitality.

Mark Twain describes well in *The Innocents Abroad* how, on a visit to the subcontinent, he and his party 'bore down on the people with America's greatness until we crushed them'. But even from his position of assumed cultural superiority, Twain found the natives entrancing. 'We took kindly to the manners and the customs,' he wrote. It is a country where the old world meets the new in a cacophony of sound and clashing symbols, where carts drawn by horses or bullocks joust for space in a noisy race with rickshaws and BMWs. Pakistan's inherent kindness, the hospitality of its peoples and its viability as a nation were all put to the test with the Soviet invasion of neighbouring Afghanistan.

The two countries have always been closely linked by history and geography. Outside the hotel at which I normally stayed in Islamabad, near Rawalpindi, a road sign indicates the way to the Afghan capital of Kabul and helpfully tells the visitor that it is approximately 300 miles from the centre of Islamabad. After the Soviet invasion that sign in Islamabad was a pointed reminder of the proximity of war.

For centuries Pakistan and Afghanistan together formed part of the long frontier across which ancient invading hordes crossed deeper into Asia. The famous Khyber Pass, which links the two countries and which only became part of Pakistan alone in the late nineteenth century, has been witness to some of the great movements of history. One of Alexander the Great's commanders probably used the Pass on his way south. Arab and Turkish Muslim armies in turn came through it. In the thirteenth and fourteenth centuries Genghis Khan and Tamerlane marched through at the head of invading forces attempting to reach the heart of the subcontinent, and the Moghuls arrived in the sixteenth century. Much later, the pass, with its winding road and steep defiles, had stirred the emotions of Victorian Britain, evoking scenes of gallant soldiers defending the might of the Raj against the fearsome Pathans, stout-hearted fighters with long memories. British garrisons fortified the pass to prevent the Russians from using it as a route for the conquest of India. After that the Khyber became what it is today – an obvious route for smugglers, gun-runners, drug dealers and roaming tribesmen. The Pathan tribes straddling the border still cross to and fro as though the border does not exist.

With the invasion of Afghanistan on 24 December 1979, the relationship of the two countries acquired a fresh dimension.

Pakistan was given a sharper profile in America's perception of its geopolitical role. In one of those enduring clichés of international diplomacy, Pakistan became a 'frontline state, resisting Soviet expansionism'. In such high-sounding phrases lie the seeds of new political partnerships and Pakistan was to be no exception. In the course of a few tense days, towards the end of December in 1979, Pakistan and its President, General Muhammad Zia Ul-Haq, whose titles included Army Chief of Staff, Chief Martial Law Administrator and President, were about to witness a change in their international status. To reinforce its new-found political respectability, Pakistan was to receive massive American aid. Thus, in the early 1980s, as the Soviets struggled to enforce their tenuous hold on Afghanistan, the Senate Foreign Relations Committee in Washington concluded: 'Our commitment to Pakistan's security is given both real and symbolic shape through the existence of our six-year, three-point two-billion-dollar programme of security and economic assistance and through our willingness to contribute to Pakistan's military modernisation programme.'

However, that 'military modernisation programme' was destined to have a disastrous effect on Pakistan: in a very short time it helped to make the country ungovernable. Lawlessness increased, guns became Pakistan's currency and the heroin trade its most important international distinction. Caught in the turbulence of Pakistan's new role, the authorities were powerless to stop the country sliding into anarchy. The 'military modernisation programme' was, in the end, the cause of Pakistan's destabilisation. It was to be supplemented by $200 million a year to help Pakistan cope with the millions of refugees who crossed the border when Soviet tanks rolled into Afghanistan and who were squatting on Pakistani soil. Relying on the hospitality which is such an essential ingredient in the philosophy of Islam, the refugees made no secret of the fact that they intended to remain in Pakistan until their homeland was delivered from the hands of the Soviet aggressors.

For Pakistan's General Zia the change brought about by the Soviet invasion was nothing less than dramatic. Only a few months before Zia had turned down appeals from a score of nations around the world, including one from President Jimmy Carter, to spare the life of Zulfiqar Ali Bhutto. Zia had been a protégé of Prime Minister Bhutto, but, when Bhutto failed to extricate his administration from charges that he had rigged Pakistan's general elections and had been implicated in the death of political opponents, Zia led an army take-over, jailed Bhutto and condemned him to death. The West had never been unaware of Bhutto's failings as a leader and his arrogance had been well publicised by Western diplomats, but Zia's conduct in taking control of the country under a military dictatorship and putting Bhutto on death row seemed to go beyond the pale of civilised behaviour.

Many years later, on my visits to Pakistan, I came to know one of the doctors who had attended Bhutto in prison in his final days, before the doctor himself had been forced to flee to the West via Kabul. (It was ironic that the doctor should have found his way to safety in the West through the country which had been overrun by Communist tanks.) The doctor told me about the appalling conditions in which Bhutto had been kept before his execution. His spirit held but his health had deteriorated, his blackened teeth had been loosened in their gums, and his sight had begun to fail. On 4 April 1979, eight and a half months before 100,000 Soviet troops went into Afghanistan, Bhutto was hanged.

Zia ignored the protestations of the world, even when they were made explicitly on humanitarian grounds, and in refusing to yield

Beginning in Trinidad. At the local radio station I was news reader, continuity announcer, disc jockey and later sports commentator.

Reporting northern Ireland in the 1970s at the height of the 'troubles'. I had insisted that ITN send me there and it was my first big television story.

I finally caught up with Colonel Gadaffi after a two-day chase across the desert. He greeted me in the grounds of his house in Tripoli and sat down to talk in his famous tent.

I talked to the Nicaraguan leader, Daniel Ortega, in a jungle hideaway. We lunched on iguana which he had shot from a nearby lake. His wife acted as translator.

*After months of negotiations and false starts, Yasser Arafat agreed to
see me at a Non-Aligned conference in Zimbabwe. I was not accredited
to report the conference and a Zimbabwean soldier threatened to shoot
me on my way into Arafat's hotel.*

*On the dividing line
between rival
militias in Beirut. I
am trying to explain
to a television
audience back in
Britain the
complexities of the
war in Lebanon.*

More than a million refugees from Afghanistan crossed the border into Pakistan when Soviet tanks rolled into Kabul. They settled mainly near Peshawar in the North West Frontier province.

I saw a lot of the late President Zia during the years of the Soviet invasion. He always asserted that it was Pakistan's duty as fellow Muslims to take in the refugees. After his death, Prime Minister Benazir Bhutto came to see the Afghan refugees much more as a threat to Pakistan's social order.

One of Pakistan's biggest problems is the trade in heroin. Under guard, I was taken to Landikotal where in the town's subterranean markets the trade in dangerous drugs flourished.

I always enjoyed talking to the former Zambian President, Kenneth Kaunda. He was a stalwart of African politics, a great supporter of the Queen and the Commonwealth, and a firm believer that sanctions against South Africa would eventually help to bring about change.

Jesse Jackson was the great campaigner in American presidential politics. He tried to instil pride in black Americans, but his electoral appeal was to a broader rainbow coalition. His constant refrain to black voters was: 'the hands that once picked cotton can now pick a President'.

Working out of the ITN office in Johannesburg on my first visit to South Africa.

Chief Mangosuthu Buthelezei in his garden in Ulundi, capital of the Zulu homeland.

I was the first journalist to interview Nelson Mandela after his release from prison.

Television technology had undergone a revolution during his long incarceration. He expressed great surprise at how small lapel microphones were.

The Presidential guesthouse the night before my interview with Saddam Hussein. The long period of waiting had its moments. I shared them with Angela Frier, Peter Heaps, Phil Bye, our London-educated Iraqi minder who had fond memories of Trafalgar Square, and Jim Dutton.

Our formal interview over, President Saddam Hussein treated me to a long lecture on the evil of the Kuwaitis.

President Bill Clinton in the Roosevelt Room of the White House. He defended his policies on Bosnia, Somalia and Iraq.

Newscaster of the Year 1993.

on an issue which seemed susceptible to compromise, he was universally vilified. After the invasion of Afghanistan, though, everything changed. Zia's political morals had to be weighed against the fact that America desperately needed a frontline state to help in the fight against the expansionist designs of Leonid Brezhnev. Thus a military dictatorship which had just executed the Prime Minister of its country was given the assistance and respect usually reserved for a fully fledged democracy. A political pariah had become a cherished ally.

The Pakistani left-wing writer and polemicist Tariq Ali had this to say about the speed of Zia's international rehabilitation:

> The Soviet entry into Afghanistan provided the Pakistani dictator with a new lease of life. This could be seen most clearly in the sudden change of attitude displayed by the Western press. The sordid hangman of an elected Prime Minister was soon transformed into the plucky defender of the frontiers of the Free World. Prior to the Russian invasion, most Western observers had been in favour of a return to civilian rule, but this theme virtually disappeared in the years that followed.

In my conversations with Western diplomats after the invasion there was a marked reluctance to condemn Pakistan's military dictatorship. There was a great deal of talk about the 'order and stability' which Zia had brought to the turbulent politics of a difficult country. There were sickening whispered comments about what had come to be seen as 'the failures' of the democratic process under Prime Minister Bhutto. I was given minor lectures which would have done credit to the American academic and Ambassador to the United Nations Jeane Kirkpatrick, who had argued in well-publicised papers that authoritarian regimes need not always work in ways which are inimical to American interests.

There is a fictional, but wonderfully hilarious story of how the news of the Soviet invasion was greeted in Pakistan. It comes from

Salman Rushdie's novel *Shame* and the scene is set in the house of the Chief of Staff in Rawalpindi, whose name is Raza Hyder, and is a thinly disguised caricature of General Zia Ul-Haq. Rushdie writes:

> They had just told Raza that the Russians had sent an army into the North-West Frontier and, to their astonishment, the President had leapt from his chair, unrolled four prayer mats on the floor and insisted that they all give thanks, pronto, fut-a-fut, for this blessing had been bestowed upon them by God. They had been rising and falling for an hour and a half, developing on their foreheads the first traces of this bruise which Raza wore with pride, when he stopped and explained to them that the Russian attack was the final step in God's strategy, because now the stability of his government would have to be ensured by the great powers. General Raddi replied a little too sourly that the Americans' policy was centred on staging a dramatic countercoup against the Olympic Games, but before Raza could lose his temper, Raddi's friends, Phisaddi and Bekar, began to shake each other's hands and congratulate themselves noisily: 'That fat-arsed Yankee,' Phisaddi shouted, referring to the American ambassador, 'he'll have to pay the bills now,' and Bekar began to fantasize about five million dollars' worth of new military equipment, the latest stuff at least, missiles that could fly sideways without starving their engines of oxygen and tracking systems that could detect an alien anopheles mosquito at a range of ten thousand miles.

Rushdie's fictional characters are remarkably close to the reality perceived by Pakistan's military high command. In the years after the Soviet invasion Pakistan became awash with all kinds of military hardware. It has been convincingly argued that the American policy of arming General Zia was a tremendous economic fillip to the big American arms manufacturers and, therefore, of great benefit to the American economy. Of that I know very little, but what I did see from my visits to Pakistan was the effect the flow of weapons from the West had on the country. Long after the Soviet invasion American policy may have conferred political respectability on General Zia's regime, but in the process it drove large parts of Pakistan to the brink of collapse.

I remember discussing the point one evening in the city of Peshawar in the North-West Frontier province. My host, who was a prominent politician, began by explaining that, after 24 December 1979, Peshawar, only a few hours by car from Kabul, had become the main centre for Afghani refugees, indeed the city had been overrun by Afghans. 250,000 of the $3\frac{1}{2}$ millions who crossed into Pakistan to escape the Soviet tanks headed for Peshawar and stayed, defying the attempts of the Government and of aid agencies to disperse them over a wider area. Now the better off lived in mud huts, while the majority were to be found in sprawling camps on the edge of Peshawar, dependent on hand-outs from some of the forty aid agencies who descended on Peshawar as well as on the goodwill of their fellow Pathans.

Peshawar has always had the look of a wild frontier town, where the old world meets the new, where present and past collide with surprising harmony, and where modern sophistication rubs shoulders with ancient tribal ritual. It has been described by one writer as a meeting-place between Kipling's India and Bogart's Casablanca. However, what concerned my host most of all was the lawlessness which had engulfed the city.

Peshawar has never been short of guns, for only twenty-five miles away is the dusty town of Darra – known as the 'town of guns' and in reality an enormous gun bazaar. On either side of the main street are countless factories where skilled craftsmen turn out anything from small pistols or guns in the shape of large fountainpens to anti-aircraft weapons. The shops of Darra display pictures of almost every rifle and pistol ever made and, for a frighteningly reasonable price, the visitor can have any weapon made to order. Suddenly, though, newer and much more deadly hardware began to appear. In the most popular hotel in Peshawar visitors sat down to afternoon tea with their sub-machine guns tucked almost casually under their chairs. Anyone who was anyone seemed to be protected by a brace of gun-toting funtionaries.

My host told me the story of how he had gone to a wedding in one of the most rural parts of his constituency, where even the natural gaiety of the occasion had failed to conceal a certain tension between two leading families. It had not been easy to discover the source of the trouble, but he had persisted. Eventually he was told that there had been a dispute over the ownership of a rocket-launcher. This had come into the possession of one family who, unable to appreciate its value, had agreed to sell it to another for a small price. These were not city people; they were farmers. When the real value of the weapon came to light, the original seller demanded the return of the rocket-launcher. The purchaser refused and an almighty row had ensued. It had threatened to disrupt a wedding. The thought of two families up in the bush on the North-West Frontier arguing about the ownership of a rocket-launcher amused me, but my friend, the politician, found little in it to laugh about. He went on to tell me that more and more domestic disputes were being settled by sub-machine-gun shoot outs more deadly than anything that went on in the American Wild West. As a consequence the police found themselves easily outgunned by assailants, and law and order had broken down.

The focus of Peshawar's problems centred on the presence in the city of the Mujahadeen, the heads of the guerrilla organisations committed to driving the Russian troops out of their country. To anyone who would listen they preached loudly that they could, with the proper quality of assistance, make it terribly uncomfort-able for the Soviet occupiers of their country. In the course of time arming the guerrillas became Western policy despite the fact that there were two views about the Mujahadeen. Some American undercover arms suppliers saw them as Jeffersonian democrats fighting for the freedom of their country, while others saw them for what they were – a disparate band of squabbling groups as anxious to tear their movement apart as they were to get the Russians to leave their country.

This tension between the various factions spilled over into Peshawar life as open warfare. The Mujahadeen, frustrated for many years by being trapped across the border in Pakistan, became involved in extortion, gun-running and worst of all in the drugs trade. At the height of the Soviet invasion a senior figure in the Pakistan army confided to me his high command's view that, of every ten weapons passed on to the guerrillas to fight the Soviets, seven ended up in criminal hands in and around Peshawar. He told me that some Afghan guerrilla leaders had become the 'Godfather' figures in the region's criminal culture and had joined the heroin trade.

Nor were the Mujahadeen's gun-running activities confined solely to Peshawar and the North-West Frontier. During a visit to Karachi, I discovered that it was possible, at a cost of no more than a few pounds, to rent Kalashnikov rifles by the day, and a roaring trade had developed. People would rent them in the morning, settle their disputes by that same night, and return the weapons the following day. Civil unrest of this sort, accentuated by the policy of flooding Pakistan with weapons, was of minimal concern to the Americans or the other Western arms suppliers. There was no such equanimity, though, about the effect this lawlessness had on the burgeoning trade in heroin. There was good reason for that. Ninety-five per cent of the drugs manufactured in the country was destined for the overseas market. At one stage during the 1980s drug enforcement agencies estimated that between eighty-five and ninety per cent of the heroin which reached the East Coast of America and which came to Western Europe originated in Pakistan.

Long before the trade reached such proportions American Congressmen had zeroed in on Pakistan's role. Pakistani Government officials were not always pleased at the suggestion that they were not doing enough to stop the growth of the heroin industry. On my first visit to the North-West Frontier province Pakistani drug enforcement officers delighted in telling me the story of a visit to the region by New York Senator Daniel Patrick Moynihan.

The Senator, who knew the problems caused by drugs his metropolis, was clearly shocked by what he had seen of the heroin trade in Pakistan, so much so, in fact, that he suggested to the Pakistani Government official who toured the country with him that perhaps the only way to arrest the growth of the trade was by the introduction of the death penalty. He felt it should be mandatory for anyone found guilty of the manufacture or distribution of heroin. While Pakistanis have always taken umbrage at the suggestion that they do not do enough in their own right to try to halt the trade, they have perfected the art of accepting advice from foreigners with studied equanimity. So, the Pakistani official's reply to the American Congressman was this: 'Of course, Senator. What a good idea. I tell you what – you bring in the death penalty for drug smuggling in New York and I assure you Pakistan will follow the day after.' The Senator saw the point. The trade in heroin flourished not only because of the manufacturers and distributors in Pakistan but also because it was sustained by demand in America and in Europe.

For more than 500 years the peoples of Pakistan have grown poppies and made opium. Part of the trade was allowed for medical purposes, but it was soon overtaken by the illegal trade. It is grown chiefly in remote villages along the border with Afghanistan and especially in the so-called 'tribal areas', which are technically part of Pakistan, but are allowed sufficient local autonomy to do much as they please.

I once spent a week with drug enforcement officers in the North-West Frontier acquainting myself with the magnitude of the problem. The drug enforcement people were realistic. Heroin manufacture is virtually impossible to police. Opium extracted from poppies is cooked and pressed into large sticky blocks, and the process of manufacturing heroin from such blocks is rudimentary. Under strict security, late one evening I was taken to the outskirts of Peshawar, to a large, secluded and heavily guarded warehouse containing hundreds of bags of raw heroin. It had not been through all the manufacturing stages, was brown in colour, and seemed a most impressive haul, but I was told that it represented only a small fraction of what was actually being produced in the region.

Defeating the manufacturers in the inaccessible parts of the territory was never an easy job, but by the 1980s they had become increasingly sophisticated in their operations. Fully aware of the pressure on the authorities to show some success, they would occasionally 'invite' the police to 'discover' and 'close' a particular factory. The manufacturers would happily give a written undertaking to the effect that the operation would from that day be discontinued – in fact I was shown files from the previous weeks including such undertakings. In many instances the people giving the undertaking could neither read nor write, but had affixed a thumb print at the bottom of the official order. I was taken to see factories which had been closed in this way. They were basic in the extreme – rubber tubes, pipes and a number of large pans and chemicals – much like a rustic, old-fashioned chemistry laboratory. Every time one of these closed, the owners packed up and moved to a new location to begin the operation all over again. The police faced a phenomenon of unstoppable force. The biggest drugs bust in Karachi in the 1980s had been organised by the drug barons themselves. The police had merely been invited along for the ride and then made to look inept because what they had been told to expect was not there by the time they arrived.

Whatever success the Pakistan authorities achieved before 1979 was quickly dissipated by the effects of the Soviet invasion. The North-West Frontier, always wild and with a tendency to lawlessness, went slowly out of control. One afternoon I went to the village of Landi Kotal, close to the border with Afghanistan. The experience was quite surreal. I was kept waiting at a checkpoint until a suitable escort could be arranged. A dozen armed policemen accompanied me into the village and yet there were drugs on sale in the underground markets and bazaars everywhere. Some stallholders made a pretence of concealing their supplies when the police approached, while others, understanding their impotence, merely smiled disarmingly and did absolutely nothing.

Drug enforcement officers in Peshawar talked openly about the role of the leaders of the Afghan resistance movements in the drugs trade, yet for the political leader whose position owed so much to the Soviet invasion there was hardly a murmur of concern. I had at least half a dozen formal interviews with President Zia shortly before he was killed in a helicopter crash.

Everything about his manner was in stark contrast to his reputation as an unbending disciplinarian and a political brute. To me he was courteous in the extreme, on one occasion separating me from my crew and insisting that, when I came to see him, I should always use the ambassador's entrance. Neat in appearance, he managed to project humility perhaps because, although he was five feet seven inches tall, his poor man's dress of the *shalwar kameez* encouraged the impression that he was much shorter. But his eyes were alive and blazed with interest. One Opposition newspaper in Pakistan advanced the thesis that Zia had perfected the pretence of being a small, ordinary man to a point where his manner seemed obsequious. According to this paper, he had mastered 'the style of the double handshake and the triple embrace', always accompanied by liberal lashings of hugs and bows. On such occasions it was wise to remember that this was the same man who had denied Bhutto mercy and who had relentlessly hounded his political enemies.

In our interviews Zia never managed to hide his pleasure at the fact that he had become, because of the Soviet invasion, an ally of the United States. He preached the need for order and security in a manner that put me in mind of Henry Kissinger's paraphrasing of Goethe: 'If ever I had to choose between disorder and justice and injustice and order, I would always choose the latter.' This meant that any conversation about whether military rule was good for Pakistan immediately became a judgement about whether abstruse concepts like 'justice' had any place in a Third World country struggling to survive on the edge of a war the Soviets were waging right next door.

This had a strangely disorienting influence on our conversations. When, for example, I pointed to the enormous social and civil disruption American influence had caused in Pakistan, and when I mentioned the problems of drugs, guns and crime, Zia was anxious to appear tough enough to deal with them, at the same time insisting that none of these problems was grave. He had developed the knack of appearing to be a hard man while arguing there was really very little to be hard about.

Questions about Pakistan's role in the international drugs trade elicited nothing about how the trade had become uncontrollable, but a recitation from the Koran about the un-Islamic nature of narcotics.

In 1979 General Zia had announced a prohibition order which extended the ban on alcohol to narcotics. He banned the production, distribution and the use of opium, invoking the authority of the Holy Koran to support what he had done: 'Satan's plan is to excite enmity and hatred between you with intoxicants and gambling, and hinder you from remembrance of God, and from prayer. Will ye not then abstain?'

Zia refused to admit that the Mujahadeen had become involved in the illegal trade in drugs and played down the effect the trade was having on the people of his own country. He talked about it as a problem to be managed with the help of good public relations aimed, of course, principally at America, who kept pressing countries such as Pakistan to take a tougher stand on drugs in their own countries.

Conscious of the international benefits Pakistan derived from the Soviet invasion of Afghanistan, Zia was happy to act as

America's spokesman in the Far East. Unlike many of his coun-trymen, he felt that all would be well in Pakistan once the Soviets had been driven out of Afghanistan and the refugees had returned home. He was wrong.

Today, Pakistan continues to pay a heavy price for its pivotal role in America's policy to arm the guerrillas fighting the Soviets in Afghanistan. American aid ended when the Soviets left and in 1990 Pakistan's relations with the United States sank to an all time low, because of Islamabad's nuclear weapons programme. But at the height of America's involvement the CIA funded Muslim fundamentalist groups in the country to the tune of some $10 billion. When Soviet troops disappeared, the guerrillas remained, still passionate about Islamic fundamentalism and looking for new battles to fight. At least a fifth of the 25,000 Arab fundamentalists who went to Pakistan to fight on behalf of Afghanistan stayed on when the Soviets left. They fanned out across the country and later began to infiltrate Egypt, Turkey, Libya and Morocco, their influence even spreading to the United States, where they have become linked to the group thought to be responsible for bombing the World Trade Center in New York. The guerrilla fighters so ardently courted by the West are now criminal gangs trained in bombing, assassinations and the heroin industry.

In neighbouring Afghanistan, where a fractious rebel Govern-ment has little control outside the capital, Kabul, the UN today estimates the production there of 2,000 tons of opium. This has led Pakistani ministers to conclude that the rapid expansion of poppy production in Afghanistan renders it impossible for them to contain the problem, especially since they admit that, during the war against the Soviets, poppy cultivation in Afghanistan was totally ignored. It is now too late. In 1990 two of Pakistan's biggest drug barons were elected to the National Assembly, the powerful lower house of Parliament. Pakistan admits that it has little influence with the fiercely independent tribal warlords in the North-West Frontier, and the country's position as a major transit point for heroin remains unchallenged by drug enforcement. The tribesmen and their warlords carry semi-automatic weapons, rocket-propelled grenade-launchers and sophisticated communications equipment, and are prepared to kill to protect their crops. Heroin passes through Baluchistan to one of several smuggler ports along the 1,500-mile Mekran coast with the Arabian sea or takes an overland route through northern Afghanistan into Iran or across the former Central Asian republics into Russia and the Ukraine.

I had only one long conversation with the President about the opposition leader Benazir Bhutto. Zia was condescending about her hold on the public's imagination. I shall never forget the manner in which he referred to her as 'a young girl aggrieved at the loss of her father'. Any suggestion that she might be able to mobilise national support across Pakistan was rejected. Like all dictators, he insisted he was anxious to see his functions assumed one day by an entirely civilian government, but thought that Benazir Bhutto would never lead such an administration. She lacked political experience, he told me, and her campaign to lead her country would be overwhelmed by a chorus of acclamation for the order which martial law had brought to Pakistan. President Zia was wrong and was either unwilling to accept it or he had become so insulated from the pulse of normal life that he was genuinely unable to see the change taking place.

I found out for myself how far off the mark he was when I joined a Benazir Bhutto motorcade from Lahore to Gujranwala one Sunday morning. Gujranwala is about forty miles away, but the Bhutto bandwagon gathered so much support along the way that the journey took over six hours. At first the police tried to harass Benazir Bhutto and her supporters into not making the trip, but, faced by the swelling crowds along the way of several hundred thousand people, they eventually gave up. Her popularity seemed very real to me.

I had gone to Pakistan to pursue the story of the way in which the war in neighbouring Afghanistan and the flood of refugees had made the country ungovernable. In the pursuit of that story I chanced upon another, which had been the subject of diplomatic whispers for years. Substantiating it seemed impossible and yet it never went away. It was the question of Pakistan's nuclear capacity. I saw it as an example of just how far America had gone in courting Pakistan as an advance post from which to hound the Soviets out of Afghanistan, and my interest was sharply revived by an argument I heard one drunken evening in Peshawar. Attending a party at which there was a large group of foreigners, Americans, English, French and a few others, I fell into conversation with someone who I was told had once worked for the CIA. This was interesting, but not entirely surprising since Peshawar, by virtue of its proximity to the border with Afghanistan, was awash with agents, spies, bag men and a plethora of foreign operatives of all kinds. As thick on the ground as hail stones in a winter storm, they generally masqueraded under guise of aid workers, guides or salesmen, and deliberately sought out the foreign journalists. Not that they had to try to hard – after all, we wanted to talk to them as all scraps of information were useful. Sometimes the process of mutual seeking out worked so well that we would have found it impossible to miss each other even if we had tried. They were a peculiar assortment, who looked so obviously out of place; their attempts to make themselves inconspicuous had the opposite effect. One of these 'guides' once talked about taking me into Afghanistan secretly. His proposition, as I saw it, had two inherent problems: I would have to trudge some forty miles in waist-high snow, and he was slightly unsure about how quickly we could get out again. I was not impressed and declined, thanking him profusely.

That evening in Peshawar the whisky was flowing freely and I fell into conversation with an 'ex-CIA' man who told me he knew for a fact that Pakistan possessed the ability to put together at least half a dozen nuclear bombs. I was dismissive of the idea, partly as a way of enticing him into saying how much more he knew. He did not convince me, but, in the course of a long, rambling disquisition, he enunciated a theory which I had long held dear. He said that the Reagan administration had become so obsessed with the presence of the Soviets in Afghanistan and were so keen to keep on 'using' Pakistan to supply the Mujahadeen and maintain a watch on Soviet planning that they were willing to ignore whatever Pakistan did. He told me the arrangement worked to the satisfaction of both parties: Pakistan could develop its nuclear weapons, although the Americans knew it, and America would be given whatever facilities it needed in Pakistan in its anti-Soviet campaign. From everything I had observed over many years in connection with weapons and drugs what the inebriated ex-CIA man had let slip made sense. I was especially fascinated by his suggestion that, even before the Red Army tanks rolled into Kabul, Pakistan had been used as a forward position by American intelligence keen on spying on the Soviet Union. He told me the Americans had been given what he called 'listening facilities' in Pakistan for years.

In my meetings with President Zia earlier I repeatedly raised the subject with him. I never expected an honest answer and he never gave me one, for he had perfected what passed for a response to such questions, which in the time-honoured tradition of Whitehall civil servants was economical with the truth. The President employed a form of words which suggested that Pakistan's peaceful intentions towards the rest of the world, were at odds with the possession of an aggressive nuclear capability, thus making such a capability unlikely or unnecessary. Interestingly, he never actually reached the point of categorically denying it. There was nothing I could say to push President Zia further. For one thing my question was based only on hints, scraps of information from third parties and on my own uninformed suspicion, and for another I knew the form. Realising this was rather unfruitful ground, I never pressed the question, but resolved to enquire elsewhere.

In attempting to do so, I had an unexpected stroke of good fortune. On one of my visits to Pakistan I went to see a well-known journalist to do a wide-ranging political interview. Long after the formal part of our conversation was over he began to sound me out about the possibility of finding a job in England. I gave him the benefit of my view, but I was puzzled about why he wanted to leave Pakistan at what seemed to me to be the pinnacle of a very successful career. Adjourning to another room, he explained his reason. It was a fascinating story, and it concerned Pakistan's nuclear capability. A high-minded young man, he was in dispute with his newspaper about a story his editors had refused to publish; their decision made his position at the paper untenable, although he had evidence that the editors had been leant on 'by the highest authorities in the country'. His unpublished story was based on a conversation with Dr Abdul Khan, who, he told me, was the man in charge of Pakistan's nuclear weapons facility. I had never heard Dr Khan's name before. He told me that he had seen Dr Khan, who had given him sufficient information to enable him to conclude that Pakistan could deliver a nuclear weapon and he had surmised, in his unpublished piece, which he then showed me, that material for Pakistan's nuclear weapons programme had come from Germany, Britain and the United States. Pakistan, he said, had been acquiring the material over many years. Contrary to what President Zia had earlier vouchsafed about Pakistan's peaceful intentions towards its neighbours and the rest of the world, this journalist explained that, having lost a part of its country – the part which became Bangladesh – the Pakistani High Command was obsessed with preserving its territorial integrity. The main worry was India, as he had discovered from separate conversations with Pakistani army generals, who were apparently convinced that India would always be a threat and was only waiting for a suitable opportunity to humiliate Pakistan. At the time I was able to take this story no further.

Several months later, though, on a subsequent visit to Islamabad,

I tried to seek out the journalist to discover how he was faring. Not finding him at the paper, I enquired his whereabouts from a friend who had put us in touch in the first place. I was told he had been fired from the paper, put under house arrest for a time and, even when that period ended, his movements had been restricted. He had since left the country. I became convinced that his nuclear weapons story had annoyed the authorities because it was true and decided that the next time I met any Pakistani generals I would confront the issue head on, confident that I had acquired sufficient information to do so.

The chance came when I spent an evening with one of President Zia's close associates, a brigadier who had kindly invited me to dinner to discuss my request for a helicopter facility to fly over the mountainous divide between Pakistan and Afghanistan. (I forget now why we particularly wanted to be given permission to do so and, in the event, to the chagrin of the proud officers of the Pakistani Air Force, we were unable to circumvent a spell of appalling weather.) However, I got on well with the Brigadier. We shared a passion for American politics, and our conversations on the subject were always lively. The bookshelf in his office was crammed with titles on Jefferson, Truman, Eisenhower, Kennedy, Nixon and Kissinger. With a keen political eye and with the interest of a military man, he had read widely about America's involvement in the Vietnam War. He knew a great deal, too, about the Civil Rights Movement in the United States and about the roles of Martin Luther King and President Lyndon Johnson. I must also confess I had another reason for liking the Brigadier. Although he was fairly abstemious himself, he had a wholly commendable interest in fine wine and excellent Cuban cigars. He kept a supply of the latter in his office and was unfailingly generous. Those were the days when it was still socially correct to light up a six-inch Havana in someone's office before lunch or in someone's home after dinner.

That evening, after a delightfully simple meal, we sat on his verandah passing the time. Like two schoolboys trying to outdo each other, we swopped stories and raked over the problems of the world. Having solved everyone else's problems, I turned to Pakistan and asked the Brigadier about his country's military concerns. He talked about the threat his country faced from India – Pakistan's nightmare was that Indian forces could create havoc in his country. I said I thought such a scenario unlikely, to which he responded by saying that military thinking required a greater level of pessimism than I had about the world. He talked about military contingencies to meet the 'worst case scenario' and tried to explain to me how much time was spent on planning to meet the Indian threat. In a moment of pure mischief it occurred to me that I could test my host on the subject of Pakistan's nuclear weapons, all the while pretending that I was doing so without much knowledge.

'Why should you worry so much about India?' I asked. 'Surely, if they have designs on your territory, you could threaten them with a nuclear response?'

The Brigadier, who had been reclining in a short hammock, sat up sharply. I quite expected him to say that Pakistan did not have such a nuclear capability, but significantly he did not.

'Who told you we had nuclear weapons?' he asked instead.

His question implied more surprise than incredulity – surprise that I should have said what I did. I replied that I had not been told by anyone, but had always assumed that Pakistan had acquired such a nuclear capability over the years. It was not a particularly satisfactory answer, but I decided to leave it at that.

For several moments there was silence. Smoke from our cigars drifted from the verandah, eventually disappearing in crazy patterns toward the garden. The break in our conversation revealed a strange quiet. Very far away in the distance I could hear the rumble of traffic. The Brigadier sank back into his hammock and slowly resumed his rhythmical swaying.

Drawing deeply on his cigar, he asked, gazing into the middle distance, 'Could you imagine the uproar if we launched a nuclear strike against India?'

It was a rhetorical question I did not respond to.

Many years later the *Sunday Times* highlighted in what seemed a well-researched story the dangers of a nuclear exchange between India and Pakistan.

In April 1993 Seymour Hersh, writing in the *New Yorker* magazine, proved conclusively that Pakistan has the bomb, that the Americans knew about it and kept it a secret, and that the secrecy was part of the pay off for Pakistan's co-operation in monitoring and fighting the Soviet occupation of Afghanistan. Hersh says that it was well known among the American intelligence community that 'many more nuclear related goods were clandestinely bought inside the United States by Pakistan than by Saddam Hussein's Iraq', and went on to say in the same article that there is 'indisputable evidence that Pakistan has been able to escape public scrutiny for its nuclear purchases because the Reagan and Bush administrations chose not to share the intelligence about the purchases with Congress'.

The start of the Soviet withdrawal from Afghanistan meant that Pakistan's flagrant violations of rules which had been set by the American Congress could no longer be ignored, however. According to Seymour Hersh, Prime Minister Benazir Bhutto found that out during her short term in office, when she was told by the CIA in no uncertain terms that America knew precisely the size of Pakistan's nuclear arsenal and that, unless steps were immediately taken, America would have to blow the whistle on its one time close ally. Mrs Bhutto was given the chance to buy F 16s instead.

With the departure of Soviet troops from Afghanistan, Washington's need for an ally in Islamabad had disappeared. It was time to place the relationship between the United States and Pakistan on a newer, more realistic basis.

Pakistan was discovering that.

And as the problem of lawlessness and the trade in heroin grew, the Americans were discovering the true cost of their earlier policy.

8

Worms in the Bud

It was the best of times, it was the worst of times...
It was the spring of hope, the winter of despair.
CHARLES DICKENS, *A Tale of Two Cities*

NOTHING is more invigorating to a journalist than the opportunity to watch the process of political change because it is like having a seat at the window of world history. The process of political change may not always be sufficiently obvious to be instantly understood for key elements in the process can, on occasions, be obscured by the sheer speed and turbulence of events. At other times revolutions simply fail to reveal themselves for what they really are. The French Revolution was like that – the scope of the sweeping change it would bring about was not always clear.

Alexis de Tocqueville records that, despite his political acumen, Frederick the Great 'had no inkling of what was in the air'. As de Tocqueville says, 'He was very near to the Revolution, yet he failed to see what was happening under his eyes. Even he failed to perceive the signs of the long impending storm.'

Edmund Burke tried, but failed, to put his finger on the true significance of what was going on. He saw the revolt in limited, negative terms: it would, he concluded darkly, totally destroy the France everyone knew and the new France, the one which emerged from the ashes, would be impotent – it would lack significance as a force in the world. 'We may assume,' he suggested, 'that for a long time to come France need no longer be reckoned with as a military power. Indeed she may be destroyed, as such, for ever and men of the next generation may repeat those ancient words, '*Gallo quoque in bellis floruisse audivimus*' [We have heard say that the Gauls too once excelled in warfare].'

That seems to be taking matters too far, but it was typical of the scathing and almost dismissive view Burke had of events in France at the time. English diplomats could not boast that their judgements were much better, indeed in some respects they thought even less of it than Burke did, for they were convinced that the French Revolution was nothing more than a little local difficulty, a strictly domestic phenomenon with scant chance of making an impact on the world.

Journalists today have at their disposal much more information on which to base their assessments, though that is not always a guarantee of accuracy. As the Diplomatic Correspondent at ITN, I recall, to my horror, trying to convince one of our programme editors that the invasion of South Georgia in the Falklands by a reckless band of scrap metal merchants would never in a thousand years lead to armed conflict. I even offered a wager. Worse was the fact that my view changed hardly at all when the Task Force set sail from Portsmouth on a sea of national pride and on a wave of emotion.

At other times, though, fortunately for us, events which are harbingers of political change are too dramatic to misread.

I witnessed and reported the build up to the passing of unpopular systems in South Korea, where military governments fought street battles to defy the popular will, in the Philippines, where a corrupt dictator was finally banished from his palace by people power, and, perhaps most significantly of all, in Eastern Europe.

The changes in Eastern Europe were so profound that they prompted a wholesale reappraisal of foreign policy by Western Governments. It all began, perhaps, with the coming to power in the Soviet Union of Mikhail Gorbachev and very quickly it spread to the Soviet Union's closest Communist allies. The effect was at times nothing short of high drama. In October in 1989 the Soviet President, Mikhail Gorbachev, made an important visit to East Germany. Long before he got there, Gorbachev had set the Soviet Union on a course for irreversible change. In public he embraced his country's staunch ally, the East German leader Erich Honnecker, although by that time Honnecker had become one of the most embarrassing relics of an age quietly sliding to oblivion. Gorbachev's was no ordinary visit. He had gone to draw the line on how far Honnecker and East Germany could count on support from the Kremlin in future – support for which Honnecker had always been desperate. Overall manager of an obnoxious and repressive regime, he had locked East Germany into a outdated and decaying order and needed help. At a time when East/West relations were improving in giant strides, East Germany remained a chilly, forbidding fortress of the past, frozen in the tedium of the Cold War.

The Soviet Union had sustained East Germany for forty years, 300,000 Soviet troops had guaranteed the determined political obsolescence of Honnecker and his hated Stasi secret police, but by the autumn of 1989 the old Soviet Union had already changed almost beyond recognition. It had all but torn down the barriers with which it had shut itself in. Reform was the word on everyone's lips. In some sectors of Soviet life it was more of a concept than a recognisable movement, but the country had broken its addiction to the ideology of Marxism and was busily engaged in an ardent courtship with the West.

If Honnecker had ever bothered to look up from the isolation of his political bunker, he too would have caught the changing mood in his own country, but that, it seems, is not in the nature of authoritarian regimes. Their survival is based on introspection and rigid thoughts about the need for order, the *status quo* and what is generally perceived as its stability. All these things are diametrically opposed to the concept of change. However, in the summer of 1989, tens of thousands of East Germans started to force the pace and it began with their determination to leave their country. Prevented by the barbarity of the Berlin Wall and by its notorious gunmen and guard dogs from crossing into West Germany, they presented themselves instead at Hungary's door. For a moment the world held its breath. What would the Hungarians do and what would the consequences be for those attempting to flee Honnecker's repression? That fateful summer the Hungarians struck an important blow for change. They opened their frontier and, by doing so, signalled immediately that Mr Honnecker's days were numbered. He was about to be overwhelmed by the will of his people and by the progressive forces he had so studiously ignored. Hungary was not the only focus for East Germans on the move; Poland and Czechoslovakia were too. In September a tidal wave of some 6,000 East Germans hit the Federal Republic's embassy in Prague. The East German authorities responded in the only way possible, short of firing up an instant revolt: they began to make arrangements for the orderly transfer of people to the West. The tide had proved too great.

By the time Gorbachev arrived in Berlin in October the Honnecker regime was in its death throes. Not even Gorbachev's troops could save it without the most unthinkable bloodshed. People demonstrating in their millions in Leipzig, Dresden and Erfurt literally drove the unmourned Honnecker out of office.

As the Soviet troops remained in their barracks, ordered to make no hostile moves by their superiors deep in the Kremlin, East Germany fell to the noise and passion of an unstoppable revolution. In November one million demonstrators forced the East German Government to resign. On 22 December, after a torrent of high-level diplomacy, the Brandenburg Gate itself was opened in Berlin. It was an event of earth-shattering political significance and a moment of epiphany. As Timothy Garton Ash, one of the most brilliant commentators on Germany, wrote of that time, 'It had a Pentecostal quality ... Ordinary men and women found their voice and their courage. These are moments when you feel that somewhere an angel has opened its wings.'

I arrived in West Berlin at about three o'clock one morning after Germans from East and West had decided in a frenzy of celebration and relief to do what the authorities had willed. They began to pull down the Berlin Wall. Every tool imaginable was pressed into service. Pick-axes by the hundreds materialised from nowhere. The entire city seemed to move and heave on a constant rolling tide of humanity. There was an almost palpable feeling of relief mixed with incredulity and joy. East Germany had crossed into West Berlin and Honnecker's children were wandering about the city as if they had discovered the glories of an old family treasure chest. An epiphenomenon which impressed the West Germans who witnessed it was the sight across the city of hundreds of thousands of East Germans queuing outside West German banks. They were guaranteed a small sum of money by the West German Government and lines had begun to form from four o'clock that morning after the Wall fell, some five hours before the banks were due to open for business. The cost of breaking down the Wall would only later come to haunt German politicians.

Beyond that, though, there was a sense that something profound had happened in Europe. It was a moment of history and destiny. It felt as though an entire nation had broken through a huge subterranean dungeon and had glimpsed the light of a new dawn breaking through from the other side. Suddenly a new world and a new life seemed within the grasp. I have seen few political events which encouraged such ecstasy. The look on people's faces told the story – it shone with the privilege of having witnessed a momentous event.

Western politicians were caught on the hop, unprepared to deal with the implications of such an event. For decades the West had been calling for the dismantling of the Berlin Wall. It had become the kind of political statement with which Western leaders enhanced their international credibility as when John F. Kennedy on a famous visit to Germany suggested no one who knew Berlin could fail to understand the very concept of freedom and declared himself a Berliner. Later Reagan driven, as always, more by tough anti-Communism than by fine, philosophical concepts, urged Mr Gorbachev to 'tear that Wall down'. In Britain Mrs Thatcher did the same. However, now that the Wall had collapsed and Germany was about to be reunited with Berlin once again at its centre, grave reservations surfaced.

The Americans were worried. The French, rather untypically, had been caught off guard and hesitated for what seemed an age before committing themselves. Mrs Thatcher called a meeting at the Prime Minister's country house, Chequers, to discuss the implications of what had happened. Germans, too, had reason for concern as they remembered Schiller's warning about the futility of Germany ever trying to make itself one cohesive nation. The ensuing national debate about the glories and dangers of uni-fication split political parties and intellectuals, dividing statesmen and peasants, but by then it was all academic. It was too late to control the revolutionary force of what had occurred. The people had willed the destruction of the Wall which divided their country and their people. Politicians could but respond.

I SAW a similar revolution begin in South Korea in 1987, although it had none of the global significance of the fall of the Berlin Wall. The case for the reunification of the two Koreas was less a factor in the general climate of discontent than it would prove in Germany two years later. In almost every other way, however, it threw up the same determination of a people to confront and eventually to overwhelm an authoritarian regime. For decades South Korea was ruled by military governments, who had done very much as they pleased. South Korean governments had enjoyed Western respect-ability and support only because the proximity and the latent hostility of Kim Il Sung's Communist North Korea made it an absolute necessity. Kim Il Sung runs one of the most isolated and autocratic dictatorships anywhere in the world, having effectively cut his country off from the rest of civilisation. While other parts of the world looked on in awe at Soviet *perestroika* and *glasnost* as instruments of economic and political change, Kim Il Sung took his country in the opposite direction. He closed it down, set his face like stone against the possibility of any outside influences and drilled into his people the need for rigid, unquestioning uniformity. In addition he fashioned the 'cult of personality' into the salient doctrine of a godlike creed, its strength eclipsing potent political ideologies such as Stalinism. Kim Il Sung's other characteristic was that he was beyond embarrassment. For example, he claimed with monotonous regularity that in routine plebiscites he got, not ninety, ninety-five or even ninety-nine per cent of the vote, as more reluctant demagogues might insist, but all one hundred per cent. Statistical freaks are unable to puncture the deep introspection and myopia of a man who rules without a trace of dissent, confident that his role as the Great Leader is an article of faith.

South Korea has always had its failings too, but they are vastly different from the one-man show in Pyongyang. On my visit to South Korea I was taken to see the no-man's-land which separates the two Koreas. Twenty-five miles north of the South Korean capital of Seoul is the truce town of Panmunjom, where the agreement ending the Korean War was signed at the site of the ridiculously named Demilitarized Zone – the DMZ. There, across a barren landscape, $1\frac{1}{2}$ million soldiers face each other in a posture of constant readiness. It was a stark reminder that, in the remoter reaches of our political universe, there are all the resonances of a nasty old-fashioned Cold War confrontation. From the Demilitarized Zone, I looked through binoculars into the North. What I saw appeared to be outlines of a fairly quiet town. A tower of enormous height dominated the landscape, on top of which was a large North Korean flag. There were substantial administrative buildings and much smaller houses, and, according to our guides, at various periods in the morning a trickle of people could be seen heading purposefully to work. A peculiar puzzle was the noise that came from the town. It was a non-stop diet of old pop music, which was annoyingly broadcast to the South, firstly as an irritation and secondly to indicate that life in the town was thriving beyond reproach. On closer examination, though, the whole town was a facade. There was a series of 'fronts' of buildings and the sound of outdated music, and nothing else. In the truce town itself things were no different. The large building in Panmunjom facing North Korea was also a one-dimensional structure, a facade with nothing of the depth suggested by its outward appearance. We stood looking at the North Koreans and they looked back at us. Against the advice of our hosts, we waved at them, and they responded with quizzical looks. One country and two distinct systems separated by megalomania and an ideology born in the world of the 1940s.

South Koreans talked about reuniting with the North, but Kim Il Sung's regime had done everything to temper their optimism with caution. When I went to Seoul in 1987, I found there was still a great deal of North/South paranoia. South Koreans were genuinely worried that their Northern brothers were devising huge dams to destroy the South by flooding. When I made the mistake of not taking such a possibility seriously, I was shown detailed diagrams of the dams on the North Korean side, their capacity and the extent to which the water from them would submerge even the tallest office blocks in the South. It would be invasion by water torture – which did not seem feasible, but was somehow impossible to dismiss altogether. In the end I became convinced that Kim Il Sung lived in such a hermetically sealed world that perhaps his enemies were right to assume that the most far-fetched schemes to destroy the South might be possible. It was not easy to avoid the profound feeling of distrust although, before the Olympic Games in 1988, South Korea entered into talks with the North about sharing a few of the events. Never a very practical suggestion, it came to nothing. To remind me that there was hard evidence North Korean agents had been sent South to reek havoc on Seoul and other major South Korean cities, I was taken to see a number of tunnels, which suggested that North Korea had at least at one stage set its heart on trying to invade the South. The whiff of conspiracy had grown strong enough to envelop the place.

Much more real were the grievances of the people of South Korea against their Government. They clamoured for greater democracy and, to make their point, took to the streets.

In 1987 South Korea was preparing to host the Olympics in the following year. The country was flushed with pride at having been chosen for the Games and had employed the best American public relations minds to help them shape the image they wanted to present to the outside world. In downtown Seoul, huge computers marked off the days and hours to the opening ceremony. The democracy protesters, seeing a chance to press the authorities for radical reform, decided to make good use of the period when the attention of the world was focused on Korea. The South Korean Government, already supported in its quarrel with the North by the presence of 40,000 American troops, indicated that it might be ready to discuss change, but on its own terms and not if it was goaded by street protests. The battle lines were drawn. The Government wanted to show that it had the will and ability to keep the protesters at bay. The protesters saw the months before the Games as their last chance to force concessions.

Every afternoon, just after lunch, an eerie calm descended on Seoul; people disappeared off the streets as the demonstrators prepared to march. The security forces had their hands full: at one stage there were up to a dozen big demonstrations in different parts of the city every day. The Government tried to lay down firm guidelines about where the marches could go and what they could do, but, sensing that their protests were gaining a momentum in the country, the democracy protesters refused to follow the rules.

The street battles which ensued were fierce, the more so because the authorities had decided on this occasion to take a tough stand and partly because troops sent out to confront the demonstrators knew no other way to behave.

In 1980 the security forces had charged into a peaceful demonstration in the provincial city of Kwangju. Somehow, even in the words of the official documents of the time, the whole situation had got out of hand and by the end of a violent and bloody evening nearly 200 civilians lay dead. The closest the South Korean military and the Government ever came to admitting culpability for the massacre was in an admission that perhaps a mistake had been made in sending a crack regiment to Kwangju to deal with a provincial problem. The regiment in question had been trained to deal with incursions from the hostile North and was not equipped to cope with local disturbances.

Now in a variety of locations across the South Korean capital they prepared to do battle once more with the demonstrators. The aim of the security forces was to keep the marches away from the main city thoroughfares and especially away from the big international hotels crammed with foreign visitors. Their main weapon was a pernicious brand of tear gas and I discovered to my cost how bad it could be.

One afternoon we followed a large crowd of demonstrators about 5,000 strong which began heading into the city centre. As they turned to march down one of the main streets, the police and troops – about 300 or 400 of them – drew up in a solid attacking formation about 400 yards away. Their weapons for firing tear-gas canisters resembled crude, oversized sub-machine-guns; some were armed with long clubs. They looked a formidable lot in their Darth Vader uniforms and gas masks, which, on top of their heads, went up into a futuristic triangular shape, completely obscuring their eyes and making them look strangely inhuman. There was no chance of communicating with them; they seemed like angry creatures from another planet hell bent on pacifying the troublesome natives. When they advanced, they dragged their feet in unison across the ground. Whatever the military purpose of this exercise, the sound of 600 or 800 large, heavy boots made an abrasive and menacing noise. It did not deter the marchers, however, who kept moving towards the inevitable confrontation.

Only fifty yards separated them, when the troops fired their first volley of tear-gas canisters. More volleys came hurtling through the sky towards the marchers, many of whom were equipped with gas masks, so the tear gas failed to halt their progress. The marchers seemed to be taunting the impotence of the police and troops when the clash occurred. The security forces waded into them with clubs and batons, and a fierce battle ensued. The tactic of the marchers was to hit and run. It did not work. The police gave chase and inevitably caught up with them. The biggest setpiece battle took place right in front of one of the larger downtown hotels. When some marchers tried to take shelter inside from the troops, the latter broke through a pane of glass to drag them out. Many demonstrators emerged from the conflict with blood streaming from their faces.

I was very badly affected by the gas because we had arrived in town only the day before and had failed to take local counsel by providing ourselves with gas masks. As the battle raged outside the hotel, my eyes burned painfully. They became much worse later, when I washed the tear gas out of my hair and back again into my eyes. Local rumour had it that no other government used tear gas of that kind in trying to repel marchers. It had apparently been developed for use by President Marcos in the Philippines, but he thought it too dangerous. It was certainly unpleasant. At the height of the confrontation, my face felt as though a blow torch had been held to it and I thought I was about to lose my skin – nasty red blotches appeared on my forearms. Unable to see clearly, and in deep discomfort, I slipped and fell. In doing so, I knocked my head and took some time trying to regain my footing. Just then I felt a helping hand on my shoulder – it was one of the men in his

Darth Vader uniform, coming to the aid of someone who was obviously a foreigner.

As soon as it became evident the South Korean authorities could not contain the protests by force, demonstrations sprouted in every part of the city, university campuses erupted and professors championed the cause of their students. The Government let it be known that it recognised the need for change, but it failed to convince the students and other demonstrators that it was really committed to a new political order. South Korean ministers were not accustomed to accounting to the press for their actions and, whenever they did so, they chose to stress instead the need for order and for due regard to be paid to authority. It was too late for that. Eventually President Chun Doo Huan was forced to admit defeat. He was allowed to go into retreat to contemplate and to repent for his misdeeds, but, before he did so, I saw him make one last stand at a party conference. The faithful applauded him, the country did not.

His successor, another military man, was allowed to assume office only after giving a pledge that the process of setting in place a more representative democracy would begin. Several influences were at work in the eventual change in South Korean politics: the protests of the people, the students and the other demonstrating South Koreans played a crucial part, while political leaders who had been shut out of the process re-emerged to take their place.

A MUCH longer battle for change had been under way for many years in the Philippines, a country with a tradition of presidential elections. Although these elections were free and Opposition candidates were not prevented from standing, during the long tenure of President Ferdinand Marcos dark suspicions had fallen on their results and many Filipinos had long ago come to the conclusion that the elections were rigged.

I first went there after the bizarre assassination in 1983 of the

Opposition leader, Benigno Aquino, who was killed seconds after he stepped off a plane from the United States, where he had been in exile for many years. Although he had become a significant figure in Filipino politics, there had been no plans for him to be given a civic reception on his return. In fact, the contrary was true. He had been warned by the Government, by President Ferdinand Marcos himself and by his wife, Imelda, that it might be unsafe for him to return to Manila. Indeed, Marcos had said flatly that he feared Aquino might be harmed and suggested the Government might be unable to do anything to protect him, and Aquino was only too well aware of all that. Minutes before his plane touched down in Manila, he gave an interview to the journalists who accompanied him in which he acknowledged the danger of attempting to return to Manila. Moreover he did not shrink from speculating that he might be killed. Tragically for him, Aquino was proved right. Walking down the stairs from the aircraft, he appeared to be met by a police and army escort, who he must have assumed were there to protect him. Many years after the incident there is still a mass of conflicting evidence about precisely what happened or who pulled the trigger, but, as the officers approached Aquino, he was shot and killed in what seemed a confusing blur of distressing, frantic images. It was chilling to watch so dreadful a prophecy come to pass, like witnessing the terrible apotheosis of some powerful ancient curse.

It has never proved possible to pin Aquino's assassination firmly on the Marcos Government. On the day he was killed, Mrs Marcos was lunching with a party of local film producers at a restaurant near Manila Bay. They had barely finished the soup course, when a call to the First Lady from the Chief of the Armed Forces, General Ver, broke up the party. Mrs Marcos hurried back to the Malacanang Palace.

Sweeping through the palace gates, she rushed not to the main part of the building, but to an annexe, which in earlier years had been intended as a guest house for foreign visitors. Now, unknown even to the President's closest associates, it had been transformed into a hospital wing. Containing the most up-to-date equipment and well staffed by nurses and doctors, it was out of bounds to palace staff and its existence was never disclosed to the country. Marcos was ill. Although there were rumours to that effect, no one knew precisely how ill he was; a conspiracy of official silence surrounded any speculation about the President's health. He had moments of strength and lucidity, but he very frequently needed constant attention.

When, therefore, having spent fifteen minutes with her husband, Imelda Marcos emerged and declared, 'He's dead,' everyone in her entourage who knew of Marco's illness naturally assumed she was referring to the President. However, she quickly cleared up the confusion by explaining that Benigno Aquino had been shot.

The President's Ambassador to London and the European Community, J. V. Cruz, remembers saying at the time that the Marcos administration would be hurt by the killing: 'If this was done by our friends, it was stupid and we would pay dearly for it. If it was done by our enemies, it was brilliant because we would pay dearly for it.'

Ambassador Cruz was right. Benigno Aquino's death plunged the Philippines into chaos and precipitated a sequence of events which would ultimately bring down the Marcos regime.

Anti-Government protests began timidly with some offices in the business district of the city organising Friday afternoon demonstrations. At first they sought no confrontation with the authorities. Many never even left their offices, but at the appointed time showered confetti from office block windows. Gradually, though, more and more office workers joined in and a fledgling protest movement was born. The confetti-makers quickly became so efficient that their handiwork filled the sky with a million pieces of drifting paper. It became quite a sight.

The drivers in the road below were next to join in, slowing traffic into a grid lock. And that is when the marches began, as spontaneous expressions of disgust at the way Aquino had been gunned down. The demonstrations grew in numbers as the protests came to represent the wider resentment of a hitherto silent majority about Government isolation, mismanagement and corruption. The most persistent charge was that Marcos had been in power for such a long time that he had lost touch with the people who had elected him and had done little to address their most pressing economic concerns. At first the demonstrations were confined to the business area, but, as they broke out in the rest of the city and began to spread to other parts of the country, the authorities began to take notice. The response was typical of the way Marcos had settled protests against his administration in the past. He simply ordered that rules and regulations be tightened, and strict guidelines were issued about where marches could go. By then it was already too late.

Filipinos are known more for their hospitality than their public anger, but, once roused, they can be extremely resolute in defence of their interests. They had had a prickly, painful passage through history, first at the hands of the Spaniards and then the Americans. Their Spanish colonisers saw them merely as docile, ungrateful, indolent imbeciles; they enjoyed Filipino hospitality and then abused them. The real tyrants were the Spanish friars, who gave the Philippines the full treatment. The Augustinians arrived first in 1565, followed in rapid succession by the Franciscans in 1577, the Jesuits in 1581, the Dominicans in 1583 and the Recollects in 1606. The hapless Filipinos were hardly given the chance to catch their breath: they were battered into submission by the crushing force of aggressive religion. The islands' Spanish masters in Madrid bore their Far East colony no ill will and, in fact, proclaimed a number of sober, benevolent decrees, but the local religious fanatics simply ignored them. They developed the perverse policy of agreeing to obey, but failing to execute the orders they had been given – '*Yo obedezo pero po cumplo* ... I obey, but do not execute.'

Filipinos were denied access to the Spanish language and were kept in an educational twilight. When one of them, Jose Rizal, proved too brilliant for the Spanish friars and taunted their lack of care with his brilliant literary caricatures, he was banished and later executed. Rizal's true sin was that he was too clever for his country's tyrannical rulers.

When, much later, the Americans became involved in the Philippines they began by expressing the desire for a partnership, but it was quickly replaced by America's grand imperialistic design and Filipinos once more had to wage a battle to retain their national identity.

The Filipinos over whom Marcos ruled for nearly two decades had long ago developed a philosophy to deal with the pain of colonisation and now it was to prove useful in surviving the worst excesses of his regime. It was a sense of fatalism coupled with the vice of resignation. They learnt to face disaster with equanimity and to appear indifferent in the face of graft and corruption. Marcos profited from that immeasurably.

The main problem of the Marcos years was that they went on too long. The government had become fat, uncaring and arrogant, detesting challenge and making the dangerous miscalculation of beginning to think of its political opponents as enemies of the state. It maintained sound relations with the Americans, however, who had at Subic Bay a naval base considered crucial in observing what the Soviets were up to in the region. Marcos's strongly pro-Western credentials kept criticism of his domestic policies in check. It was felt that the Americans would go to great lengths to keep their Far East ally in place. So used to power had the Marcos Government become that it was genuinely caught off balance by the growing spirit of the demonstrations in the wake of Aquino's killing.

When I arrived in Manila the state was already finding it impossible to put a lid on the growing chorus of anti-Government protests. The demonstrators showed an ominous propensity for ingenuity and survival. When they were driven off the streets, they sought refuge in the precincts of the Catholic Church, which remained the strongest influence in the life of the people of the country. In church they could not be touched, not even by their all-powerful leader. He, too, professed devotion to the faith to such a degree that he once had to be stopped by the Vatican from constructing a massive cathedral in his impoverished country to mark a visit by the Pope.

With the Church supporting them, the demonstrators gained strength. I covered numerous marches which either began or ended in churches decked out in the colours of the Opposition and where the sermons were not all apolitical. Gradually the Church of Rome became the political champion of the poor, the downtrodden and the political protesters seeking change.

What the protest movement sorely lacked, though, was a leader. One of my first calls in Manila was on the widow of the assassinated Opposition leader, Cory Aquino. I remember the meeting well. She was not keen to see visitors, but our persistence paid off. We were helped by her brother-in-law, who had taken to acting as part keeper of his brother's political memory and who, I thought, seemed well aware of the political capital to be made out of his brother's death – unlike Mrs Aquino.

Going to meet her for the first time, we were shown up a flight of unlit stairs, in an office block which appeared half empty. The modest office Cory Aquino used was only half lit. To complete the general ambiance, she was still in mourning and dressed in black. She spoke softly and with feeling, her pain still fresh. Her voice, never strong, sounded positively fragile, lacking the authority needed by a politician. It also had an unattractive whining quality. Her eyes filled with sadness at the mention of her husband. Never all encompassing, her grief was proper and practical, somehow carefully limited, never overdone or incapacitating. Politics never having been her first discipline, only when she was pressed did she attempt to address political issues. She did not think she would become involved in any political race, but she was keen to make sure her husband's death had not be in vain.

I recorded in my notes that Mrs Aquino looked frail and hurt. Although she did not have an overtly political persona, she showed flashes of steely determination. I felt she was an amazingly strong woman and I left her not as convinced as she appeared to be that she would concentrate in her husband's absence on caring for her family. I felt her strong dislike of everything the Marcoses had come to represent would propel her into the political arena. She was dismissive at the mere mention of the word 'Marcos' and I thought I detected real hatred there – she spat out the word with more than a hint of challenge and, it seemed to me, with a contempt you could almost feel. What convinced me this might not be the end of the Aquino story was the fact that, despite all her protestations, she was, even in the sorrow of bereavement, holding court. She was seeing people on her own terms, apparently reluctantly, but in carefully controlled settings. Doing her mourner's duty and vigorously denying that she was doing anything else, she had in fact begun to set herself up as a rival to the Marcoses. I felt that the key point in assessing Cory Aquino's future actions was that she was not afraid of the Marcoses and would secretly relish taking them on. She believed the Aquino family, steeped in wealth on its own account, was socially superior to the Marcoses. The two families were, in fact, not all that dissimilar and in other circumstances it would have been easy to imagine the tables turned with Marcos fighting the incumbent Benigno Aquino for the presidency of the Philippines.

It was therefore not entirely surprising to me when, only a few months later, Cory Aquino allowed herself to be propelled into becoming the standard bearer of the millions opposed to the re-election of Ferdinand Marcos. The grieving widow made the transition to political activist and presidential challenger.

Marcos's political campaigns were traditionally nasty affairs, their dominant characteristics being hand-outs and intimidation.

At election time money would shamelessly appear for people in need. It was never much, but there was no ingratitude among people who had so little for many Filipinos were poor. I have visited many developing countries where people struggle to survive, but I have seen few places where the gap between the rich and the poor is so wide. We filmed in a ghastly district of Manila called Tondo, where people eke out disease-ridden existences by scavenging for scraps of food on malodorous rubbish dumps. Old-fashioned diseases were rife – measles, diphtheria, whooping cough, tuberculosis and, of course, malnutrition. Uncomfortably close for anyone with the smallest social conscience is the luxury of Forbes Park, a majestic, serene area with broad, tree-lined avenues for foreigners and Filipinos with money. I spent some time in Forbes Park, too, and I have never been closer to such obvious trappings of wealth. So near to the poor of the district of Tondo, I saw Forbes Park as a kind of revolutionary trigger. I thought the stark divisions between the haves and the have nots and the faltering economy would be serious election issues.

I believed the main issue, though, would be the President himself and the way he managed to stay in power.

Ferdinand Marcos was by any standards an extraordinary political figure. He came to power by skilfully building a coalition of his country's corrupt elite, who felt they would be left undisturbed to make their millions, and the hapless poor, who for a long time saw Marcos as the champion of the dispossessed. President Marcos did this with the strong backing and encouragement of the Americans, the key to whose support lay in Marcos allowing them important military facilities on Filipino soil. Chief among them was Subic Bay, a natural deep-water harbour and a vital naval installation in the uncertain era of the Cold War. Marcos cleverly used America's need for the bases to construct a relationship of mutual dependence. He enhanced it further by convincing Washington that his Government was also involved internally in putting down Communist insurgents. That there were some Communist insurgents was undoubtedly true, but, when I talked to so called Communist leaders in the Philippines, what they complained about had more to do with economic hardship and Government corruption than with the ideology of Marx and Lenin.

Marcos moved quickly in his first term, in 1965, to establish an unshakeable hold on power, influence and on the country's purse strings. With perverse devotion, he salted away hundreds of millions of dollars in secret bank accounts in the financial capitals of Europe. The sums involved beggar the imagination – even at their most profligate Marcos and his family would have been hard pressed to dispose of it all had they survived for a hundred years. It was greed on a massive scale, obsessive and obscene. Rumour had it that the President once spent 2\frac{1}{2}$ million restoring a church in Illocos Norte for his daughter's wedding.

The extent to which the Marcos family and the Government were steeped in corruption was well known by Marcos's friends in the White House. Yet, in the loftier interests of keeping him on their side in the international crusade against Communism, American Presidents ignored all this and travelled regularly to Manila to pay court to their ally and accept his lavish gifts. As one former American President is said to have put it, Marcos was 'a son of a bitch, but at least, he was America's'.

According to dossiers built up by Filipino senators, Marcos was more than ably assisted by his wife. Imelda Marcos was the great imperatrix in the court of Filipino politics, where I watched her for many weeks during the election campaign. She had presence, but she wanted to show that she had style too, and she took her position as First Lady seriously. A large woman, she would never simply enter a room – she made an entrance, sweeping in like a battleship under full power pursued by a flotilla of attendant flunkeys. Commands were given almost imperceptibly by a nod of the head. Obedience was instant, her bidding never questioned because she inspired fear in those attending her, especially in public. The subject of hate and constant rumour – almost all bad – her opponents charged that the First Lady had acquired a staggering portfolio of commercial interests in New York and in other parts of the United States including real estate, old master paintings and valuable artifacts. At home the First Lady presided over a lavish life style in the presidential palace. Malacanang was transformed into a kind of Shangrila. She was obsessed with shoes – she had more than 1,000 pairs. She indulged herself in expensive designer clothes and vintage champagne. Caviar by the kilo was the staple diet.

Evidently Imelda could also be generous to friends, acquaintances and visitors alike. On her orders a small mosque was built in the grounds of the Malacanang Palace in anticipation of a visit from the Libyan leader, Colonel Gaddafi, whom she apparently liked. The unpredictable Colonel, however, failed to repay this touching act of friendship and faith – he never turned up. Mrs Marcos was not deterred: she went on sedulously cultivating others from abroad – film producers, artists, writers and some political commentators – many of whom repaid her friendship by praising the enlightenment of the Marcos Government even at times when its actions were indefensible.

The long arm of corruption grossly distorted the conduct of all political debate. At election time no section of public or private life escaped the need to show support for the Government; every sector was mobilised to get the President re-elected at all costs. I was astonished to discover how far the Marcos Government writ ran on these occasions. The staff who ran our downtown hotel so efficiently were all forced to wear campaign colours, but they entertained no questions about politics or about the campaign. One evening, in a joke which almost went badly wrong, I pretended to chastise a young room service steward for not wearing his Marcos colours. The poor man went pale and so shook with terror that I feared he would suffer a heart attack. Even the members of the pleasant chamber orchestra which played in the hotel lobby had been told they must show loyalty to Marcos. The orchestra's conductor was not amused by my questions about their campaign stickers, and his members were terrified to answer any political questions. I discovered just how scared people were to whisper any dissent when I went to the hotel doctor one morning. Breezily I asked him how he thought the elections might go, after he had shown more than a passing interest in what I was doing in Manila. In the traditional all-knowing way of travelling journalists, I told him I thought Marcos was on the way out and was on his last political legs. The doctor, believing I had passed his litmus test (he was opposed to Marcos, but terrified to say so to the wrong person), spirited me into his private office, closed and locked the door, and then began to pour out a tale of woe about everything the hotel staff were required to do to help ensure the President's re-election. He tipped me off about plans for what was supposed to look like a 'spontaneous pro-Marcos rally' by hotel workers the following day. They were all required to be there – musicians and doctors were not exempt, for Marcos needed the artists and the middle classes too. He could certainly count on the official media for total support.

Marcos ruled by fear and most terrifying of all were members of his entourage, his praetorian guard.

There were days, of course, when the President was lucid and even brilliant in his political discourses. Having a much better grasp of international politics than Ronald Reagan, he could speak for an hour without a note on the Soviet threat to the free world or the failure of Western economic policies and could make a convincing argument for his country's relationship with America and the West. Afterwards he would answer questions from journalists with great skill. On bad days, though, he made no sense at all. He rambled, his tongue seemed like an unhelpful weight in his head ignoring messages from the brain, and his speech was as slurred as a boxer who had taken too many blows to the head. Thoughts drifted into the realms of fancy and never reached logical conclusions. You could always tell which kind of day it was likely to be simply on seeing him. When he was unwell, his face, usually quite alive, looked like a death mask, waxen and puffed up, while his eyes, usually bright with interest, seemed dull, vacant and unfocused, scanning the crowd with the fear of a frightened child. On such occasions he had clearly been pumped full of pills and life-saving injections, and had to be helped to his place on the platform, almost as the dying Brezhnev used to be, while his guards were at their most ruthlessly attentive.

I tried to get close to the President one lunchtime, as he made his way through the lobby of our hotel. We were caught in an almighty crush. The men charged with looking after Marcos wore dark reflective glasses – you never saw their eyes – they had evil faces and lashed out at anyone who came close. Television reporters were treated as possible assassins. I was caught a glancing blow to the face for no other reason than that I was edging nearer the President to try to put a question to him and at one stage I was almost strangled by a microphone cord. It left a nasty bruise. Our sound recordist was less fortunate: one of the President's men forced his fingernails painfully into his forearm and, when my colleague managed to wrench himself free, there were four deep indentations on his forearm, all covered in blood. It was a small, perhaps insignificant, but frightful and cowardly crime totally in keeping with the manic obsession which characterised the campaign to get the President re-elected.

I am not quite sure when the Marcos family realised the seriousness of the Aquino challenge, but for me the realisation dawned one Sunday morning in church.

The Roman Catholic Church was even more influential than Marcos and Filipinos were more devoted to it than any other people I know. The Archbishop of Manila, the gloriously named Cardinal Sin, had sanctified as a part of his morning service the candidacy of Cory Aquino and her reluctant running mate, Salvador Laurel. In a solemn ceremony, such as would be employed for high evangelical reasons, the Archbishop blessed their political challenge to Marcos. To a casual observer it looked for all the world as if Mrs Aquino and Mr Laurel were being given the sacraments of marriage. The Church, which played such a dominant part in Filipino life, had made its choice.

A few days later I arranged to see Cardinal Sin at his residence. The Cardinal's popularity with the faithful was fully justified: he was a wonderful ambassador for Catholicism and a gracious host with a ready, easy smile. I liked him instantly. I enjoyed the fact that he laughed loudly, and when he did, his entire frame seemed to join in the fun.

I went to see the Cardinal with the intention of trapping him into an admission that the Church had decided to dump the Marcoses and had begun to campaign actively on behalf of the President's opponents. For several minutes we fenced around the matter of the 'political marriage service' involving Mrs Aquino and Mr Laurel. The Cardinal dealt with my questions easily, explaining with immense patience that all the Church was trying to do was to ensure that the people of the country had a proper, democratic choice in a crucial presidential election. It was at this point that I sprang my trap: I quoted from an article in the archbishopric's weekly magazine written by one of Sin's assistants, Felix Batista, in which he openly encouraged people to vote against Marcos. It was there in black and white. The Cardinal was cornered.

I moved swiftly to end the encounter with a deadly thrust. 'Does this not prove conclusively that the Church is up to its neck in political manoeuvring? Here were the words of Mr Batista, who answers to you as one of your assistants.'

The Cardinal looked at the offending article and then at me, his eyes twinkling. 'I think from what you just showed me I will have to have a word with Felix about this,' he said, his face wreathed in smiles.

With the support of the Church, implicit or otherwise, Cory Aquino's crusade swept across the country. Her campaign colour was bright yellow and it sprouted everywhere. People flocked to hear her speak in Rizal Park in downtown Manila in their tens of thousands. The Marcos campaign could only match those numbers by bussing in people from outlying districts. Once in the park, his supporters frequently had to be content with stand-ins for the President or highly controlled appearances of only a few minutes' duration because Marcos was ill and his strength seemed to falter as the campaign went on. Much stronger was the Marcos creed to win at all costs and, if that was not strictly possible, the next best thing was to retain power by any means. The news that an international observer group would travel to Manila to monitor the conduct of the campaign, the voting and the counting of votes, was a body blow to the President's team. Now, at least, there had to be a semblance of fairness. Among the international observers was the Northern Ireland MP John Hume and they were led by Senator Richard Lugar, who was then Chairman of the Senate Foreign Relations Committee in Washington.

Those who had the courage and the fearlessness to say what they thought, expected Marcos to lose and to cheat to keep his job. That was the form. With enviable cynicism and hopeless resignation Filipinos had grown used to it. Few believed Marcos could win convincingly in a fair contest, although, in my one face-to-face encounter with Mrs Marcos, she confidently predicted her husband would win by a landslide.

Even before election day Manila was swept by an overpowering sense of *fin de siècle*. While the Marcos supporters struggled to keep their composure, the Aquino camp boasted about preparing for a political revolution, though there was much uncertainty about how such a revolution would occur. Beating the President at the ballot box was one thing, but would the Marcoses and their family then pack their belongings, bid farewell to their assembled staff and quietly drive out of Manila? On that possibility all opinion coalesced – it was not on. Marcos would never do that; his wife and his partisan generals would never allow it. Marcos had been there for much too long. He had led the country since 1965, had won his second election four years later, imposed martial law in 1972, lifted it in 1980, won yet another presidential term in 1981 and now, in 1986, he was seeking re-election against Mrs Aquino. There were too many black holes in his presidency, too many secrets, too many skeletons, too much political baggage, too much evidence of Marcos misrule to be buried simply because the President lost the popular vote. I remember how easy it was to tease political operatives in the Aquino camp about the transfer of power. I had only to ask them to sketch out for me how they felt Marcos's hand-over ceremony would go. Where should our cameras be, I asked. How would the thing actually occur? Those questions touched an exposed nerve, for they saw the point all too clearly. Marcos would decidedly *not* pack up and leave town.

It was in this atmosphere of suspense and uncertainty that the great day dawned.

I travelled up country to watch the first votes cast and then gradually picked my way back through a score of polling stations into Manila again. A quiet but discernible tension gripped the country. Army and police patrols fingered their weapons nervously. Soldiers and police, as unsure as anyone about the next forty-eight hours, reacted to even the most basic question with unease, suspicion and even unaccustomed truculence.

Election day and night, and the week that followed passed in an ever-rising tide of controversy and confusion, beginning with reports of election day irregularities and drifting on relentlessly into election night. The count was chaotic and slow, its erratic progress arousing fears of foul play. At one stage Channel Four Television suggested that the delays in declaring some results were quite normal: 'What foreign observers fail to realise,' it concluded, 'is that the Philippines is a nation of some 7,000 islands. It takes a long time to collect the ballot boxes.' That would have been regarded a fair point had it not come from Channel Four, the Government mouthpiece, which broadcast Marcos's propaganda without the slightest twinge of embarrassment or shame. Coming from that Channel, the explanation only reinforced deep suspicion.

True to form, the Marcos-led official media and the Government election commission put the President in the lead. Significantly no one believed them. The so-called National Movement for Free Elections put Mrs Aquino ahead. Some people who were engaged in the count, arguing that there had been widespread election fraud, staged a highly publicised and politicised walk out with the specific aim of undermining the President. The air was thick with claim and counter claim, allegations of cheating and an expanding body of evidence of bad faith. American observers were genuinely surprised by the fury unleashed by the election. It felt as though the campaign and the voting had lanced generations of pent up frustration and fury; now it was spilling out on to the streets and seemed to be running out of control. Senator Richard Lugar and spokesmen at the American Embassy in downtown Manila, so frequently a target of anti-Marcos, anti-American demonstrators in the run up to the election, were at first very guarded in their comments about election day irregularities. It was a holding position maintained with difficulty for several days, while no conclusive result was declared. Then, from Washington, President Reagan dipped his toe into the troubled waters. Questioned about widespread claims of election fraud, Mr Reagan was equivocal, refusing to condemn his friend, but suggesting that, if there had been irregularities, they had probably come from both sides and Marcos could not fairly be asked to accept all the blame. In Manila the President's comments were read as a message of support for the beleaguered Filipino President. Reagan's comments enraged the American press reporting the campaign, who had pretty well made up their minds that Marcos had lost and said so loudly. Now they rounded on Senator Richard Lugar. He had been genuinely alarmed at Reagan's indelicate intervention and sought to restore some dignity to his country's position by making a more authoritative judgement. When I interviewed him after the Reagan statement, the Senator had gingerly begun to distance himself from the doomed Marcos cause.

Marcos himself had no reason to be totally discouraged. One count – the Government election count – had declared him the winner and at a session boycotted by the parliamentary Opposition he was duly sworn in as President for another term. Following another low-key swearing in ceremony at Malacanang Palace, Marcos began laying plans for the continuation of his reign. He summoned his ambassadors, many of whom had returned to Manila to assist the President in his fight for re-election. They were now to go back to their posts to reassure the countries to which they had been accredited that all was well. This was lunacy, self-delusion and farce on a grand scale, and entirely typical of Marcos.

Washington's next move did not crown the Reagan presidency in diplomatic glory. Phillip Habib, a State Department trouble-shooter, turned up in Manila, ostensibly to sort out the mess. In private he tried to gain an agreement between Mr Marcos and Mrs Aquino that they would share power. Mrs Aquino's advisers treated the suggestion with contempt and derision. In that fateful week Mrs Aquino's distrust of American policy was born. It was to cost both sides dearly.

It was at this point I unwisely left Manila, believing that my cynical prophecy had come to pass.

Marcos had not been swept convincingly back into power, indeed he had probably lost the election. No one could say that with absolute certainty, though, because one count had made him the winner, and apparently presidential possession counted for everything. With allegations of cheating swirling around him, Marcos was back at the palace and it was business as usual. The Opposition was beside itself with rage, but, in the absence of firm American pressure on Marcos to pack up and leave, there was nothing Mrs Aquino and her friends could do.

By the time I rushed back to the Philippines the noise of 'people power' was threatening to shake the President from his political sleepwalking. I felt it was a significant moment in the country's history. Something had snapped in people's minds; the country had experienced psychological sea change.

To people overcome by cynicism, to those who have been ignored by the system for ages, and to those who have suffered because of its whims and its indifference the sudden realisation that they may after all be able to exert some influence on the way they are governed provides a motivation of blinding force. So it was in the week following the Filipino presidential election. There was a growing sense, perhaps even a reckless one, that Marcos was not invulnerable. Over the next few days, fact, fiction and rampant rumour merged into one to create an unstoppable momentum. First of all the Army got off the fence. The Defence Minister, Juan Ponce Enrille, acting, he said, to pre-empt a move by the President to charge him with treason, barricaded himself in an Army camp and persuaded the Chief of Staff, General Ramos, to join him. Then the Church made its move. The smiling Cardinal Sin played a steady hand: instead of urging people to go home and stay off the streets, he encouraged the population to go to the support of Enrille and Ramos, and, if necessary, to block any Marcos tanks with their bodies. It was the exhortation Filipinos had waited twenty years to hear.

Holed up in the presidential palace, Ferdinand Marcos embarked on a series of bizarre television appearances. The press corps could get nowhere near the palace, but the President was hardly off the television screens, since he could cut into the national network at will. He had little to say, did not look too well and rambled on, defending what he had done, trying to talk about the future and how he might survive the present crisis of confidence. He had even more pressing concerns, he said. At one point he told his television audience that the palace was being attacked by the Air Force, but dissipated the high drama of that announcement by gathering round him, in the full glare of the television cameras, his children and grandchildren as a way of pleading with the attackers to spare young lives.

On another occasion his Chief of Staff and military adviser, General Ver, broke into a presidential speech on camera, requesting permission from Mr Marcos to fire on the attackers. 'The palace is under attack,' said a flushed and bothered General Ver, 'do you wish me to order a full scale military response?' To his enormous credit Marcos refused to turn the guns on his people and waved the general away.

At one point he responded to Ver's request by suggesting that he might consider returning fire with water hoses. It was a poor attempt at a joke, but a significant one – the spirit had gone out of Marcos. The desire to stay and fight to survive the encircling turmoil was leaving the old man. Perhaps his opponents had realised all along that this was how it would end, having planned to sap the energy of the old regime. Mrs Aquino's campaign slogan had been the Tagalog word 'laban' – in English it means 'fight.'

The beleaguered President had one last card to play. His wife, who felt that she had developed as close a relationship with Nancy Reagan as her husband had with the American President, kept urging him to call the White House. Her reasoning was that Ronald Reagan would never leave his old friend in the lurch – he would issue an episodic statement of support and, in one dazzling flash of trans-oceanic diplomacy, the redoubtable President of the Philippines would be saved. What Mrs Marcos had no way of knowing was that the Reagan administration had always been divided on the question of President Marcos and crucial sectors of it were now engaged in a rearguard action to stand clear of the impending wreckage. George Shultz in the State Department had long thought that Marcos was a crook; there would be no tears there over his demise. Caspar Weinberger at the Pentagon treated with Marcos only in so far as it was necessary to retain American military bases in Manila and at Subic Bay. Now Weinberger kept his head down.

In that deeply sad and chilling moment in international diplomacy when the bridge cementing relations between countries is pulled up for good and former allies are condemned to the fate of their own making, Marcos's calls to his old pal went unanswered. He made more than a dozen calls, but he was never put through to Reagan. In the end it was Reagan himself who took pity on him. Told by his advisers that another Marcos presidential term was not viable and that the time had come to abandon him, Reagan asked a mutual friend, Nevada Senator Paul Laxalt, to deliver the *coup de grace*. Laxalt called Malacanang and told President Marcos tersely that the game was up. Marcos tried to argue, pretending he had not grasped the message, but deep down he had. Marcos had never been a fool; he just did not want the conversation to end. Laxalt did not need to say it twice – it was all over. Encircled by hostile forces at home, Marcos had now been dropped by the world power which had lavished praise on him and given him succour. He was, as the Shah of Iran had found out six years before, cast to the winds of that especially vengeful fate reserved for former allies.

From our vigil in downtown Manila, we knew nothing of Paul Laxalt's final message. The city had succumbed to a strange atmosphere of puzzling calm. There was no hard news, no overt hostility, but tempers had been rubbed raw by uncertainty and by choking suspense.

I returned to my hotel about seven one evening, when someone came rushing through the corridors with the news that Marcos 'has gone'. At the suggestion of our cameraman, Peter Wilkinson, we headed immediately for the palace. We had been trying to get there for days – if Marcos had, in fact, left, we might be able to get close.

Suddenly the streets were overflowing with people. This made finding a route to the palace difficult, compounded by the fact that Filipino drivers, even at ordinary times a race apart, swerving across lanes at speed with manic flair to the perpetual sound of blaring horns, were now excelling themselves in jousts with death. We managed to come to rest, safely, a long way from the palace. The last half mile of the journey had to be negotiated on foot and the entire population of Manila seemed to be heading in the same direction. It was, for the most part, an orderly procession, though occasionally fights broke out, presumably between pro- and anti-Marcos supporters. In one instance we came across a fight of elemental brutality between two men. One of them was wielding a large club, while his opponent, armed with nothing but his wits, was doing badly. He had been struck several powerful blows across his face, head and shoulders and was bleeding profusely. Blood had run down into his eyes, so that he was no longer able to defend himself. Undeterred, his attacker continued to rain down telling blows. Usually I avoid fights, but it was more than I could bear to watch. I tried to drag the man with the club away, after giving him a short, sharp lecture on the Queensberry rules. I thought I was doing well until my colleagues shouted to remind me that old scores were being settled all across the city and that I was a mere reporter, not the national referee.

By the time we reached the palace, the gates seemed on the point of collapse as they were stormed. Some were shaking them violently, determined to force their way in, while others were attempting to climb over the top. Everyone was shouting and screaming. The noise was ear-splitting and the frenzy incredible. The first shots from inside the palace grounds brought instant, terror-struck silence. From where we stood I could see chunks of tarmac being thrown up by the force of bullets. It was happening only a few feet away. Not quite wanting to believe the obvious, I asked Peter Wilkinson whether they looked like real bullets. There was hardly time for him to respond before another volley crackled into the air. The crowd made frantic attempts to find cover, but there was none. They dropped down from the top of the gates and into the open roadway. I fell to my knees, shaking with fear, behind a small aluminium ladder I had been carrying for our camera crew and behind a small tree. With a thoughtless lack of diplomacy, an Australian colleague pointed out to me that it would take only one bullet to blow away ladder, tree and me. I took his point. The bullets kept flying, but now they seemed to be aimed over our heads. I had to move further away. Nobody dared lift his head, so, crawling on my stomach, I dragged myself away from the palace gates for some fifty yards. Only then did I think it safe to break into a run.

This was how it ended. The gunfire from the palace grounds came from the disorganised and frightened remnants of the Marcos palace guards, who could not continue for long. Even to them the full meaning of the turn of events must have been clear. Their time had gone – they were bit players now, bit players with guts, but footnotes in history. To the sound of gunfire and celebration, the presidency of Ferdinand Marcos had spluttered to an end.

By the time we had arrived at the palace gates that evening, Marcos and his wife Imelda, together with an assortment of children, grandchildren and others too close to the regime to survive the anger of the revolution were already on their way out of the country. With some difficulty, the Americans had convinced them it was time at last to leave. The Marcoses had tried to clear the palace of their belongings, but they had not been given enough time. As a result of their hasty departure there was enough evidence to show the transcendental obscenity of their excesses.

Two things troubled me about the prospect of the Aquino presidency long before it even began.

The morning after Marcos and his entourage were helicoptered out of the country, I drove through the impoverished district of Tondo. The residents of the area had abandoned the municipal garbage dumps and were driving wooden stakes into the ground in an empty field. The stakes were joined together by yellow ribbons to mark off roughly rectangular plots of land. Yellow had been the Aquino campaign colour; 'Tie a yellow ribbon round the old oak tree' had been the campaign song. I was puzzled, so I stopped the car and got out. A quietly spoken, gentle man explained to me what he and his friends were doing. During the campaign, he told me, Mrs Aquino had promised that her administration would give land to the peasants. The people of Tondo had simply resolved to help the new administration keep its word by indicating the bits of land they wanted. Their explanation made me profoundly sad. I sensed that the problem for anyone following Marcos would be breaking the dam of expectation. After twenty-one years of Marcos rule, the future was now burdened by too much hope. Mrs Aquino would have too many promises to keep; there would be disappointment and resentment. One Spanish philosopher elevated such thoughts into something of a political certainty when he had suggested that he or she who makes the initial revolution is doomed to be swept away by the tidal wave of change.

My second observation worried me even more, and fortified me in what I believed was the lesson of the first.

Throughout the campaign Namfrel (the National Campaign for Free Elections) had acquired a reputation built on its rigid impartiality and independence. We journalists had suspected all along that Namfrel would do the Marcos Government no favours, but that did not worry us too much. Given the level of corruption in the Marcos presidency, we told ourselves that a certain anti-Marcos bias was essential to restore the balance. On that fateful election night we went along with the belief that Marcos had lost the election because the Namfrel count said so. We had no other evidence. But the fever of the election had barely cooled before the head of the rigidly independent and impartial Namfrel accepted a top cabinet post in the Aquino Government. A great body of hope died with that appointment. The haste to accept the reward for political services granted seemed indecent and suggested that the departure of Marcos had not made all things new. Political back scratching endemic and cancerous in the body politic of the country, was already eating its way into the presidency of Mrs Cory Aquino.

9

Shooting Stars and Politicos

*Once they talked of us [Palestinians] only as numbers ... Now
we have become a cause.*

YASSER ARAFAT

JOURNALISTS have always been fascinated by the idea of the
big interview. There is good reason for that – at their best, they
can make a difference to the way people think. James Cameron's
interview with Ho Chi Minh changed perceptions about the
Vietnam War, confronting the Americans and the West with the
unpalatable reality that the North Vietnamese were not about to
turn tail and run. Robin Day's televised conversation with Gamal
Abdel Nasser at the time of the Suez crisis initiated a new age in
the conduct of international relations by giving the Egyptian leader
an audience in the opposing camp and thus a difficult issue, which
had divided Britain, acquired a new and challenging dimension.

Through interviews, bogey men, monstrous nationalists and all
round political pariahs held in contempt and isolated by our
distrust and disdain could talk to us directly through our newspapers and claim our attention through the television sets in our
living-rooms. When I became a reporter in Trinidad, nothing so
significant rested on the interviews I conducted. My job was simply
to get hold of regional politicians and diplomats, international
entertainers, conductors and screen celebrities passing through the
island on their way to Guyana, Venezuela or to other parts of the
Caribbean. Fortunately Trinidad benefited from the fact that it
was a recognised jumping off point for other countries in the

region, so we reporters enjoyed some benefits too.

The fact that I relished doing these big setpiece interviews was recognised by the radio station for which I worked and I was made a special events correspondent. It was a title dreamt up to fit the job, which was to make sure I always knew who came through the international airport whatever time of day or night it was. Thus it was that on a soporific Sunday afternoon I met one of my political heroes, the American diplomat and sometime presidential aspirant, Adlai Stevenson. Although I recorded a long radio interview with Stevenson, what we talked about is much less memorable for me than the fact that throughout the interview Stevenson never stood still. His egg head pointing resolutely to the floor, he paced the tiny VIP room restlessly, as I pursued him with my questions and a very old-fashioned and bulky tape recorder.

Stevenson had been regarded by many of his political counterparts as a brilliant Democratic prospect for the presidency, so some of the loftiest ambitions of the Democratic Party perished with his failure to win the presidential nomination. When he later became American Ambassador to the United Nations, President John F. Kennedy had kept him in the dark about America's role in the disastrous Bay of Pigs invasion of Cuba. The episode had exposed Ambassador Stevenson to the ridicule of his opponents at the UN, and the White House had made no attempt to save him from deep personal embarrassment. None the less Stevenson, demonstrating the great dignity for which he was justly famous, had bounced back, but he laboured under a political cloud. The fact that the more worldly Kennedys had privately poked fun at his honour and his lack of political guile made me admire the man all the more, however. As I recall, he fielded my questions about American policy in the Caribbean and Latin America thoughtfully and with ease, pacing about all the time, thinking literally on his feet. The place had fortunately been quite deserted, so few witnessed the comic side of our roving encounter.

Of celebrities passing through I saw a great deal. In a crush of fans, airport workers and people from the cultural section of the American embassy in Port of Spain, I once managed an interview with the great singer, actor and all-round entertainer Sammy Davis Junior. I remember worrying that he might be over-run in the squeeze of the tiny VIP room. My interview featured prominently on the main news bulletins and, suitably edited to include some of his music for an entertainment/current affairs programme the following day, produced a decent feature. In similar circumstances I interviewed, among scores of others, racing driver Juan Fangio, Sir John Barbirolli, Johnny Mathis, Sam Cook, Sarah Vaughan, The Platters, Helen Hayes and Burl Ives.

Burl Ives asked if he could be interviewed lying flat on his back in bed as he had had a long flight and was very tired – it was, I felt, a nice counterpoint to Adlai Stevenson's endless pacing. And I came to admire the Guyanese politician, now Prime Minister Cheddi Jagan, for having the good grace to keep a plane waiting in order to not to break his promise to talk to me.

WORKING for ITN, especially when I became Diplomatic Editor, my targets changed. Having uncertainly pursued the PLO leader Yasser Arafat through Lebanon, I had always wanted to arrange a long sit-down session with him. The lack of certainty with which I chased him around the world is most easily understood not by his unwillingness to co-operate, but by the peripatetic nature of his job and by the level of security which clouds his movements and which, against the odds, has kept him alive. For a number of years Arafat's aides developed the unsettling habit of setting impossible deadlines for our meeting. They would, for example, call me late at night in London to suggest that Arafat would be delighted to see me the following morning in Tunis. Their failure to comprehend the difficulty in getting to such a meeting was partly my own fault, since I had rather allowed them to believe that I could meet the Chairman whenever and wherever he chose to. My boast, though, made no allowances for planes and airline schedules, and it took me many months to explain to Arafat's aides that scheduled flights leaving Heathrow or Gatwick were not entirely under my control. Gradually I became more realistic and began to plead for more time to make it to any appointed meeting.

Then, one day, they came back with a reasonable proposition. Arafat was due in Harare in Zimbabwe for a weeklong meeting of nonaligned states. The PLO leader had committed himself to attending several sessions over three or four days at least and he would see me there. This gave me the time I needed to get there, even though it meant talking my way at short notice on to an Air Zimbabwe plane.

On arrival in Harare late one evening, I was guilty of an unforgivable error: I had failed to obey a fairly direct order that I should seek proper accreditation because the city was about to be flooded by scores of prime ministers, presidents and other heads of governments and their ministerial entourages, and security was tight. I was allowed out of the airport only on the condition that I present myself to the Ministry of Information to be fully accredited to the nonaligned conference. Unwisely, I decided to forgo what I regarded as a tiresome formality because my interview was promised for the following morning and I reckoned I would be in and out of the country much more quickly than the time it took to get accredited. I was wrong.

Next day I made contact with Arafat's people, who promised they would come to take me to the Conference Hotel later that morning. But, in the event, it was late afternoon before an Arafat aide arrived. He had a businesslike, no nonsense air and did not say very much, avoiding all conversational pleasantries. His job was to bundle me into his car and take me to the meeting with his boss – nothing else concerned him. In his impatience he literally bounded out of the hotel, so I never discovered whether he felt the chore of collecting me was somewhat tedious and unworthy of him, or whether his attitude had something to do with the fact that he appeared to have left it terribly late to collect me. He chose not to explain, and I thought it might be impolite to ask. My judgement that we were running very late was reinforced by the fact that I had insisted the interview be done within twenty-four hours of my arrival and, to emphasise the point, I had told the PLO leader's people that I had booked myself on a flight back to London that same night. Of course, I had not done so, but it had appeared the only way to make the case that I did not have a week to spare hanging around Harare waiting on the PLO Chairman.

Once we had left the hotel, we carved our way through the traffic to the consternation of other road users. An ITN camera crew, trailing us in the car behind, found it difficult to keep in touch. In no time at all we arrived at the Intercontinental Hotel, which was ringed with security. Half of Zimbabwe's Army seemed to have converged on the place. Serious looking men in camouflage jackets wore big boots and carried large guns with an expression which seemed calculated to convince you that you had come to the wrong place. They made you feel unwelcome, guilty to be alive, let alone be there. As our car swung into a parking bay and as we hurriedly followed the Arafat aide to the hotel entrance, guilt weighed heavily on my mind. I pondered my predicament: I was probably the only person within forty miles of the Intercontinental Hotel who had not been properly accredited to the meeting. I edged as close as I could to my guide, hoping that by some extraordinary process we would become as one and I could sneak into the safety of the hotel lobby undetected. During our frantic dash to the hotel, I explained to Mr Arafat's man that I was not accredited. He waved his arm in what seemed to be a dismissive gesture. I took it that he was not the kind of man to be preoccupied by such trivialities.

All too soon my moment of truth arrived.

The local ITN crew, festooned with all their proper badges and rosettes, were ushered in. Arafat's man grabbed me by the arm and together we marched forward. We came face to face with a soldier armed with a sub-machine-gun. I decided to leave the talking to the expert. I do not think Arafat's man had contemplated anything else. He was the first to speak:

Arafat's man: This man is a guest of the Chairman.

Soldier with sub-machine-gun: Where is his accreditation?

Arafat's man: He has none, but he doesn't need it. He's a guest of Chairman Arafat.

Soldier: He can't go in without accreditation.

Arafat's man: The Chairman wants to see him and, if the Chairman wants to see him, he goes in.

Soldier: I am telling you he can't. I don't care who he's going to see.

I thought I detected a slight hardening of attitudes here, which I did not find particularly enjoyable. To make his point the soldier pushed his sub-machine-gun with some firmness into my stomach and added for effect: 'And if he takes another step, I'll have to shoot him.'

I did not relish the sound of that and it seemed to me that the stage had been reached in the bargaining which bore all the hallmarks of what is known in diplomacy as an impasse. With a sub-machine-gun digging into my ribcage, I was eager to admit defeat. In the heat of the moment I even concocted a plan. It was self-serving, simple and cowardly. I would apologise and retreat, make a dash for the Ministry of Information, beg for the required passes because of the urgency of the situation, and return, properly accredited, to confront the same obstreperous security guard in my moment of bureaucratic triumph.

Arafat's man was having none of it. The scenario he had worked out in his mind was not remotely close to mine. Where mine was timid and escapist, his was bold and confrontational – he had decided to stand toe to toe with the gun-toting soldier and slug it out.

'Look,' he said to the Zimbabwean, all the while gripping me by the arm even more forcefully, 'if the Chairman wants to see this man, that's the only authority he needs. He's coming with me. You can't stop us.' And almost in the nature of an afterthought he added, 'Do what you like, shoot if you like, but he's going with me.'

I positively hated the sound of that. I loathed being talked about almost as if I wasn't there – and I worried how much longer I would be.

I found myself in the unenviable position of being pulled painfully by the arm in one direction, but hindered by the menace of a weapon which strongly suggested I should head the other way.

After a few seconds which seemed a life time the tug of Arafat's man proved the more resolute. With my stomach scraping its way past the sub-machine-gun, my eyes not daring to meet those of the soldier – if I am about to be shot, I would prefer not to watch the trigger being pulled – I was dragged with immense relief into the hotel lobby. It felt fifteen degrees cooler. Arafat's man, trying to make up for lost time, but outwardly unflustered by our *contretemps* with the Zimbabwe Army, dashed for the lifts. The crew and I followed. They had found the whole episode amusing, while I was only very slowly beginning to recover. My legs showed disconcerting signs of having lost most of their blood and a great deal of their ability to keep me firmly upright.

For the first time since I had met him about half an hour earlier Arafat's man allowed himself a smile. Showing me to the delegates' bar, he offered, 'Have a Scotch. You could probably do with one. I'll go to check if the Chairman is ready to see you.'

We made a conspicuous group: we obviously did not belong, we looked ill at ease and we were not a part of the political ambience, waiting with more than a little anxiety, in the delegates' bar at one end of the delegates' lounge. It became abundantly clear to me, even with the benefit of the most fleeting spot check, that we were the only television crew to have broken into in this inner sanctum. Somehow I felt only Arafat would have ordered it in this way. He had become accustomed to being treated like a head of state, but his aides lacked the skill and experience to deal with journalists. Had we found ourselves in the Oval Office in Washington or in the President's office in the Kremlin, I could not have been more surprised. In all my years of reporting international politics I had never been allowed so close to so many of the main players as an exclusive right, and yet here I was, without even the necessary pass to get into the hotel car park.

As I took huge gulps from my tumbler of Scotch and soda, I quite expected to be shown to an anonymous hotel suite, where we could set up our cameras and wait for Arafat. Instead, the Chairman's aide returned and advised us that we should be ready to do the interview in a few minutes. We should set up in a corner of the lounge – the Chairman was on his way. I could not believe my luck, especially after the nightmare of my entry into the hotel.

Some fifteen minutes after we had positioned our cameras as far away from the delegates as we could, Yasser Arafat arrived. Apologising for having kept us waiting, he fell into a deeply cushioned armchair and signalled that he was ready to begin.

Just then a sudden rush of activity sent a tiny knot of people crashing relentlessly in our direction. It happened much too quickly for me to assess what was happening. By the time I had, I was standing face to face with President Robert Mugabe, the Conference host, and a clutch of officials. Apologising for his intervention, the Zimbabwe President approached Arafat. A few whispered words were exchanged and then more loudly I heard Mr Mugabe say, 'I'll be gone only half an hour or so.' I got a vague idea of what had been said and for the second time in less than an hour I felt a sickening feeling in the pit of my stomach. Getting out of the armchair, Arafat explained to me, as the Mugabe delegation disappeared as swiftly as it had arrived, swallowed up in the mêlée of the delegates' lounge, that Mr Mugabe had been called away from the Conference on urgent business and that he, Arafat, had been asked to take the chair for part of the afternoon session. He would only be gone for an hour or so and we were to make ourselves comfortable until he returned.

I cursed my luck, confronted by fact that we had no choice but to do as we had been asked. It had, nevertheless, set up an amazing evening. Arafat did not return for another four hours and in the meantime, trying to make myself as unobserved as possible and failing to do so, I watched a procession of world leaders slip by, many of whom I had met before and all of whom were surprised to find me trying to blend into the comfort of the delegates' lounge. It always happened in the same way. A rush of feet would signal the arrival of another head of state and his entourage. General Zia passed close enough to see me, walked on and then did a double take when his Foreign Minister, who was a former ambassador to London and a friend, stopped to enquire: 'Trevor, what the hell are you doing here?' I explained to the General and his minister that I was awaiting the return of the PLO Chairman. They looked quizzically, wished me well and moved on.

Next President Kaunda hurried into view, stopped to chat and, as was his custom when we met, wished God's blessing on me and on my assignment. Never did I need it more, I thought.

Then, the time came for Colonel Gaddafi to enter the lounge. We were asked to make room, so we retreated to the furthest corner, as the Colonel wanted to have a small meeting with his associates and needed some of the space we had appropriated for ourselves. Gaddafi was dressed in a flowing white robe, his hair wildly long. Four women attendants similarly attired followed close behind. They were feminine, but looked formidable, and had caused a stir in Harare by insisting on keeping their guns while they flanked their leader making his setpiece speech to the Conference. President Mugabe, no antagonist, had not approved, but had given in to avoid an unpleasant ultimatum. We watched Gaddafi's little circle meet and we watched it disperse after about half an hour.

I will always remember the next little cameo. Whispers went round the room and the Cuban leader, Fidel Castro, swept into the delegates' lounge. I had never before seen him up close: he was every inch as large as the images of him I had seen on films. He stood cigarless, not very far from where we sat – by this time we were trying desperately to pretend we did not exist – talking to his aides. Almost all the pictures I had seen of Castro showed him displaying his political machismo, hurling insults at his opponents, exhorting his countrymen to abide by the principles of the revolution, and lecturing workers for many hours on the need for increased production in the face of worsening economic conditions in Cuba. Now, in the subdued atmosphere of a conference of nonaligned countries in faraway Zimbabwe, gone was the look and sound of the demagogue. Castro's face had shed the stress of leadership; the hard, angular edges disappeared. He seemed transformed into a much gentler man. Relaxed, confident, even unassuming, his features softened and his long beard looked more the consequence of an ascetic life than the concomitant of revolutionary rage. He appeared much older than I remembered, almost avuncular. As he talked in tones which were hardly audible, from the little Spanish at my command, I could just about make out that he was expecting to be joined by some other delegates. We were not kept waiting long.

A very tall, slim young man hurried to meet the Cubans in long, easy strides. He wore khaki and green trousers, a plain brown shirt and a black cap, slightly askew. My ITN colleagues based in Harare identified him as Thomas Sankara, the leader of Burkina Faso. Not yet thirty, he had taken control of his country in a military coup. Sankara and Castro began an animated conversation, although they seemed to have no common language. Castro was speaking Spanish, Sankara replied in what sounded like French, and no one in the group ventured a common translation. The bilateral seminar was expanded and became much more animated with the arrival of President Samora Machel of Mozambique. He breathed dynamism into the proceedings and talked quickly, employing elaborate, almost manic gestures to make his points, while his eyes shone with an intensity which seemed to send his eyeballs into a constant rolling motion. His linguistic skills moulded the disparate group into a functioning unit. Machel spoke to Castro in Spanish, responded partly in English and in Spanish, and addressed Sankara in French. He talked about the conditions in Mozambique and about what the nonaligned meeting should decide, and in response to Fidel Castro's invitation to visit Cuba, he suggested that a date should be fixed soon.

I never met Samora Machel and can hardly judge the kind of man he was, having seen him only in those extraordinary circumstances, but his enthusiasm and verve left a lasting impression on me. What he exhibited that afternoon in the delegates' lounge must certainly qualify for the much abused term 'charisma'. When, some years later, he was killed in a plane crash, I was overcome by a strange sense of loss. I felt that in one all too brief encounter, I had come to know him. He seemed too full of life to die.

By the time Yasser Arafat returned for our interview, the slanting rays of a glorious Harare sunset had begun to stream through the large room and we had been in the delegates' lounge too long to care about our embarrassment.

The Chairman of the PLO was more than suitably apologetic. He answered my first question by making a spirited defence of his organisation's position on the possibility of talks with Israel. He was unbending, he told me, in his determination to see a homeland for the Palestinians. He excoriated what he saw as the double standard applied to the search for a Middle East solution by the United States and he expressed his frustration at the inability of the United Nations to pursue the full force of resolutions intended to curb Israeli territorial ambitions. He said time and time again that he simply could not understand the policies pursued by the Reagan administration. When he waved the olive branch, he said, everyone thought the PLO had become a spent force. When Palestinians defended themselves or hit back at their aggressors, they were branded as terrorists. He did not deny PLO terrorism, but rather too glibly suggested that the Palestinians had been pushed to the brink, where they were forced to defend themselves. Arafat made his arguments powerfully, if in frequently fractured English. This had the effect sometimes of preventing him nailing down his conclusions. When I tried to make him focus on all the obvious difficulties of the PLO, its political splits, and its internecine battles for control of the leadership structure, he was almost dismissive. From what I had read, he had been much more forthcoming on those issues in the past. However, I thought I could understand the reason for his attitude when I saw him. This, after all, was not the Yasser Arafat on the run from the Israelis and his numerous other enemies, and making surprise appearances in the orange groves of secret fields in Lebanon. In Zimbabwe he was being fêted as a leader worthy of the support of the nonaligned nations. For him, Harare and every similar international forum represented triumphs. In this international climate he could play statesman, leader, head of state. I pressed him on how the PLO intended to conquer deep Israeli distrust.

Before we switched our cameras on, I had recounted to him my experience of how potent that distrust was. On a visit to Jerusalem, I recalled, covering a Middle East tour by the then Foreign Secretary Lord Carrington, we had been taken round the Holocaust Memorial Yad Vashem. Its profoundly moving images of the suffering of the Jews under Nazi Germany had gripped us all, but, when Lord Carrington, confronting a picture of Chamberlain's infamous 'piece of paper', suggested to the curator of the memorial that it was possible to be too harsh on Chamberlain and on that period in Britain's prewar history, the Israeli museum curator had turned to Lord Carrington and broken the solemnity of the occasion with the brutal observation, 'No, it's impossible to be too harsh. There's no misunderstanding on our part. The same mistake you made about Hitler, you're making about the PLO now.'

'So,' I said, 'in the minds of some Israelis, you are to be equated with Adolf Hitler.'

Arafat thought about my story and said after a while, 'I'm sure we can convince Israel of our good intentions. But the rights of my people cannot be negotiated away. We must fight for our rights. We cannot be passive when our people are suppressed.'

His finest response was made to what I hoped would be my best question. I pointed out to the Chairman that after all the long years of hardship and of running, of internal squabbling and lack of progress in negotiating with Israel, that the PLO had, in fact, got precisely nowhere. It had acquired an international profile, but had done no significant political deals; it had collected magnanimous backers along the way, but had succeeded in accumulating no real political clout. In a sense the PLO still had no real status, for it depended on friends and backers such as Egypt and Syria to take up its political cudgels and Saudi Arabia, Kuwait, Libya and Iraq to give it money. Despite it all, the Palestinian Diaspora was nowhere near realising what it had come to regard as its manifest destiny – a Palestinian homeland. My question was shaped to be deliberately provocative because responses to those are often sharper and thus more memorable. Arafat did not disappoint.

This time his answer flowed as he took me on journey through history. He reminded me that Syngman Rhee, one of the earlier Secretary Generals of the United Nations, had once derogatorily described the problem of the Palestinians as 'a refugee problem'. According to Arafat, Rhee, confronted with the overall Palestinian problem had apparently said, 'Tell me the numbers, give us the figures and we'll try to provide a solution to the Palestinian problem.'

'That is what we were,' Arafat told me, sitting bolt upright, his eyes blazing with passion, his finger pointing directly at me. 'That is what they said to us. Tell us how many of you there are and we will try to house you. Figures, numbers. That's how they saw us then. Now you ask me what we have achieved. I'll tell you. Once we were a problem of numbers. Now – we are a cause.'

It was a fair and eloquent description of what the Palestinian problem had become. Despite all its shortcomings, the PLO had mobilised world opinion to the belief that a solution to the status of the Palestinians was a crucial element in any Middle East peace.

The Chairman departed with my thanks. He had instructed his aides that we should be found a meal and accommodation for the night, having apparently been taken in by my pretence that I was due to fly out that night. Had that been the case, I would have easily missed my flight. Declining this offer of hospitality, partly because I was dying to escape the restrictions of the delegates' lounge, proved something of a problem. The same aide who had pulled me through the Zimbabwe security cordon, because the Chairman had requested my presence, now insisted that we have a meal on the same specific instructions of the Chairman. I decided to try for a compromise. I told him that a bottle of champagne from the bar would do very nicely. Impressed or horrified by the cost of it, he allowed us to drink it quickly and take our leave. Honour of a kind had been satisfied.

Arafat had been right to focus on 'the cause'. It had developed an undeniable permanence, being at once elusive and at the same time very real. It had been sustained by a grim determination, cast in the crucible of pain and fed by a crying sense of injustice and shame. Among the Palestinian Diaspora that sense of injustice burned fiercely enough to dispel a multiplicity of doubts and questions about the PLO's leadership and its credibility. The death of old international alliances such as those in Eastern Europe, for example, and changing political moods in the United States and in Britain had forced the PLO and its leadership frequently to alter course, to appear inconsistent, pursuing mutually contradictory goals. Arafat's United Nations speech about the 'olive branch and the gun' was neither a political gimmick nor a paradox pressed into service by the politically inept. It expressed the fundamental dilemma which tugs at the organisation's heart and divides its soul: where to go, what to do to end this trial of dislocation. In the end Arafat survived, stumbling constantly through bewildering policy changes, because he came to represent the cause, one much more powerful than himself or his leadership.

DANIEL Ortega, President of Nicaragua, like Arafat, had a cause too. I was determined, when I went to Managua, to try to see the Sandinista leader. I discovered very quickly it was not going to be easy.

On every single visit to the Ministry of Information in downtown Managua I was assured that Ortega would see me, although no official was bold enough to hazard a guess at when our meeting might be possible. Showing that wonderfully relaxed attitude to what might in other parts of the world be regarded as a slightly pressing matter, many of my Nicaraguan interlocutors went as far as suggesting that my two weeks in the country were not nearly long enough to try to see the President. I persisted because I wanted to meet the man who had been excoriated by the Reagan White House, but who, from what I could see, had a fairly loyal following in the country. That loyalty went far beyond Ortega himself and seemed to embrace the idea of the Nicaraguan revolution, its desire to break free of strong regional influences and to forge an identity of its own.

One afternoon we were driven many miles into the hinterland to meet a number of English men and women who had volunteered to pick coffee in Nicaragua. There were about twenty or thirty of them in a dreadful state, when I saw them, living in what I felt were appalling conditions and all suffering from a variety of debilitating stomach disorders. In Nicaragua such illnesses were virtually assured once contact had been made with the water. Yet they all made passionate declarations of support for what the country was trying to do. Nicaragua's freedom from American domination had become an international *cause célèbre*.

I never ceased to wonder just how possible freedom from American domination was. If Nicaraguans were inclined to be angry at American hostility, popular nonpolitical sentiment in the country was very pro American, so much so that I formed the view that the Sandinista revolution, its zeal notwithstanding, might have occurred too late. The country had already been colonised. It was struggling manfully to undo that, but I felt it would be difficult. History had not been on the side of the revolutionaries. The big regional superpower had done its business effectively, for Nicaraguans in the street craved everything American and everyone talked of Miami as a kind of capitalist and cultural Mecca. The American embassy seemed to me to be the focal point in the city. It had done such a splendid job of ostracising Ortega and his Sandinista Government that, on my plane into Managua, I was shocked to find Americans still travelling to the country. Nicaraguans played baseball and watched it on American television by the bucketful, and in a country anxious about basic economic survival the power of the American dollar exercised a fatal hold on the minds of Nicaraguans.

Nicaraguan economists were not shy of admitting the problems the Sandinistas faced in trying build a viable country. My interest in meeting Ortega was to discern where he saw the silver lining in what seemed to me to be a depressingly gloomy landscape.

Called to the President's house in Managua one Sunday morning, we planned how we would shoot the interview as we waited in the lightly guarded grounds. Before long, with not the slightest word of explanation, we were asked to join a convoy of jeeps, which soon left the grounds of the house and the city, and headed out on an open road into the country. Only then did we begin to surmise that probably the Nicaraguan President had not been in his house and we had gone there to *rendezvous* with our guides. After what seemed an hour under the full glare of the noonday sun, we turned off the main road and on to a gravel track, but never altering the furious pace at which we were moving. Clouds of dust flew up around and behind us, at times totally obscuring the ambient view. Our vehicles had known better days and rattled loudly.

Before long the gravel ran out and we turned into the bush. There was no path here that I could discern, no visible evidence that anyone had been this way before, and no attempt was made by our guides to convince us they knew where they were heading. The bush thickened into light forest. The ground became uncomfortably uneven and the clatter of our convoy increased into a fearsome commotion, puncturing the deep stillness of the countryside. Thankfully, even where the ground was at its most uneven, it was firm.

The leading drivers, still making no concessions to the terrain, began to play a disturbing game of dodging the trees. The game has no future in countries where there is respect for Landrovers and trucks or for the lives of their occupants, but, even so, it had its moments. We would head for a stout tree trunk at speed, never varying our course, until the very last moment, when we would suddenly be thrown out of our seats and into the air by the prominence of the tree's roots, and down again.

Each time I thought I detected a clearing in the forest and felt confident enough to predict that our adventure was nearing its end, I was wrong. After a while I gave up, and succumbed instead to lugubrious intimations of mortality. The mind can encompass only such a measure of unpredictability and then it gives up, if only in the interests of its own preservation. Mine had begun to lapse into that state when we began to ford a huge river. Heading into the bush again, I was almost beginning to feel relieved, when we started to climb a long winding hill. Heading down on the other side, with a precipitous fall on either side of our meagre track, I came to the firm conclusion that, even if we managed the downward slide in safety, we would never make it out again. It is utterly depressing to think that, even if you do survive, you may be lost for ever in some nameless Nicaraguan forest.

It was a chastened group which dismounted the jeeps at a

clearing in the forest. Here the vegetation slipped away to reveal the shores of a peaceful lake. Gradually, as the noise of our arrival subsided, soldiers, dozing in their hammocks or sleeping in the bushes, got up and shook themselves awake. I was grateful that we were so clearly expected.

Ortega was out on the lake shooting iguanas for our lunch, a proposition which held scant interest for me because I have a deep-seated aversion to green reptiles, even before they reach the lunch table.

The Sandinista President was preoccupied with his regime's war against the Contra guerrillas. He felt the Contras, despite the backing of their American friends, would never win the war, but were capable of inflicting serious damage to the economy. Ortega had no clear solutions for turning the economy round, realising the extent to which it had been crippled by American sanctions. In nearly all his answers to my questions he relied on the inherent need, as he saw it, for the Nicaraguan revolution which his Government had helped to bring about. He emphatically denied that Nicaragua was interested in spreading revolution throughout the region. He had few real answers to any of his country's crushing problems and relied almost entirely, it seemed to me, on his faith in the idea of a socialist revolution, which would reverse the horrors of the past.

Close up, in a clearing in the jungle, eating iguana and surrounded by his wife and family, Ortega hardly looked the zealot the Americans frequently described. His speeches were never as potent in fervour as those of his brother, Defence Minister Humberto Ortega. He had no plan dramatically to improve the lot of his people and he had no idea how the debilitating war would end. Politically he seemed at a dead end. The shadow cast by America's influence was much too long to allow Nicaragua genuine freedom. For a time the country had basked in the approval of a disparate group of intellectuals and artists, and had become the great political cause – that was obviously a help – but it had never succeeded in helping the country in its day-to-day life. Ortega spoke calmly and softly, never exaggerating the difficulties his country faced, but never totally dispelling a feeling of resignation.

A few days later he invited us to his modest house in Managua for tea. It was pleasantly overrun by children and toys, and sparsely decorated with splendid examples of Nicaraguan art. As we were leaving, he explained that the house had once been owned by a wealthy industrialist and had been taken over by his Government since the revolution. I could not help feeling that, for the Nicaraguan revolution to be a success, the redistribution of available resources would have to be much wider.

THE circumstances which led me to seek an interview with President Saddam Hussein of Iraq were entirely different from my reasons for wanting to meet Ortega or Arafat. We wanted to go to Baghdad because the world seemed to be drifting towards a potentially catastrophic military conflict and Saddam Hussein was at the centre of it all. More to the point, he had started it.

In August 1991 Iraqi forces, having waited near the border for several days, marched into neighbouring Kuwait. For reasons, never satisfactorily explained, the American CIA and other Western intelligence agencies had chosen to believe that the Iraqis had no hostile intentions towards Kuwait. In the specific case of the Americans there had been, some weeks before the invasion, a meeting – later the subject of some controversy – between the American Ambassador to Baghdad, Mrs April Glaspie, and President Saddam Hussein. At that meeting Mrs Glaspie had appeared to signal to Saddam that Washington was much too interested in good American–Iraqi relations to be overly concerned about Baghdad's quarrels with Kuwait. The State Department at first denied it, then said that the content of the meeting with the Iraqi President had been misreported, then sent Mrs Glaspie into seclusion and much later attempted to pretend it all might have been her fault anyway. This might explain why Iraq's invasion occasioned such disbelief, shock and anger. Obvious signals had either been missed or misread.

Events moved swiftly. Securing unprecedented United Nations support for a number of strong anti-Iraqi resolutions, Western Allies, led by the Americans, amassed a formidable coalition force to turn back his invading army. Of particular significance was the fact that some Arab nations had joined the Western-led coalition against President Saddam. The United Nations had hardly ever in its existence been so effective; Iraq had been isolated by the international community. The Iraqi President had seen less than a handful of journalists since the invasion and none from Britain.

Our attempt to secure the first British television interview began at the office of the Iraqi Cultural Attache in Tottenham Court Road in London. I paid my first visit there one morning in the company of our Editor in Chief, Stewart Purvis.

Our Iraqi contact, Naeil A. J. Hassan, looked the most unlikely person in the world to set up a meeting with Saddam Hussein. He appeared frequently disorganised and his office looked more permanently so – it was the desk which gave it away. Mr Hassan found it impossible, even when he summoned the assistance of a secretary, to find anything when he wanted it. His desk was an untidy jumble of what looked like several stacks of unrelated papers, and half-empty coffee cups and Coke cans, all clumsily and haphazardly tossed about, jostling uncomfortably for space. They might have found some papers were it not for the centrepiece of the mêlée – an oversized ashtray crowned by a mound of ash and cigarette butts. Mr Hassan was never without a cigarette, yet, in that abiding paradox of many chain-smokers, he did not seem to care much for his brand; too many cigarettes had been abandoned after they had only been partially used. Smoke from his lips and from his ashtray curled around the room in crazy, meaningless patterns. In time it enveloped the place and lingered clingingly. Very quickly I discovered that all visits to Mr Hassan's office left their mark. Mr Hassan's room was badly lit and was always overrun by noise. Only with great persistence, which meant making it quite clear several times that you could hear little of what he had said, did we succeed in persuading Mr Hassan to turn the sound down from two large television sets, which were usually tuned to different channels and were never turned off. I found it amusing that the Iraqis were carefully monitoring all the nasty things being said about their President and their country on television.

The chaos was rendered bearable by the fact that Mr Hassan's staff were the epitome of politeness and good manners. Indeed, despite the actions of their President, those qualities seemed part of the Iraqi nature. To enter the semi-dark, noisy, messy room was to be embraced by genuine kindness expressed in repeated offers of strong, dark, viscous coffee and biscuits. The disorganised Mr Hassan, too, was never less than gracious.

By the time I had made half-a-dozen visits to the Iraqi cultural office, a different look had been forced upon it. For a while it had been under siege. Sections of the London community, unimpressed by what President Saddam had done to Kuwait, broke down the outer doors of Mr Hassan's office and smashed the glass in some of the windows. The wooden frontage was replaced by a large steel contraption not unlike the doors to a bank vault.

Alerting the Iraqi guards to the fact that you were attempting to get in was not always easy. I soon found that the knuckles of my hand were inadequate to the task of attracting the attention of the security guards and always carried about my person a large coin or a small piece of metal.

Mr Hassan was forever encouraging about arranging for me to see his President. 'You'll get the first interview, I promise. I have made my recommendation to Baghdad,' he would say. He needed to be reminded, though, and very frequently, and I made sure of that by seeing him most mornings of the week. Our setpiece dialogues were invariably the same:

Me: 'Any news about the interview, Mr Hassan?' trying desperately not to sound too repetitive, or to betray too much anxiety.

He: 'Not yet, but I'm talking to Baghdad this afternoon and I will send another telex.'

Although I was not required to, I found it difficult not to test Mr Hassan on his views about the prospect of an Allied war against his country. He was contemptuous of the American-led alliance against Iraq and, although he was never quite specific about how it might be accomplished, he suggested that the Allied campaign was doomed. I implied that he was very optimistic and left it at that.

One morning Mr Hassan startled me with a chilling prediction. We were talking about the role oil played in bringing Iraq's quarrel with Kuwait to a head. Mr Hassan reminded me about Kuwait's virtual isolation at the OPEC meeting that July, when the contentious issue had been overproduction, and he repeated the Iraqi claim that over the years the Kuwaits had been systematically stealing Iraqi oil by employing the technique of lateral drilling. Then, still shuffling through the mountain of papers on his desk, and hardly looking up as he spoke, Mr Hassan said, 'Why are the Americans so concerned about Kuwait oil? If war starts, it will all go up in smoke. We have mined all the oil fields and, as soon as the invasion begins, we'll blow them all up.'

I was horrified. It was one of the mornings on which I had taken a colleague with me for company and I looked around to see if what we had heard had made the same impact on him.

At that point Mr Hassan looked up from behind his paper mountain and broke the intervening silence. 'That's the fact, Trevor. We've mined those oil fields, we've put the explosive charges there, and we'll blow them *all* up.'

Mr Hassan had always been very friendly in our discussions about the possibility of an interview and had shown flashes of a well-developed sense of humour. On those rare occasions when his good humour had deserted him I had put it down to the fact that he seemed to suffer with great regularity from the effects of too many naughty nights on the town. Mr Hassan talked a great deal about late-night parties and, from what I observed, was clearly not teetotal. From my earliest meeting with him and from his many invitations to a 'good lunch', he obviously enjoyed a drink. He was sober, however, that morning when he told me about the mining of the oil fields in Kuwait, and he had lost his ready smile.

I made a serious effort to avoid it, but on future visits to his office I always had in the back of my mind his warning about blowing up Kuwait's oil fields. One Sunday morning I was poring over a stack of newspapers at home, all predicting as inevitable an allied *blitzkrieg* against Iraq, when my telephone rang. It was Mr Hassan suggesting that maybe the time had come for me to present myself to his colleagues in the Ministry of Information in Baghdad.

I had not always retained faith in Naeil Hassan's ability to get me an interview with his President and, now that it looked a distinct possibility, I found it necessary consciously to reactivate my interest in the project, to begin to steel myself mentally for the possible encounter. That was not very difficult. My Editor in Chief, Stewart Purvis, who had worked so diligently on the project, was delighted, and helpful, as were my other ITN colleagues. No British journalist had got near President Saddam Hussein. ITN would be first.

My response to Mr Hassan's suggestion that I should go as quickly as possible to Baghdad did me no credit. I complained feebly that I did not possess a valid visa and that my understanding of the process of getting one was that it took time. Mr Hassan's humour returned; he laughed loudly over the telephone and chided me by saying that, since it appeared he had made some progress in at least positioning me in Baghdad for a possible interview with his President, then perhaps I should also entrust to him the relatively simple task of getting me an Iraqi visa.

'Come to my office at ten thirty in the morning, and you'll have your visa' – still with the sound of laughter in his voice.

Three days later I was in Baghdad.

10

Facing Saddam

We are prepared for ... the mother of all battles
SADDAM HUSSEIN *before the Gulf War*

HARDLY had I arrived at my hotel in Baghdad before I was summoned to the Ministry of Information for the first of many meetings. Bearing in mind that the Americans and the other members of the coalition were in the final stages of putting together a massive military force to humiliate Iraq, the capital looked remarkably assured. It is true that, as a rule, ordinary people in Iraq know little of what is really going on in the rest of the world, but on the eve of the Gulf War there was more to it than that. Baghdad had had its fill of war – it was sated by long years of military attrition, had grown sick of anxiety, air-raids and uncertainty, and had decided instead to make the most of the meagre benefits of mere survival. The war against Iran had been fought over a period of eight years. Several times the city had been threatened by destructive bombardments and the disruption to the life of its people had been immense. The scars were never far from view. Now a stubborn pride was asserting itself, based almost solely on the fact that Baghdad had not been crushed. It had survived, and resilience shone in people's faces.

Across the city, when the bustle of the day gave way to evening, Baghdad took on a look of near normalcy. The pulse of life quickened and people flooded downtown to the markets and restaurants. Stall-holders along the banks of the Euphrates enticed passing motorists with their fish baked on charcoal. The larger hotels did a roaring trade catering for parties and weddings. There was nothing extraordinary in the fact that people were busily getting married in Baghdad, it was simply that the jollity of such festivities seemed at odds with the more sober temper of the times. But the fact that its army had gone into neighbouring Kuwait at the start of what might be another long-drawn-out military adventure played little on the mood of the people. Whatever their leaders thought, Iraqis had become weary of war.

The Director of the Ministry, Naji al Hadithi, was delighted to see me, but he evinced none of the quiet assurance of Naeil Hassan about my interview with the President. Not that the possibility of an interview was gone by any means, but a series of problems had arisen. In the three or four days immediately preceding my arrival those difficulties had been dealt with with great confidence, skill and untiring zeal by my colleague Angela Frier. Angela had done sterling work as ITN producer in Baghdad and my early arrival was intended to give her additional support.

It was not easy to get to the root of the difficulty, because Mr al Hadithi was nothing if not a diplomat. Despite the fact that his country was on the brink of another potentially serious conflict (we had talked a great deal about the ruinous effects the protracted conflict with Iran had had on Iraq, and al Hadithi had shown me just how close Iranian bombs had come to demolishing his office), his serene good humour could never be punctured and, in the tradition of his countrymen, his kindness could not be faulted.

I was distressed to learn, though, that the interview was being talked about only as a probability and, worse, as a probability with strings.

The cause of the trouble was the BBC. They, too, wanted an interview and were not happy about the fact that it seemed to be moving ITN's way (my arrival in Baghdad had been confirmation of that) and they had launched a sustained campaign either to have the decision reversed or to be included in the interview facility. Under the guise of good-natured, gentlemanly conduct

and professional probity, they began an undercover fight to convince the Iraqis that giving such an important interview to ITN
would be a mistake. They argued that fewer people watched us, a
claim that was easily dismissed. Their other charges against us
were either little white lies or clumsy distortions, and the Iraqis,
with our guidance, eventually found them so. Confronted by
any fresh, inaccurate BBC claim, my response to the Ministry of
Information was simple: I advised them to check with their man
in London. This proved effective, and we came to the view very
quickly that the BBC never had a chance of success. Much later, I
was amused to hear them peddle the line, born understandably
perhaps out of failure and disappointment, that they never really
wanted an interview at all, their *post facto* reasons being that
they found the conditions attached to the facility journalistically
intolerable. That is not remotely true. On the ground, in Baghdad,
they pressed Mr al Hadithi relentlessly. He bore the tribulation
of our contending entreaties with great stoicism, but with an
embarrassment which he found difficult to conceal. It led him to
attempt to find a diplomatic solution.

In terms of the agreement I thought we had struck in London
about an exclusive interview, none of this made any sense. Angela
Frier and I, therefore, decided to fight it vigorously. We thought
we detected in the course of our many long conversations that Mr
al Hadithi had not been given any instructions from his Minister
or from the President's office to seek a compromise between us
and the BBC. He simply felt it was the decent thing to do. We,
therefore, resolved to listen carefully to all his suggestions about
a compromise and to state quietly, but unequivocally, that we
could not and would not agree. The first suggestion we turned
down was that we should allow the BBC correspondent to join in
the questioning of the President. The second involved the BBC
simply being there, so that they could use a part of the interview
of their choosing. We turned that down on the ground of its
absurdity, since no one wants to share an exclusive worth the

name. Either the Iraqis thought sufficiently of an interview with their President or they did not. It was rather more difficult, though, to combat Mr al Hadithi's third suggestion. For some reason, he sought our agreement to allow the BBC to do an interview with the President at the same time as we did ours, on the explicit understanding that theirs would not be broadcast until some forty-eight hours after ours had been used. This was almost farcical. We pointed out to the Iraqis that such an idea would not be in their interests. Assuming the role of diplomat, I suggested to Mr al Hadithi that President Saddam's popularity ratings were not sufficiently high in Britain to sustain two interviews in quick succession, and that they might well be doing themselves a disservice by agreeing to a second. I made the point in our own interest, of course, but there was more than a little truth in it.

We had discovered that a number of people in Britain felt very strongly that President Saddam Hussein, a man who had sent his armies to crush Kuwait and who at the time of my visit was still holding British hostages, should be given no time on British television. Although we had no real trouble in fighting off this view, we were aware that to many viewers Saddam Hussein had assumed the characteristics of a monster. To them we employed the general argument about our responsibility as journalists. We said it was imperative that we were seen to be challenging the Iraqi President about his international conduct. No inquiry of this kind should be excluded from the public's right to know, especially when British troops were being mobilised to fight what was generally perceived to be the Iraqi menace, but we were sensitive to people's feelings. At one stage, to emphasise our point, we said that, had we been around at the time, we would certainly have tried to interview Adolf Hitler. It is a judgement I make today.

Back in Baghdad Mr al Hadithi began to sense that his efforts on behalf of the BBC would find no favour with us; his zeal to obtain a compromise was diminishing.

At one meeting, as I paced impatiently in Mr al Hadithi's office,

I was sharply reprimanded by Angela Frier. I remembered, to my shame, Kipling's fateful epitaph: 'A fool lies here who tried to hustle the East.' Kipling was writing about the Far East, but his warning applies as much to the conduct of affairs in the Middle East. I was glad I remembered it then for the real tests of our patience were yet to come.

I shall never forget the point at which I thought we had successfully fought off the BBC's attempt to share the interview. Mr al Hadithi invited me to dinner and not until the last moment did I realise that a similar invitation had gone out to all the other foreign media representatives in Baghdad. It was an elaborate affair: three venues were offered to us, all in the one hotel and the honour of choosing one of the three fell to me. 'You make the choice,' said Mr al Hadithi, 'this dinner is in your honour.' And then *sotto voce* with a conspiratorial smile, he added, 'It should be in your honour because you're doing the interview. You sit near me; I'll put the BBC further down the table.' And my BBC opponent was placed further away.

During dinner and in the days that followed I talked to Mr al Hadithi a great deal about the prospect of war. He thought little of the American attempts to build a coalition against his country and seemed puzzled by the fact that the Americans, in particular, had taken such a line; after a while I came to believe he felt it was an occasion more for sorrow than anger. In the light of what has since emerged about the West's policy of arming Iraq with the most sophisticated weapons of mass destruction at a time when Iran was perceived as the greater enemy, it is possible in retrospect to understand some Iraqis' reactions to the growing anti-Saddam coalition. Al Hadithi felt none of it made diplomatic sense.

I tried to say to him numerous times that his country's invasion of a neighbouring independent state had put Iraq beyond the pale and that the international consensus, very visible at the United Nations, demanded the aggression be brought to an end. Mr al Hadithi would have it, although, in the nature of diplomats everywhere, he seemed to suggest that 'all things are possible by negotiation and not by threats'. Never far from the surface of what he said was the fact that a proud nation like Iraq, which had survived the convulsions of a war against Iran, could not be expected to back down publicly in the face of an attack by Western Allies. At one point he seemed to be saying that President Saddam could simply never do that and remain the leader he is. Stripped of all the rhetoric, Iraq's position, as explained to me by Mr al Hadithi, came down to this: the American-led coalition would not attack – it was just too improbable and made no sense. Nothing I said could change Mr al Hadithi's mind. It was not part of my remit to argue with Iraqi officials, but I did try to draw to Mr al Hadithi's attention to the fact that President Bush appeared hell-bent on smashing Iraq. The noises coming out of Washington, I told him, sounded determined and truculent. He told me that the Americans would be too terrified of getting 'bogged down' in Iraq; he felt the first body bags would inspire such revulsion in the United States that Mr Bush would be forced to back down.

I was slightly surprised to discover that Iraq's view of what Mr Bush might do appeared locked and frozen in the memory of America's psychologically bruising experience in Vietnam. They were sound on American social history, but they seemed to lack real appreciation of more contemporary American diplomacy. Nothing I said about the inevitability of an Allied attack unless Iraq withdrew its forces from Kuwait could dent Mr al Hadithi's apparent confidence in his assessment of America's intention. One evening, after another dinner of many courses spread unhurriedly across a canvass of interminable debate and several hours, Mr al Hadithi revealed what lay behind his country's plans for meeting an allied attack.

He had taken me on a tour of the city, and across several of its bridges. 'If the Americans attack,' he said with some urgency, 'we shall be forced to bring Israel into the war. What happens if we do that? We'll bring Israel into it. How will the coalition fare then?'

This was the unanswerable point and it had obviously been uppermost in the minds of Iraq's military command. It was at once their fall back position and their plan of attack; it was the core of their strategy. Suck Israel into the war, they reasoned, and Arab support for the anti-Saddam coalition would trickle away. Once that happened, according to the Iraqi view, the coalition's international respectability would begin to disappear. It was Iraq's masterplan: if the Allies attacked Baghdad, Iraq would launch missiles at Tel Aviv and Jerusalem.

For once I did not contradict Mr al Hadithi. Machiavelli himself stressed that his description of how the Prince should conduct the affairs of state was never intended to be a lesson in political morality, and I felt sure that bringing Israel into the conflict would add a new and explosive dimension to a war.

It was shortly before one o'clock in the morning when we drew up outside the al Rashid Hotel. I was fairly anxious to get some sleep, but my host pointed out that a news bulletin from the Voice of America was due on the hour and suggested that I might like to hear it, so I stayed. The content was predictable. The first five minutes of the news were devoted to the continuing storm of international protests against Iraq and the gathering clouds of war. Day by day and with meticulous care the Allied coalition was making its plans and getting its forces into position. One of the biggest military campaigns of modern times was about to begin. Seen from Baghdad, the auguries were bad. I do not know what Mr al Hadithi had expected of the Voice of America, but the news caused him some distress. He shook his head in disbelief, bade me goodnight and arranged to see me the following morning at his office.

In my several meetings with Iraqi officials one point seemed to recur: given the level of Western co-operation the country had enjoyed when it had been at war with Iran, there was genuine incredulity at the precipitate suspension of all contact since the invasion. One afternoon an official struck up a conversation with me about the hostile undertones of a visit to Israel by the British Foreign Secretary, Douglas Hurd – it had been done with a purpose. He asked: 'Why doesn't your Foreign Secretary come to Baghdad? We could settle a lot of issues and he'll certainly be treated much better here. Tell Mr Hurd he's welcome here any time.'

I am sure that was true. Iraq, I concluded, was as concerned about a possible war as it was by its diplomatic isolation. I became convinced in some of my conversations in Baghdad that, in the course of an uneven diplomatic effort to justify the unjustifiable, Iraq flirted with the idea of a face-saving solution to the impasse. Its key point would have been a formula to tackle what the Iraqis continued to describe as their 'legitimate grievances' against Kuwait. Under a cloud of international 'mediation', the Iraqis would have then begun to make some small concessions about withdrawing its troops from its neighbour's territory.

Long after the Gulf War had been fought and conclusively decided, I had a conversation in London with the Assistant Secretary of State for Defence in the Reagan administration, Richard Perle. In exchange for a description of my visit to Baghdad before the war, he agreed to talk about the mood in Washington before the Gulf War. I floated the view that had Secretary of State, James Baker, gone to Baghdad at a certain point, the Iraqis would have fallen over themselves to try to strike a deal and avoid a showdown. I said I had no idea whether it would have succeeded, but given the pragmatic, nonideological approach Mr Baker took to Foreign Affairs and his reputation as a 'political fixer', it would not have been impossible to imagine a ceasefire of some sort. Until that time I had had only the word of a few minor Iraqi officials to support my hunch, but Mr Perle added considerable weight to it. He told me that in the run up to the war he had been a central figure in an informal group of diplomats around Washington who were determined that Secretary of State Baker should not go to Baghdad for that very reason. Mr Perle told me that his group, too, had been worried about a possible deal and felt that, had Mr Baker gone, enough of a fudge might have resulted to give Saddam a chance to edge away from a confrontation. Mr Perle's group had tried to make sure that this should not happen because they felt the Iraqis should be punished for their aggression and given no opportunity to escape the consequences of their reckless behaviour. If President Saddam made any serious calculations about American public opinion, he had misread the importance of the 'hawkish tendency' in Washington. Mr Perle, who had acquired the unofficial title 'prince of darkness' had been just as passionately uncompromising about striking deals with the Soviet Union.

When, on my fourth day in Baghdad, I was summoned to see the Minister of Information, I hoped for a fuller discussion on the consequences of Iraq's invasion. However, the appointment had been arranged as a courtesy only and we sat at either end of a long leather-covered bench, merely exchanging pleasantries. The sole virtue of the encounter was that it confirmed to me and to my colleague Angela Frier that we would meet the President.

One afternoon, just after lunch, the informal, almost leisurely atmosphere at the Ministry of Information changed abruptly. The entire ITN team was asked to attend a meeting to discuss how the interview would be shot and how its translation would be handled. A ministry clerk laboriously took details of all the technical details in long hand. Even so, maddeningly, any question about when the meeting with President Saddam Hussein would take place or the mere mention of the interview as a fact was met by a stony-faced expression which gave nothing away. After several such sessions, I concluded in one of my darker moods that the preliminaries were meant only as a tease: the interview had never been anything but a fiction and, as a consolation, we were being made to go through the motions, although no presidential meeting would ever occur.

I knew I was wrong when, after yet another session at the Iraqi Information Ministry, we were asked, without explanation, to return to our hotel and to remain in our rooms. Two hours later a man from the Ministry asked us to assemble with our equipment and our overnight bags in the lobby of the al Rashid hotel.

We had all given almost constant thought to the shape the interview should take. For me it had begun in London in discussions with several of my colleagues and had continued throughout our visit to Baghdad. On one point we had all agreed: the interview had to be demonstrably tough. We could afford no other, and always at the back of mind was the fact that many people felt we should not be interviewing Saddam at all. A 'soft' interview would be a disaster of enormous proportions. That thought never left my mind. There had even been a suggestion that, if the interview did not turn out as we hoped, it might not be broadcast. For me the consequences of that were too grim to contemplate. Before I left London, Stewart Purvis had said to me, only half jokingly, 'Don't think about it too much. The only things at stake are ITN's reputation and your job.'

A big problem for me was that so few people had met Saddam Hussein. I had met no one who had even been near him, and officials in his own ministry were so vague and unhelpful that their President might well have been inhabiting a different planet. This was compounded by what appeared to me to be the elements of respect and fear; the mere mention of the President's name was enough to stop all conversation dead in its tracks. Some years before, at the end of celebrations to mark Shaka Day in South Africa, I had almost been lynched by a drunken crowd of Zulus for mentioning the name of Chief Mangosuthu Buthelezi. Talking about Saddam did not cause the same anger, but encouraged a wary, opaque silence – people just said nothing. That is why, on a visit to the British Embassy in Baghdad, I was anxious to find out how diplomats there thought I should approach my task. One afternoon, at the end of a very pleasant conversation with Ambassador Harold Walker, I asked whether I could try my proposed questions to the Iraqi President on him.

I said my first question would be: 'Mr President, is it in the tradition of Arab hospitality to invade and rape a neighbouring country?'

The Ambassador almost fell out of his chair. Looking at me as though I had taken permanent leave of my senses, he said: 'You're not going to say that to him, are you?'

For a second I froze at his response, then tried weakly to explain that, whatever I said, I would be obliged to take a no-nonsense approach.

Walker made it clear that he thought I would be guilty of a grave tactical error. He tried again. 'Have you done anything like this before?' he asked.

By this time I was so worried by his initial response that I almost failed to remember the names of any of the many senior diplomats or heads of state I had met and interviewed over the years.

As I haltingly mentioned the names of a few, the Ambassador said in a tone of unmistakeable resignation, 'I suppose you know what you're doing.'

I felt sick at the thought that I had so misread my assignment, but regained some confidence when I asked the Ambassador how he might begin the interview. He suggested a general question about the President's hopes for his people and his country. Trying to make light of our exchange, I said, 'Ambassador, if I said anything like that, I'd be sacked before I even got back to London.'

Even so the significance of our conversation was not lost on me. Ambassador Walker had stayed on in Baghdad long after many of his Western diplomatic colleagues had left. He was in the first division of British diplomats and was not the type to be easily intimidated, but was concerned about me and about my proposed opening question. He was, I sensed, advising me to be careful. My worry returned: should I be more cautious in the way I approached my meeting with President Saddam?

Back at the al Rashid Hotel, two cars had arrived to take us to an unknown destination. An Army major got in with Angela Frier and me. He was pleasant, but said little. In fact, it was to prove a fairly silent journey. We had been asked to get in the car and we had, with never a word about our proposed meeting with President Saddam Hussein. Iraqi officials, I told myself again, were still treating the interview with the same unspoken detachment as the search for an unidentified flying object. The Major sat next to the driver and it soon became clear that the driver had no idea where we were headed. Driving towards the outskirts of Baghdad, we came repeatedly to large roundabouts. Our driver, looking straight ahead, would slow his vehicle to indicate that he was unsure which way he should go and was awaiting an instruction. He evidently did not want to speak to the Major out of deference to a superior and kept his eyes on the road, even though he had no idea where he was supposed to be taking us. It seemed unreal, but it was the only conclusion I could come to. Neither was the Major keen to say anything to put the driver out of his misery before it was absolutely necessary. Only at the very last moment would he say tersely, something like 'second turning on the left'.

We went through about a dozen roundabouts and the same thing happened every time. The driver never said a word; his role in the Iraqi revolution was to drive and to keep his mouth shut. His restraint, under the circumstances, left me in awe, though I found it bizarre and tried to say so with a rather poor joke. To Angela Frier I remarked, 'You know, I've come to the conclusion that you and I are absolutely crazy.'

Angela, deep in thought, did not respond, so I persisted. 'Have you ever before willingly got into a car in a foreign city with not the slightest idea of where you were being taken?'

The point touched a nerve. Angela, looking as though she did not want to be reminded of what we had just done, sat staring straight ahead, not even attempting a weak smile, while the Major kept up his terse instructions to our speechless driver.

After about forty minutes we turned into the compound of two or three well appointed houses. We had escaped the noise of the inner city, but only just. At the entrance to one of the houses we were greeted by a smiling, dapper figure in Army uniform, and inside by a man in a dinner jacket, who seemed to combine the jobs of house manager and *maître d'hôtel*. It was about five o'clock in the afternoon.

The formality of all the greetings concluded, the *maître d'* figure showed us to our rooms and then promptly asked what we would like for breakfast. Rather stupidly, I thought that his English was poor and that he really meant to ask what we would like for dinner. But no, he meant breakfast next morning. I have stayed at a variety of hotels and guesthouses in countless world capitals, but I had never before been asked that question at half past five the previous day.

'Does this imply,' I foolishly enquired, 'that the interview will definitely not take place tonight?'

For this the house-manager-cum-chef had reserved his most comprehensive smile. With it went a shrug of the shoulders and a studied silence. He had, his expression seemed to say, no idea what I was talking about. He would have been much more forthcoming if I had made the more reasonable request of asking him to help me unravel the mysteries of the universe.

Our evening in President Saddam's guesthouse passed, like the progress of a wounded snake, with deathly slowness. We were well looked after, but not knowing what is happening in a strange, unknown location is alien to journalists. We tried to cheer ourselves up but, after we ran out of jokes capable of crossing international cultures, our laughter assumed a hollow ring. I recalled T. S. Eliot's brutal line about 'the laceration of laughter that ceases to amuse'. We had stopped being able to amuse ourselves; uncertainty rendered our cheerfulness a pale imitation of the real thing. We all felt as though we had been locked away in a cocoon laden with enough supplies to survive, but cut off from reality.

The Iraqis had thoughtfully provided a companion for our

evening's entertainment – an information officer in the Ministry and one of the few I had not met before. He had been to university in England, was mad about the London theatre, missed St Martin's Lane for some reason I fail to recall, and loved to walk around Trafalgar Square. The Iraqi Ministry of Information was crammed full of Anglophiles. He showed passion for the performances of my favourite football team and his, Tottenham Hotspur, so we talked about football a great deal, and then about our families and about books (I even promised to send him some) until I stopped rather abruptly, when I thought about the unreality of it all.

Compared to some of his more reserved colleagues, it was difficult to keep a rein on our companion's conversation. One thing silenced him – any mention of 'the interview'. Our information officer had no information about that. To all intents and purposes he had been sent to spend an evening with us solely in the interest of keeping international relations alive. A man of some intelligence, he saw nothing odd about that. I took leave of him just before midnight, marvelling again at how effective President Saddam's regime had been in preaching self-restraint. He was there again next morning at breakfast.

'Any news?' I asked him.

'No,' he replied, seeing no need to elaborate.

His other Iraqi colleagues in the room, the guest-house staff who spoke little English, would occasionally ask him to translate my questions about what I kept referring to as 'the interview'. He would do so, and they would look at me and smile. It was, I felt, a smile of genuine pity.

I was disturbed by the fact that, although there were phones in the house and although one of them rang with regularity from what I took to be the kitchen area, we were told it was impossible to make calls out. The paradox was never explained. Without a telephone, I could give no comfort to my anxious Editor in Chief, Stewart Purvis, in London, I could not connect with the world outside. I desperately needed a fix of reality. We spent a long day, sitting idly, reading, talking discursively, waiting.

Nothing would persuade our Ministry of Information companion to say anything about the prospect of our meeting with the President. The phone kept ringing, people responded in Arabic, put it down again and said nothing to us. By four o'clock that afternoon I could tolerate the suspense no longer. I approached one of the occupants of the house who seemed to vary his dress from civilian to military throughout the day for no reason clear to me. With all the politeness I could muster, I asked him what the hell was going on.

For the first time someone made sense of my question and gave me a reply. He told me we would be setting off any minute now.

About five thirty we were asked to make our way quickly to waiting cars outside. Our crew rushed to gather up their equipment, only to be told they must leave everything behind. We looked at each other in a state of disbelief. Our camera team had had interminable and very detailed conversations with the Iraqis about what equipment would be needed for the interview, we had given them a full list of everything we would need to take and they had agreed. Now, maddeningly and without explanation, they had changed their minds. Our equipment was to stay at the guesthouse, while we went off to do an on-camera interview with the President of Iraq. It made no sense at all. I was beside myself with rage.

I feared the worst and began to sink into deep despair. The isolation, the lack of information and the refusal even to entertain our protests about not taking our equipment began to take their toll.

We were driven off into the fading light of a Baghdad afternoon in a cloud of anger and confusion. Fifteen minutes later our convoy of cars and officials swung into the drive of an imposing building. Having decided it was important not to betray our deeply bruised emotions, our team was all smiles when we met officials from the President's office inside. After a thorough security search, we were shown where the interview would take place and sat down to await the arrival of the President.

Given everything that had gone before, the arrangements seemed ideal. We were to use cameras from Iraqi Television and technicians were there to help us make sure they worked. The room where the interview would take place was large, well appointed and well lit. Our mood began to improve, and I settled down to concentrate on my imminent encounter with the Iraqi leader.

The President's interpreter, who was there to supervise the operation, approached me. He opened by saying he knew that one of the main conditions under which the interview had been agreed was that the President would not be given a list of questions beforehand. In all honesty, this was a principled but fairly cosmetic stand on our part since it was not difficult to imagine the issues any journalist would want to raise with the Iraqi President given that he had invaded an independent country, and there were reports of the most appalling atrocities by Iraqi troops, and Iraq was holding a number of Western hostages.

'So,' asked the President's interpreter, 'without wishing in any way to contravene the terms of that agreement, may I ask if you intend to use any unfamiliar words in your questions? I ask only as an interpreter and for purposes of translation.'

I was still a bit on edge and, although I managed a smile, I told the President's man that there would be no unfamiliar words, a decision I regretted almost as soon as I said it. Feeling that I was being too defensive and that my response lacked style, I called the interpreter back. On reflection, I said, there was one word he might like to be warned of. Expressing gratitude, he asked me what the word was.

'The word is "disembowelling",' said I.

The interpreter sat up with a start. 'Why would you be using such a word?'

'Well,' I responded, 'there have been widespread reports from Kuwait about the conduct of Iraqi troops. Some reports say that pregnant women have been disembowelled. I must put that grave charge to the President.' The interpreter adjusted his spectacles, looked at me sternly for a moment and then smiled. 'Fine,' he said, 'thanks for telling me.'

As he turned to walk away, I added, 'Of course, you have an advantage on me since I do not speak Arabic, but I shall be watching the President's reactions closely when I put the question about disembowelling and, if I have the merest suspicion that you have not faithfully translated the word, I will draw an appropriate sign across my stomach to indicate what I mean by "disembowelling" to make sure the President understands.'

The interpreter smiled again and said there was no need for that, I should not worry, he would translate faithfully everything I said.

We had waited for more than an hour for the President to appear. Gradually I became aware that there were fewer presidential officials around, some had begun to drift away. About ten minutes later we were told that the interview had been postponed. In a flash the furniture which had been arranged for the interview was rearranged, in a flurry of activity. We were to go back to the guesthouse and resume our vigil there.

The news came as a blow to the solar plexus. I had mentally prepared myself for an interview in those surroundings. It is never easy to get yourself mentally warmed up and then be made to wind down again, let alone the pain of disappointment. But we could not let it show, as I quickly pointed out to my colleagues; if this was all part of a game, we should play it too. So I made a businesslike, unemotional speech saying I found the postponement very understandable in view of the President's impossibly busy schedule and that we looked forward to seeing him later on. Smiling broadly, but with well-concealed emotions, we left. Once in our cars we allowed our hearts to sink again in private, made gestures of hopelessness to each other, and made our disconsolate way back to the guesthouse.

Nothing much was said, but an offer of dinner was met with such universal disapproval that our hosts may have sensed how badly we felt.

Fortunately the interval this time was not too long. An hour later we set out from the guesthouse again.

This time everything looked and felt different. Our escort had grown encouragingly in size, our convoy was larger and everyone seemed much more serious. The restriction on our taking our own equipment remained and this time the instruction was summary, and we did not even attempt a protest. And this time the security checks began even before we left the guesthouse. I was made to empty my pockets, on the excuse that it might save time at the other end. Then, much to my alarm, all my interview notes were confiscated and my protests that they were just sheets of paper were ignored.

As we drove off into the night, I came to the conclusion that there had never been a real possibility of an interview earlier in the day; it had all been a charade – we had been used as extras in an elaborate and convincing dress rehearsal. If proof were needed, we were now on our way to an entirely different location.

If, from my position in the lead car, I was puzzled about what was going on, I was not alone. Fifteen minutes into our journey the Major who had confiscated my interview notes and crammed them into his pocket with such lack of respect for my work, and from whom I was determined not to be separated, slammed his fist on the dashboard, bringing our car to a screeching stop. The Major got out and went in turn to all the other following vehicles. At each car something was whispered, there was an acknowledgement and the Major moved to another. I was in no doubt that only then were the other vehicles told where we were heading. Our destination had been known only to the Major. Into the dark we plunged again at speed.

Turning at last off the main thoroughfare, we entered a badly illuminated road which looked long and wide enough to take a decent jet. I thought it might well have been used for just such a purpose. Half a mile along, past several groups of armed guards, we forked right into the shadow of a mammoth building. Quickly we made our way across the well-appointed grounds and were escorted up the stairs at a gallop.

The difference to the non-interview location of earlier was immediately obvious. Men in suits with bulging armpits filled the place; unsmilingly, they murmured to each other on walkie-talkies. A variety of sub-machine-guns were out in the open and there were what seemed to me to be a field of metal detectors. We were to be ushered through them all. I have never understood why so many of the things were necessary; at one stage I found it inconceivable that we would get through them all before midnight. Although the readings seemed to indicate that we were 'clean', we were then strip-searched. From an adjoining room, I could hear Angela Frier's distinctly disapproving tones as her clothes were removed. Our cameraman Phil Bye almost lost his shoes – the soles were apparently judged much too thick to be considered secure. I was deprived of my watch, my ring and my pen. If this was psychological warfare, it was working – I was terribly angry. Stop watches, until then thought essential to what we were about to do, were almost the first to go. Shorn of a great deal of dignity and much of our belongings, we were then marched, in my case protesting, along a seemingly endless corridor until we were shown into the bustle of an enormous room filled with members of the presidential staff and Iraqi television technicians. Our technical team dived for the cameras to make sure we could use them and it was as well that they did as Phil Baye identified a number of faults immediately. Peter Heaps, our engineering genius to whom no technical problem was insoluble, set out with manic determination to conquer them.

I begged for confirmation that it would all work. Heaps murmured something indecipherable. Bye, an instinctively helpful man, tried his best to put my fears at rest in terms I could understand. Jim Dutton, our sound engineer, tried to infect us all with a cheerfulness which went far beyond the call of duty and bore no relation to the circumstances in which we found ourselves. In the meantime I began, all over again, to remake the interview notes I had done in a hundred drafts ever since I left London. The atmosphere was not conducive to concentration. The frenetic rushing about and my worry were too much. Catching sight of the President's interpreter with whom I thought I had established such a rapport in our 'disembowelling' discussion, I momentarily lost my cool.

'Listen,' I said, somewhat to the alarm of my colleagues, 'I demand to have my notes which were taken away from me at the guesthouse. I want them now.'

The interpreter hurried away and came back with several sheets of blank foolscap on a clipboard.

'No, no, no – my notes taken away from me by that man,' I said, pointing rather disrespectfully at the Major.

They arrived back, rolled up as though about to be discarded, only a minute or so before the President did.

Saddam Hussein strolled into the chaos of our frantic assembly stiffly, but with the poise of a head of state.

A formal group picture with him, we had been instructed, was *de rigueur*, so we all stood ramrod straight, looking directly ahead, as the cameras flashed. Then, without further ado or any fraternal chit-chat about the palace or the weather in Iraq at that time of year, we got down to business. I introduced the members of our team and told the President we were grateful that he had agreed to be interviewed. Then, as stiffly as he had entered and as we had stood to have our pictures taken with him, we walked to our respective seats for the commencement of the interview. Scurrying in our wake were three or four cabinet ministers, a small army of interpreters and a vast array of the men in dark suits with bulging armpits. There is no chance of getting out of here quickly, I thought to myself, as I faced President Saddam Hussein.

My first impression was that he looked preoccupied, even tired. His face was creased by what seemed to be lines of worry. Presiding over a country in a moment of great crisis had not come terribly easily to him; whatever Iraq was saying to the world at large, surviving a possible Allied attack weighed heavily on the President's mind. He did not attempt to be overfriendly. He was serious without being too distant, confident without being overbearing, and conveyed the impression of being a cerebral sort of person, one who thought carefully before deciding what action to take.

As we waited for the translators and the presidential entourage to arrange themselves around us, I looked into the President's eyes. We were not very close, but our swinging feet could touch. Neither of us made any attempt at small talk. I was very aware of the presence of his cabinet members. If the President and I may be described as having been at either end of a tennis court, they sat at the net, their eyes ready to swivel from question to answer.

Ignoring the British Ambassador's advice, I asked the President whether it was a very Arab thing to invade and rape a neighbouring country.

He did better than I expected. While his ministers rocked back in their seats, he feigned amusement at the sharpness of the inquiry and asked in return whether it was a very English thing to do.

I waited and asked the question again, this time slightly differently, reminding the President of the condemnation he had brought on his country and on his people.

Saddam staunchly defended Iraq's position, excoriating the Kuwaitis for their selfishness and their greed, and berating the West for being so easily taken in. He was not boastful about the prospect of meeting the Americans and their Allied coalition partners on the battlefield, but felt the Americans would want to avoid getting bogged down 'in the sands of Arabia'. At one point he employed a lurid metaphor about American blood and Arabian sand, and was scornful of the Arab nations who had joined the coalition.

The President found it impossible to answer in a reasonable way why he had invaded Kuwait, launching instead into a rambling, unconvincing historical discourse about Kuwait being a part of ancient Iraq. Prepared for that, I said his response was unconvincing because, until the invasion, Iraq had been an independent state with a seat at the United Nations; tactfully, I pointed out that what he said made no sense at all.

When the President denied his men were disembowelling Kuwaiti women, my response was intended to elicit from him an invitation to go to see for ourselves. However, when I played my trump card by saying we had only his word for that, he agreed independent confirmation was impossible and would remain so 'because of the security situation'.

The President sounded repentant about the Western hostages he was holding. To his predictable claim that they were being well treated, I had carefully prepared the response that what the hostages wanted was not Iraqi hospitality, but their freedom. Saddam's response was interesting.

Before I went to Baghdad I had read an account by a Japanese American writer of how Japanese in the United States were incarcerated during the Second World War for no other reason than the fact that they were Japanese; the writer had strongly condemned what had been seen by Japanese Americans as the fundamental injustice of the position taken by their adopted country. The Iraqi President answered my question about hostages by saying that, in times of national emergency, actions otherwise inexcusable were sometimes necessary, as the Americans had found out in the Second World War. The words he used to make this point sounded to me like an echo of the sentiments expressed by the Japanese American writer. Something told me he had read the same book. It was a very sophisticated argument to a rather messy situation.

I tried to draw from the President the lengths to which Iraq was prepared to go to defend itself, enquiring about the possibility of the use of nuclear weapons. He was evasive and made no mention of bringing the Israelis into the war, though he did not rule it out when asked. 'We shall see,' was his reply.

The President flirted with the idea of a negotiated peace, but did not attach too much weight to that possibility. If an important facet of leadership is demonstrable resolution, Saddam passed the test. His conviction was that Iraq would keep the Allies bogged down until they withdrew. As interesting as the President's responses were the semiotics of the occasion. It seemed clear to me that his ministers had witnessed few such exchanges with their President. Their eyes lit up like beacons every time I asked a tough question and I speculated whether cabinet meetings were ever as forthright.

The President's belief in Iraq's ability to 'overcome the foreign enemies' seemed genuine. His conversation appeared in part to be that of a leader cut off from the mood of the outside world and his views about countries such as America and Britain shaped under different circumstances and in other times. Now he found it impossible to change and, even had he wanted to, lacked the knowledge to do so. Quite unable to understand Western anger at his invasion, he did not entirely believe the Allied commitment to turn back the invaders. If his ambassadors had been telling him about significant developments such as President Bush's increasing impatience with Iraq, Saddam had shown no sign of comprehending their message. One probability is that few emissaries brought their President bad news. A story doing the rounds in Baghdad, when I was there, pictured Saddam asking Foreign Minister Tariq Aziz what time it was. The Foreign Minister bows deferentially and replies, 'Whatever time you'd like it to be, Mr President.'

Immersed in the never ending intrigue of the politics of his own country and with the need constantly to keep ahead of enemies and rivals, there was scant time for any real appreciation of the twists and turns of public opinion in the larger capitals of the West. The President never fully understood the determination of the Allied coalition to punish Iraq for its invasion and for its disregard of United Nations resolutions. He and his advisers badly misread the American President. George Bush longed for a world set on a buttery smooth course of predictability, he hated surprise and Saddam had shocked him. The Iraqis understood none of that. They preferred instead to imagine Western plots and conspiracies, and to divine American-led cabals aimed at insulting Iraqi sovereignty. No arguments, however logical, could breach this barrier and nothing seemed capable of penetrating the country's self-imposed isolation. The very ruthlessness with which Saddam ran his Government and by which he had survived for so long worked against him. People were too scared to tell him the full significance of the West getting ready for war. No one wanted the job of making him face up to the possibility that Iraq was in trouble.

The interview over, Saddam got out of his chair and beckoned me to follow. I was a touch alarmed when he said, 'I want to have a word with you.' The relief that had washed over me at the end of our conversation evaporated. As he gripped me by the arm and led me to the other end of the room, I felt sure I would at least be told off for being rude in my questions. The British Ambassador's horror at my first question came back to me.

At the far end of the room the President spoke: 'How much do you know about Kuwait, do you really understand what kind of people the Kuwaitis are?'

I decided not to enter this dialogue, so I waited for the translation of the President's question, said nothing, and allowed him to continue. For the next twenty minutes or so, moving back and forth across the room, I was given a lecture by the Iraqi President about the evil of the Kuwaitis. I was told how the money the country earned from oil was squandered in the casinos of Europe.

'Should this money not be spent on improving the lot of their people?' the President wanted to know.

It seemed a fair point. I knew a lot about how some members of the Kuwaiti Royal Family spent their money. Before going to

Iraq, there had been a long exposé in an American national magazine, but I decided to keep my counsel. Sometimes to make his point the President reached for my arm, so I resolved to keep them firmly behind my back for the duration of our walking dissertation.

Saddam was appalled even at the grand houses in which some Kuwaitis lived, regaling me with the information as though it were a terrible sin that some Kuwaiti houses had separate entrances for house maids and other servants. I thought I detected a strange echo of normal, everyday envy here – envy about money. Kuwait could flaunt its massive oil wealth, while Iraq, after a bruising eight-year war, had to be more circumspect.

The President then said something which convinced me again that had an American envoy such as Secretary of State James Baker gone to Baghdad, a deal might well have been done. (Much later, on the eve of the Allied offensive, Foreign Minister Tariq Aziz did, in fact, meet the Americans in Geneva, but nothing came of their discussions. They broke down partly because it was too late and partly because only Saddam Hussein could have cut a deal and explained it to his people. Tariq Aziz had offered the Americans nothing.) Saddam asked me, 'Why has nobody come to talk to us about these problems? Isn't that the way you deal with difficulties between states? Why don't they come? They'll be welcome here.'

By that point in his monologue he had given up all hope of having me respond. Perhaps all along his questions were meant to be rhetorical. I thanked the President again for his time and we prepared to leave, having been in his company for nearly two hours.

Back at our hotel our rooms were swamped by officials from the Ministry of Information. Because I had been mentally consumed by the task of interviewing the President, I assumed they had come to ask me how it went, but no one did. Their questions were more revealing: they wanted to know what the President was like. It was not an easy conversation to have with Iraqi Government officials, so I murmured something appropriate. The words 'businesslike' and 'frank' came to me quickly, then, to my consternation, I listened to a heated debate between two Ministry of Information officials about whether the President spoke or understood any English. There had been no detectable signs that he could and I was happy to tell them so, but suitably assisted by generous quantities of ITN Scotch, the two officials continued to argue into the night. One of them thought the President had usable French; the other was sure he had heard it was English.

Although by this time I was almost too emotionally and mentally drained to register anything like surprise any more, I was amazed at the implications of their discussion. Saddam was isolated not only from the world, but from his own people. They knew almost nothing at all about him; he was a distant figure whom they served unquestioningly. Even to officers from his own Ministry of Information he was a closed book because they had no contact with him. Like millions of other Iraqis, they had never met him on the hustings; he had never sought their vote. Now I, a mere visitor, had become something of a hero in their eyes by virtue of the fact that I had been accorded a privilege they have never had. They were genuinely interested to hear my views about the man who was about to lead their country into another war. That was, in my eyes, perhaps the most damning indictment of repressive dictatorships.

I never learnt what my Iraqi contacts from the Ministry of Information thought about the interview, as I left Baghdad before they had seen it, though Mr Hassan did give me his view on my arrival back in London. Over the telephone he had told me that it had gone well. Pressed further, he would only say, 'It was fine.' I suspected that my friend was not telling me what he really thought, but did not have the chance to confirm this until many months after my return from Baghdad, when Hassan was declared *persona non grata* by the Foreign Office for statements about the possibility of a war against Iraq and hints that hostilities might spread to British cities. The Foreign Office felt such a statement was incompatible with Hassan's status as a diplomatic representative of his Government in London and he was given twenty-four hours to leave. Although I had an unbreakable office engagement on his last night in London, I wanted to say goodbye to him and so I turned up at his London flat just after midnight. A bachanalian night was in full swing. Hassan had made vague concessions to packing; half-filled bags and suitcases were spread across a wide area, and several different bottles of whisky seemed to be on the go at once. The mood was bitter sweet. Hassan's friends were putting a brave face on the fact that his tour of duty had ended, albeit abruptly and not at a time of his choosing, but no matter how hard they tried, it was more of a wake than a party. A distinct feeling of sadness hung heavily about the room.

Hassan affected a dislike of Britain, based on its opposition to Iraq's invasion of Kuwait, but he had enjoyed living in London. The night life had been his métier and the valedictory tones of his remarks left no doubt that he regretted making the statement which had sealed his fate. Just before two o'clock in the morning I thanked him for all the help he had given me in getting the interview and prepared to leave. He saw me to the door.

As I turned to go, he took my arm and said, 'Trevor, I've always wanted to say something to you – you were fucking rude to our President, you know.'

I made light of the remark, pretending that we had all had too much to drink, and left. Five hours later the man who had done so much to facilitate my visit to Baghdad was on a plane heading home. Although we had nothing in common, I had grown fond of Hassan. In his own disorganised way he had been genuinely helpful and at the moment of his leaving, I felt sad I had never found the time to accept his many invitations to long, bucolic lunches. His invitations to even longer dinners were more frequent, but I had managed to miss those too.

Several months after the Gulf War was over a few of my ITN colleagues had him to dinner in Baghdad and I was pleased to hear he had survived what I had been told was the displeasure of the Iraqi Foreign Office at the statement which had got him expelled. Before he left the company of my colleagues that night he handed over to one of them a sheaf of membership cards for a variety of London nightclubs. He was making a serious and painful bequest, cutting loose of memories which were very dear to him, resigning himself to the fact that he would never be allowed to return to London again.

11

The Politics of Black and White

Apartheid works. It may not function administratively, its justification and claims are absurd. And it certainly has not succeeded in dehumanizing – entirely – the Africans, the Coloureds or the Indians. But it has effectively managed to isolate the White man. He is becoming conditioned by his lack of contact with the people of the country, his lack of contact with South African inside himself ... His windows are painted white to keep the night in.

BREYTEN BREYTENBACH

PLATO suggested that there was more than a hint of untruth and deception in the general conduct of political affairs, and this applied, he thought, as much to elements of the process as to the people involved in ordering it.

The administrators of South African political affairs have invested heavily not only in outright deceptions and untruths but also in euphemism. Whenever, in the name of the state, their actions cried out to heaven as grave offences against the cause of civilised humanity, they reached for euphemism.

The Greeks defined 'euphemism' as 'speaking words of good omen'. Put another way 'euphemism' has come to be defined in English as a figure of rhetoric by which an unpleasant or offensive thing is designated by a milder term. In South African political life the biggest euphemism of all was the pervasive use of the term 'separate development' to define apartheid. The role of that euphemism is obvious: it was meant to disguise the basic unpleasantness and offensiveness of apartheid by suggesting that, behind a brutish and nasty political system, there was some abstruse morality. At its worst it attempted to be a poor cover for a regime which perfected human degradation to a fine art.

Even so, the euphemism 'separate development' has been amazingly resilient. Despite ritual condemnations of racism or racist policies, apartheid South Africa was never totally ostracised, trade and a variety of other contacts with the country flourished. Fine, upstanding Western democracies such as the United States and Britain made apologies for 'constructive engagement' with Pretoria, and South Africans themselves faced most critiques of their country with the response that the majority of their opponents had never fully understood the system because they had never seen it in action. Once they had, went that school of thought, once they appreciated the immense complexities of the land and its many peoples, they would understand and might even applaud the concept of apartheid. Perhaps that was one reason why I was allowed a visa to go to South Africa as a journalist. If so, it was a decision of brazen confidence.

I saw South Africa in two phases. The first phase was at a time when the country was deeply unsure of itself and when the most offensive forms of discrimination by race and colour were still law. Deep down, there may have been a realisation that apartheid was untenable for the long haul, but this was never publicly conceded and the Government focused instead on strengthening its hold on desperate people, which in turn led to violence, confrontation and loss of life. The second phase, separated by a long intervening period, was more hopeful. The Government of South Africa began to talk seriously about the possibility of releasing Nelson Mandela from prison and about the chance of far-reaching reform. This did not bring violence and confrontation to an end, but it allowed a battered and dispossessed race to dream hopeful dreams about peaceful change and about a secure political future.

I had, of course, heard and read a great deal about the country long before I went there and, indeed, before I began to work as a journalist in England. It is not always understood that the issue of apartheid has always been prominent in West Indian political life. It was bound to be so, for just as the National Party in South Africa was introducing its most draconian measures to make sure that Blacks had no part whatever in the destiny of their own country, the peoples of the Caribbean were pushing their White colonial masters for greater self-government and ultimately for full political independence. The contrast could hardly have been more stark and the political paradox was inescapable. As West Indians contemplated an age of political freedom in the 1940s, their Black South African brothers were being politically enslaved on the other side of the world. When Malan's election landslide in 1948 enabled him to proclaim that 'South Africa belongs to us once more' and when his Government proceeded to enforce racial segregation in his country by law, West Indian politicians concluded that Pretoria had cut itself adrift from the civilised world.

Few people from where I was born had ever travelled to South Africa, but the issue of racism and racial discrimination was no abstraction. Elements of both were evident in the culture of colonialism and West Indians felt deeply about them. West Indian islands, too small and too weak to take any meaningful political action against South Africa, focused instead on helping to isolate South African sport. One of the more salutary episodes in West Indian sporting life is the ferocity with which it was done. West Indian cricketers who went to South Africa to play 'rebel' cricket were, on their return, totally ostracised. Some time ago a British television film was made about the fate of those players: there is a despairing and poignant image of one promising Jamaican cricketer who had seemed set to conquer the world; following his return, he is shown drugged to the eyeballs, sitting disconsolately in a shack in a Kingston shanty town with no job, no chance of ever representing his country at cricket again and seemingly without any hope of personal salvation. As an epitaph to a sporting career, it ranks with the most capricious example of Greek tragedy, yet West Indians were unapologetic. As far as they were concerned, the player had committed the unpardonable sin of breaching the sporting ban, which carried political and emotional weight, he had gone to South Africa to consort openly with a racist regime. The ban was pursued with passion until the release of Nelson Mandela presaged a new dawn in South African politics.

The purpose of my first visit to South Africa was to report on elections to the country's first tri-cameral legislature; as diplomatic editor, it was part of my job. The fiction had been allowed to take root, that black visitors allowed to go there had to be made 'honorary Whites'. I found that to be untrue. Apartheid relied too much on doctrinaire rigidity to allow such flexibility; as a system it depended for its survival on its rocklike certainty. It could not be otherwise. The term 'honorary White' did, however, acquire some standing in order to enable the South Africans to maintain their policies of segregation by race and colour without depriving themselves of Japanese investment cash. I was aware that some Japanese industrialists had been given 'honorary White' status. It would probably have been inconceivable to treat the status-conscious Japanese in any other way, even if their money had not been so important. To almost anyone else who was not White the term made no sense and had no real meaning.

Rules are rules and regulations, once made, are difficult to controvert, so it was impossible for any Black visitor to enter a railway carriage or a hamburger parlour if neither place had been accorded what came to be known by the time of my first visit as 'an international licence'. The possession of such a licence meant that an establishment was partly exempt from the race laws and could serve foreigners of whatever colour. Without it, they could not, as Black rebel sportsmen who went to South Africa soon discovered to their pain and embarrassment. Although they were hailed as heroes by South Africans for breaking the sporting ban, they were routinely hounded out of restaurants and trains. The

South African Government had decreed that people should be codified by their race – they had enacted laws to make sure it happened. No temporary status handed out as a concession to a conspicuously non-White visitor, even if he were a cricketer of international renown, could overturn that, certainly not in the eyes of a vigilant ticket inspector on a train or a law abiding restaurateur ... as West Indian players Colin Croft and Alvin Kallicharran found out. Croft was made to leave a railway car reserved for Whites, despite the intervention of a White cricket fan who tried to convince the inspector that it meant a great deal to South Africa to have the player in the country. Kallicharran has told the story of being refused service in a hamburger bar in the town which had engaged him as a professional; he said he accepted the verdict without demur.

The South African Embassy in London thoughtfully did not stamp my passport as that might have jeopardised my using it again to enter a number of other countries who had cut contacts with Pretoria; instead, they sanctioned my permission to work as a journalist on a separate visa document. Arriving in Johannesburg, I was shown a similar courtesy. The immigration officer explained that he would make an official note of my arrival in the country on my detachable visa. I thanked him for his thoughtfulness. He responded with a half smile and said that he was doing it because of his country's unpopularity.

'Not many people in the world like us, you know,' he told me.

'Why ever not?' I asked with more than a hint of mischief in my voice. He shrugged his shoulders and handed me back my documents.

The South African Government's plan to expand its legislative process to include minority Coloureds and Indians was claimed by them to be a progressive measure or, to quote another widely used euphemism of the time, it was described as a 'new constitutional dispensation'. For the first time, Coloureds and Indians, who made up no more than twelve per cent of the population, were to be allowed to vote in elections to the national assembly. There they would have only a limited say in the way their lives were run – the phrase used to describe the area on which they could legislate was 'own affairs'. In addition, the plan had one other major flaw: it excluded, without even a promise of future participation, the majority of the people in the country. Black South Africans make up more than seventy per cent of the population, but the new tri-cameral legislature in itself foreshadowed no great alterations to the system of apartheid. On the contrary, its critics saw it as a plan designed to co-opt Coloureds and Indians into the system which oppressed the Black majority. It had sharply divided the country, which in itself must have been a bonus to South Africa's leaders, who had constructed an elaborate edifice based on dividing people into groups and rival factions.

Nothing I had read or heard about South Africa prepared me for what I saw there – nothing can. For much of the time discovering things about the country and the way it ordered its affairs put me in mind of the words of the Queen of Sheba on her visit to Solomon: 'The half had not been told me.'

Directly upon our arrival we were driven to a rally organised by supporters of the Reverend Allan Boesak, a Coloured political activist, who was prominent in a movement to encourage people to boycott the elections to the new legislature. The movement's main platform was that a derisory low turn out would render the elections irrelevant and frustrate any useful purpose the legislature might have served. Boesak argued that the so-called 'constitutional dispensation' was a nonsense.

I had always been puzzled about how the South African Government managed in such a fundamentally multicultural, mixed society to 'separate' people so effectively. The answer was that it had been accomplished through the power of a manic and bloated bureaucracy and with a fanatical dedication to detail. The concept of 'separate development' was deep rooted in the Dutch Reformed Church and in the politics of the National Party, but its survival necessitated an absurd obsession with peoples' race and the colour of their skin. So thorough had been the compartmentalisation of the races that they could be divided and subdivided into those who could live in towns and those who could not, those who could stay the night in cities and those who could not, those who could find jobs outside their allotted areas and those who could not, and now, with the introduction of a tri-cameral legislature, those who could vote with the Whites and those who could not.

My first enquiries about how the system operated in practice were almost trivial. As we drove along to the Allan Boesak rally, I asked my South African colleagues whether they could explain to me, in simple terms, the criteria by which people were classified. I chose for our experiment random groups of people along our route.

'What is he?' I would ask. 'Is he Coloured or Black?'

At first my colleagues were able to answer with confidence and, so far as I could make out, with unerring accuracy. 'Black, Coloured, Indian, Black,' they would reply.

But every so often, as I kept up the pressure of questions, they were unable to say.

'How are difficult cases decided?' I wanted to know. 'What happens if, for example, it's not possible on just casual observation to determine whether someone is Coloured or Black?'

There was a momentary silence. Then my colleagues told me about the 'pencil in the hair' test. In some disputed cases race classification was determined by whether or not a pencil pushed through the person's hair would remain there unaided or whether it would not. If it stayed, it was a comment on the coarseness of the hair and a clue as to the inferior classification. The perversity of this was not lost on any of us. It went further. Over many years South Africans had spent a lot of time and effort deciding precisely how much mixed blood a White person was allowed before his cultural identity was too severely contaminated. After much serious academic thought and deliberation, it came to be felt that seven per cent of Coloured blood was probably the limit; a greater percentage would mean a loss of cultural identity so profound that a person would slip from being classified as 'White' to 'Coloured'. The implications of such a change in status were far reaching and traumatic.

The central plank in South Africa's vision of separate development was the Homeland policy, which required that the millions of Black people living in towns or cities and in what came to be regarded as 'White South Africa' must return to their rural homelands. Not only were the Black homelands the most unproductive parts of the country but they had also been sliced up in such a way that Black South Africans, the majority people, were given the smallest patches of land. Minority Whites had the largest share of the land, whereas Blacks, who represented more than 70 per cent of the population, were given less than 20 per cent of the land. Put as another equation: Whites were given 86 per cent of the land, while a meagre 13.7 per cent went to Blacks, although they were six times as numerous.

Nor were these homelands cohesive units. They were a geographical nightmare, a disjointed mishmash of odd bits and pieces of bleak and barren territory connected by nothing but the fiction of sovereignty and a desire to drive Black people into the hinterland. One homeland KwaZulu is a jumble of ten jigsaw pieces – 'an archipelagic state, scattered across a continental white sea'. Lebowa and Bophuthatswana each have six separate areas. In these homelands Black people would be given what was called their own 'national independence' to pursue the 'freedom of their own national cultures' away from Whites. 'National independence' was meaningless, however, because the homelands were never more than puppets of Pretoria and, far from wanting to pursue the 'freedom of their own national cultures' Black South Africans were desperate about economic survival. In fact, those phrases were euphemisms for a policy intended to rid White South Africa of all Black townships. People would come to the cities to work and they would return home at night. Most important of all, though, they would become citizens of their rural homelands and have no political claim on White South Africa. South African Government ministers had never been shy about explaining the consequences of the homeland policy. One of them, Connie Mulder, saw its apotheosis and said so with exemplary frankness: 'If our policy is taken to its full conclusion,' he said, 'there will not be one Black man with South African citizenship. There will no longer be a moral obligation on our Parliament to accommodate these people politically.'

The Homeland policy was aimed at eradicating Black South Africans once and for all.

Of course, it was a total absurdity. Not even the efficiency of apartheid in all its bizarre manifestations was able to rid the towns and cities of all Black South Africans – their majority status was simply too overwhelming – but the National Party's determination had little truck with fact or reality. Its decision to pursue its policies of racial segregation to the bitter end never wavered. The Government passed a mind-boggling raft of legislation – acts, laws and regulations – designed to confound, confuse and break down the defences of Black people and to leave them lost in an impenetrable legal swamp.

Long before I arrived in South Africa, the *New York Times* correspondent, Joseph Lelyveld, put it much better than I ever could. He wrote:

> Viewed even on its own terms, South African racial law is the opposite of elegant. It is not a body of law, but a tangle of legalisms designed to maximise the power of officialdom and minimize the defences of the individual, a labyrinth of words ... Blacks are either 'qualified' or 'disqualified' for residence in 'prescribed' urban areas. Even if they are 'qualified', they must have 'authorised accommodation' in which only their *'bona fide* dependents' are eligible to live. Officials qualify, disqualify, authorise and prescribe, and ultimately decide what

all these terms mean. Even if she is *'bona fide'*, a wife can be 'disqualified' simply because the authorities have not chosen to 'authorise' an accommodation. It is a crime for a 'disqualified' Black to be in a 'prescribed' area for longer than seventy-two hours.

It got much worse when all the gobbledegook was enshrined in law. Take, for example, the Black (Urban Areas) Consolidation Act, part of which says:

> [A qualified person] means a Black referred to in Section 10 (1) (a) or (b) who is not a Black referred to in section 12 (1) and any descendant of such a Black who is a Black referred to in section 10 (1) (a) or (b) and ... also any Black who is not a qualified person but falls within a category of Blacks recognised by the Minister by notice in the Gazette as qualified persons for the purposes of section 6A and 6B and regulations relating thereto, or who has in any particular case been expressly recognised by the Minister as a qualified person for such purposes, as well as any person who has in general or in any particular case been expressly recognised by the Minister, subject to such conditions as may be determined by the Minister, as a qualified person for such purposes. Provided that the said conditions may also provide that a person shall be recognised for a particular purpose or for a particular period or until the occurrence of the particular event only.

With government-inspired language like that no reporter visiting South Africa needed to exaggerate. It was impossible to embellish reality; hyperbole and normality were one and the same.

I felt that one of my first tasks in South Africa should be to try to show how these regulations affected the lives of ordinary Black people. To police this plethora of racist legislation the South African Government needed the courts, especially the 'pass courts'. All Black South Africans were required to carry pass books, which stated where they could go and where they could not. The hated 'dompas', which went back to 1809, allowed Black South Africans to work in urban areas. Being caught without a pass or being caught in a prohibited area meant immediate arrest and an appearance before the pass courts. Police raids in towns to apprehend those who had committed pass violations were a distressingly common phenomenon.

On most weekday mornings the courts were bursting with pass law offenders. My colleagues had sought permission to film the work of the courts and were very disappointed when their request was turned down. I was not deterred. I pointed out that since we were never allowed to film in British courts, the request should probably never have been made in the first place. The refusal of the South African authorities was understandable and no real problem.

I decided our report on what went on in the courts could be done very simply: I would spend a morning listening to cases and then once outside again I would record to a camera what I had seen inside.

It was an unforgettably painful experience. The suppression of people is not unique to South Africa, but what made the pass courts so different was that the full majesty of the law was being used to deprive the people of the country of their basic right to move about as they wished.

The court was full. The White magistrate could have been no older than thirty and when he did not look bored, he exhibited an impatience which might easily have passed for efficiency. I thought he would have preferred to be doing something else and there was certainly little to suggest that the pass courts required the most brilliant lights in the constellation of South Africa's legal system. As the names of defendants were called, he looked up briefly and then sank his head in the paperwork required for each case. That was the key: checks had to be made on peoples' movements; paperwork and bureaucracy were crucial elements if this system were to be a success. Few words were exchanged before sentences were passed. Many defendants were fined or given time to get out of town, while some were bound over. Each case took no more than two minutes.

The various languages spoken by the defendants posed something of a problem. Interpreters were constantly being called and, although I could not always determine with any accuracy what was being said, it was evident that the interpreters were frequently not up to the task of translating the defendants' responses. It all appeared haphazard at best. The magistrate certainly had no way of judging what was being said, yet it did not seem to matter, for lack of comprehension made no apparent difference to the exercise of due process in this court. The numbers of cases to be dealt with meant that speed was important.

No defendant was represented by a lawyer that I could see, though some were accompanied by relatives who looked as lost, as if they were on trial too. In this court, I concluded, *all* Black people were on trial. The defendants sat, quietly, saying never a word, looking straight ahead. When they did speak, they tried to make their predicament understood; they managed to give the impression that they had absolutely no idea of what was happening to them. In many other parts of the world I had seen that same phenomenon before, of people shrinking into speechless timidity when confronted by the power of the law. Sentences were received with the same vacant look with which the defendants had entered the courts. Most depressing of all was that no one attempted to challenge any accusation; once the charge had been put there was slight chance of correcting matters of fact. They were dignified apologies, but never the slightest show of defiance.

People here confirmed a more general feeling of Black powerlessness: they had been crushed by the weight of the rules and regulations. Trapped in this legal thicket, there was no way out, no escape. It felt such a terrible distortion of what justice should be. One function of the courts and the law should be to protect the rights of all the citizens of the state, the last recourse in the search for equal and fair treatment by the voiceless and the weak. These people were weak, but they were not citizens and they had no rights, and the courts were employed to emphasise that point. Black people appearing in pass courts were made to feel how the system had ordained that they should – as the dregs of an uncaring society, cast to the winds by a feckless fate. No wonder Black South Africans arraigned before White courts wore permanent expressions of hopelessness and once again the system had triumphed. Few White South Africans even sat through a morning in the pass courts – there was never any need.

It was not easy for me to do it. A feeling of unspoken hate and oppression permeated the place, frequently to a point of physical discomfort. It was almost possible to feel guilty by simply being there. As a contrivance of social engineering, apartheid was awesome in its structure, thorough in its administration, and monstrous in its cruelty. I was on the verge of deciding I had had enough after about an hour, when a Black attendant noticed I was not wearing a tie. Without ceremony, he told me I was not properly attired and must leave. I did as I was told, longing to get into the fresh air again, but I was puzzled by the dress regulation. Perhaps totally inappropriately I remembered Yul Brynner arguing with a few crusty old locals and overfussy undertakers in the film *The Magnificent Seven* that everyone, regardless of his social status, should be able to find a burial place in that great human leveller, Boothill. Surely, I thought, in courts which demeaned every noble tenet of the law and in which people's dignity was so conspicuously shredded, the attire of visitors should not be the most important matter on the official agenda. But it was.

Outside I recorded my piece to camera, describing what I had seen in the court. I ended by saying that White South Africans have a kind of pass book too, not that it restricts their movements. They sometimes refer to it as 'the book of life'. Not surprisingly, I concluded, Black South Africans refer to theirs as 'the book of death' and with tragic good reason – sixty-nine people had been killed at Sharpeville in 1960 in a protest calling for the abolition of the pass laws. Long ago these laws had ensured their place in the demonology of South African race legislation; they were written in the blood of the oppressed.

It was while I was on the trail of how South African Blacks managed to survive the pass laws that I encountered one of many groups of brave, selfless, warm-hearted White South Africans. On the day I went to the headquarters of the Black Sash organisation, they were trying to help about fifty Black people who had found themselves in trouble with the pass regulations. The members were middle-class White women who had become persistent thorns in the sides of the system, organising demonstrations, championing protests on specific issues, and trying to find loopholes in the law through which Blacks could escape oppression. In South Africa, Black protests were another matter; at Sharpeville and on countless other occasions the authorities had developed a sure fire way of putting down what they termed 'Black civil unrest', or 'Communist-inspired activities'. They did not, however, shoot White protesters from the Black Sash organisation, though they had frequently been quite ruthless.

I was fascinated by the phenomenon of official attacks on liberal Whites. I was taken to the house of a Black Sash worker who had been the victim of such attacks. The windows of her house had been smashed by missiles, excreta had been pushed through her letterbox and she had stopped counting the death threats made over the telephone or shouted from the street late at night. When she complained, the police had tactfully stayed away.

As I learnt later from the celebrated case of Donald Woods of *Cry Freedom* fame, a system like apartheid, founded on such flimsy speciousness, had to rely on rigid adherence to survive. The fact that Woods was White was no protection for him and his family when he strayed from the apartheid line. White dissent had to be put down as promptly as Black unrest. Because apartheid could be killed off by sanity, rational thought or just plain common sense, rules had to be brutally enforced and the Government had to be seen to deal with all opponents in the same way, whether they were Black or White. Sometimes I thought Whites who opposed a system which the Government advertised as one which should be to their benefit ran a greater risk of persecution. White involvement in anti-discrimination marches and other protests certainly made the Government terribly angry.

I remember watching police charge into a group of student demonstrators outside Witwatersrand University with a fearful show of force. It was not easy to understand why the police were so tough on the students except in the context of the fact that the demonstration was a multiracial one. One of the greatest fears of the authorities always was that South Africans of all races might one day transcend all the government-imposed barriers and unite. That was the ultimate threat, for the Government had constructed a system dedicated to dividing people and keeping them apart. Any grouping of the various races, especially in protest, was a challenge too serious to be ignored.

Contacts with the Black Sash organisation left me with the strong view that the future of democratic South Africa was unquestionably a multiracial one. In many visits there, stretching over many years and at various intersections in the political life of the country, I have never ceased to be amazed at the courage of people of all races brave enough to defy the system.

I was in Johannesburg when South African papers broke the story of a young doctor who had been suspended from duty for reporting the fact that a number of prisoners she had been asked to treat had clearly been tortured. To do this, the doctor, no more than twenty-five or twenty-six, had put her career on the line. Her bosses disagreed with her diagnosis and asked her to make a retraction; when she refused, she was suspended. We tracked her down to her parents' home in Cape Town, but she would not talk to us, referring us instead to her solicitor back in Johannesburg.

I had some difficulty setting up an interview with the solicitor, but finally managed to meet him on the outskirts of the city centre. It was just before midnight when we sat down in his study. The young doctor's accusations had been committed to a sworn affidavit of seventy or eighty pages. With a young daughter sitting not far from his side, the solicitor began to read from the document. What I heard was chilling:

> Prisoner A told me that electric wires had been connected to his genitals and the electric current had been switched on. His injuries were consistent with such a description of what happened.
>
> Prisoner B had abrasions to his face and skull. There was severe bruising to the area around his cheekbones. The injuries were consistent with the prisoner being slapped and beaten repeatedly about the face and head.
>
> Prisoner C said he had been beaten with a rubber hose about the feet and buttocks. The bruising in those parts of his anatomy was consistent with his description of what happened.

The lawyer read on into the night, in a flat, clipped, unemotional voice. He might easily have been giving a historical discourse about the terror of another age. His daughter, no more than eight or nine years old, sat near by, barely out of our camera shot.

I found myself wondering whether the language of the affidavit were not too violent for the ears of a young child, but I had another cause for concern. My cameraman that evening lived in Soweto and the regulations required him to get back to his home by midnight. If he did not, he was worried that he might be picked up by police. His deadline for finishing our job and getting on his way was drawing closer. I was terrified I might be the cause of his arrest and yet was shocked into mental immobility by what I had just been told.

The solicitor provided me with all the evidence I needed for my report on the torture of prisoners in South Africa. Before we left, I thanked him for his time and help, and I offered to reciprocate

his kindness by entertaining him to lunch or dinner if he ever came
to London.

'That's very kind of you,' he said, 'but I'm afraid I won't be
taking you up on that for some time. The South African authorities
confiscated my passport many years ago, and there's no sign that
I'll ever get it back.'

That White opposition to apartheid was not more widespread
could be put down partly to the fact that the system worked so
well. It was entirely successful in keeping the races apart, a fact
that is not always appreciated by journalists, who not surprisingly
spent a large proportion of their time talking either to people in
the townships or to Government politicians. I became aware of it
when I went to a party given by a few White South African friends.
Well into a very jolly evening someone asked me how I had been
spending my time. My answer, that I had spent the last three days
in the townships, brought all conversation in the room to a sudden
halt. Everyone looked in my direction; everyone wanted to know
what I had found there. I did my best to explain what we had been
doing and my impressions of what I had seen, though surprised
that my findings excited such interest. I asked why. The townships
in question were all less than half an hour's drive away from the
house where we were that evening, but none of my South African
fellow guests had ever been there. Townships were beyond the
limits and a brilliant road system took people past them at high
speed. If they so wished, passers by could pretend they did not
exist, since there was never any serious need to turn off the beaten
track. White South Africans were effectively cut off from any
contact with the people who made up the majority of the population of their country. It was, in many ways, the greatest triumph
of the apartheid system.

Many years later, reporting the drought in Southern Africa, we
took a White farmer into a Black township in the Orange Free
State, despite the fact the man wasn't at all happy because he felt
Whites who entered Black townships had little chance of emerging

alive. When our cameramen alighted from the car and began filming people queuing for water, the farmer almost died of apoplexy. He had lived in the Orange Free State for twenty-five years and had never been into the Black township three miles away. People from the township worked on his farm, took his orders and did as they were told, but once they went back to their homes, they became part of a foreign country again, separate and deeply feared. His relief at getting out unharmed was almost touching.

He later described proudly to us how effectively he had sealed off his own home from any harmful intrusion from outside, by which he meant township Blacks. He said he slept with a gun under his pillow and that his dogs had been highly trained to detect even the slightest difference in his voice or in his family's attire, the theory being that even if an intruder managed to penetrate his system of security alarms and get to him or his family, he could set the dogs on them simply by altering the tone of anything he might be forced to say under duress. Even a change of clothes, he told me, would have a similar effect. I was baffled by this. So, by way of illustrating how effective his system was, he told me a story. His wife had recently changed from her summer to winter pyjamas and the dogs, not so sensitive to such seasonal adjustments, had gone for her. Only his timely intervention had saved her life. The man related the incident with pride, but I found the story profoundly sad. I felt it reflected the broader sadness of the country. Breytenbach was right: apartheid had isolated the White man. That was the supreme tragedy, confirming as it did Hegel's view that the relationship between the oppressor and the oppressed is such that it holds them both in the same kind of tyranny.

Township life under apartheid was tough. Names such as Crossroads on the outskirts of Cape Town, Kwa Mashu near Durban, Mameolodi just outside Pretoria, and Alexandra near Johannesburg acquired a notoriety of their own. They had come to be seen as Black blotches on the face of a White landscape. Some, like Soweto, had become well-established towns in which many houses were positively luxurious by African standards. I was once driven round Soweto in an armoured vehicle by a policeman who proudly showed me the homes of all the township millionaires. I never understood the point of his demonstration, but I had no reason to doubt him, though I did suggest that Soweto was the exception to what township life was really about. The majority of people in the townships had a more modest aspiration: they simply wanted to survive the systemic hardships.

Townships were what they were meant to be – geographical excrescences on the rump of White areas. In many of them, sanitation, where it existed, was crude, running water was a luxury and they were pockets of privation and disease – the end of the line for any hope of a dignified existence. The images I took away from these sprawling sites of squalor and despair were almost all of children trying to make the best of their young lives. It frequently occurred to me some of those scenes were not unlike many I had seen in the West Indies, Latin America or other parts of the world. There was, however, one important difference. People born into poverty in other parts of the world could by hard work, ingenuity or simply by good fortune make something better of themselves. South Africa allowed no such opportunity to its township Black people: the system institutionalised a permanent and deprived underclass. Wherever townships encroached on White areas, the Black people could choose to move or be moved. Bulldozers were sent in to persuade those who stubbornly refused. Their use inspired some of the most pathetic episodes in the frightening history of apartheid.

One morning we drove out into KwaZulu in pursuit of a story about malnutrition among young children. I had agreed to make the long journey because we had heard there were British doctors who might be willing to speak to us on the record. We found them at their hospital after a three-hour drive, but they declined our invitation to be interviewed. Sensing that we were disappointed at having wasted an entire morning, the doctors wondered whether we might be interested instead in the fact that a nearby township which had grown too large and had begun to encroach on a White area was about to be moved. I had been told that such procedures were becoming rare and I expressed surprise, so I asked the doctors how they knew the township was about to be moved. They assured me that their information was sound and suggested that, if we were up to a drive of another couple of hours, we would see the evidence for ourselves. Reluctantly, we set off.

The heat of the mid-day sun overwhelmed our car's air-conditioning and I nodded off in the back. Some time later loud gasps from my colleagues awoke me. The countryside was wild and stunningly beautiful with little evidence of civilisation around that we could see. In fact, we seemed to have reached the edge of nowhere. Ahead of us, on a distant bluff, barely visible from the car, were about thirty or forty tiny galvanised constructions. Caught in the dazzling glare of the bright afternoon sunlight, they seemed suspended from a point just above the horizon. As we drew nearer we recognised them for what they were: a cluster of portable latrines ... high on this isolated hill and in the middle of rolling, open countryside. The authorities, so I was told, were always fastidious about moving Black townships, thus one of their first acts was to make sure the latrines were in place. The sight of those structures filled me with an all-encompassing gloom such as I have fortunately known only on very few occasions in my reporting life. In shock and in the uncommunicative silence of my own thoughts, I tried to fathom the minds of men who could quietly and calmly plan so degrading a future for fellow human beings. People moved to this sad outpost of human existence would have no chance of a decent life; they were being exiled within their own country. Moved to this barren outpost, they would be outcasts for the remainder of their natural days. Wherever I go, the sight of those portable latrines never quite fades from my memory and I never cease to be moved by the horror of what they meant.

If they were to survive, township men and women were required to sell their skills to White employers in the cities, which entailed journeys of many long hours day after day. But that, too, was part of the heinous plan. Black family life was under direct threat. I have seen townships stir as early as three in the morning, by four the trickle to the train and bus stations became a flood. In those shy, reluctant hours before dawn, shadowy figures stumbled purposefully through the chilly darkness and the morning rush began.

At the other end of their journey, as the trains and buses emptied their human cargo in town, the scramble for transport went on since people still had to get to their places of work. Their long day over, the exhausting journey home commenced. People from outlying townships travelled up to six or eight hours a day to and from work.

None of this was seen by most Whites as an unbearable burden on the majority of the people living in the country. On the contrary, the horror of the Black experience scarcely impinged on the consciousness of Whites at all. A disconcertingly large number of White South Africans deluded themselves into believing that their Black countrymen were relatively happy with their lot. The more conservative among them even felt it would be wholly unacceptable for Black people to be accorded a fairer share of their country's wealth and opportunities. One heard it said with the constancy of a familiar refrain that South African Blacks were the happiest in all Africa.

What was so extraordinary was that most Whites were only too well aware that, without Black support, the country would grind to a halt. Yet, at the same time, they were happy to preserve an order in which Black South Africans were routinely discounted as human beings. South African society survived and thrived because of the involvement of Black workers; without them White communities would hardly function. I once spent a weekend in Grahamstown in the Cape area, where I had gone to report as part of a much longer story about a Black boycott of White businesses.

Grahamstown enjoyed a tradition of liberalism which went back to its English origins and it was a strange place in that the separation between Black and White areas was not as pronounced as in other parts of the country. If White South Africans could usually ignore the existence of Black townships on their doorsteps, in Grahamstown they could not. The White area virtually ran into the Black township and the Black residents had been protesting for several months about the appalling conditions in which they lived, requesting basic amenities such as running water. When nothing was done about it, they decided to boycott the White shops.

My first call in the town was on the Mayor. His anger at the action of Blacks in boycotting the commercial centre was palpable; he grew red in the face as he told me how the misguided action of Blacks was destroying the livelihood of the town. White bus operators in the unreconstructed American Deep South had shown the same testiness at boycotts organised by the young civil rights campaign of the Reverend Martin Luther King.

I suggested to the Mayor of Grahamstown that one of the failings of the South African economy was that it was forced to depend for its survival on Black custom and Black labour, trying to make the point to him that, since this was the case, some sort of political accommodation with Black South Africans was a priority. The problem in Grahamstown had been created not by the boycott of White businesses, but by apartheid. The Mayor saw the point, as did the President of the Chamber of Commerce, who I met later that day. He told me that the boycott had forced him and his colleagues into discussions with Black representatives for the first time in their lives: What had struck him, he told me, was how 'moderate their demands were' – all they sought were the basic necessities of a decent existence.

The fact that it had taken a crisis of commercial confidence in liberal White Grahamstown to agree to a meeting with Black representatives depressed me and led to an unfortunate encounter with a couple of professors from the university. One of my colleagues had arranged for me to meet them because they were interesting people, ideal for a pleasant, informative dinner. For some reason they set out to impress me. One of them told me proudly that at a recent high-level meeting of university professors it had been decided by an impressive majority that apartheid did not work and must be reformed and a statement to this effect had been enshrined in a declaration by the professors.

I was astonished and angry that it had taken the brilliant minds of Grahamstown forty years to come to a conclusion so simple and so basic. Mischievously, I decided to play devil's advocate. Helped by a generous quantity of excellent wine, I attacked the findings of the professors, arguing enthusiastically that from what I had observed apartheid had worked very well, it had done what its framers had meant it to do by keeping the Black majority firmly in its place. It had banished Blacks from White areas and allowed them in only as domestic servants or to satisfy the need for other cheap labour. It had made Black people dispossessed foreigners in their own country. And it had appropriated all the privileges of living in South Africa to the White minority. Whenever Black protests got too persistent or too noisy, they were branded Communists and put down by force. All this, I suggested, added up to a record of tremendous success by the state. Finally I ended my dour assessment by saying to the shocked professors that Machiavelli himself would have been proud of apartheid's ruthless efficiency.

My bitter reflections reduced our guests to silence and the dinner broke up shortly afterwards. I was the first to leave, regretting what I had done, but I had grown tired of back-handed apologies for a system dedicated to crushing the lives of millions of people. From my colleague the morning after I heard what the professors had thought of my lecture. 'My god,' they had concluded, 'your colleague is a gloomy bastard.'

My mood can partly be blamed on meetings with senior South African Government ministers who although always helpful in arranging interviews and unfailingly gracious with their time, were unbending about apartheid. I had a long conversation with the then Minister for Constitutional Development, Chris Heunis, who had been responsible for the 'dispensation' of the tri-cameral legislature. Mr Heunis charmingly explained to me why there could be no question of Blacks being brought into a future constitutional structure. Heunis is a lawyer with a good mind, but I failed to get him to see the stark failings of a system which excluded the majority of its own people. In a long discussion after our more formal interview was over, I offered Heunis the view that apartheid was riddled with so many illogicalities that perhaps it was harbouring the seeds of its own eventual destruction. I was interested in the fact that he did not appear to disagree too violently and gave me the impression that, faced with the inevitability of its demise, White South Africans had decided to do everything in their power to keep the system going for as long as they could.

I had a similar meeting with Minister F. W. De Klerk, later to become a reforming President, but who at the time was responsible for the Home Affairs portfolio. De Klerk sought to convince me that Black South Africans could never be seen as a monolithic force in his country's political future and that, in any event, majority rule was out of the question. He emphasised that there could be no arrangement in the country's future which gave any single group the power to dictate what the others should do. I had heard this view expressed by many leading South African political figures and never ceased to be amazed at the fact that, in stating this position, they conspicuously ignored the way in which White South Africans were dominating the lives of the majority Black population.

De Klerk and Heunis had a standard response to all questions about the future participation of the ANC (the African National Congress) in discussions on South Africa's future. There was little talk about the release of Nelson Mandela when I first went to South Africa, but to Government politicians any mention of the

ANC led to the strongest official condemnation of what was described as the organisation's support for violence. This was to become the most persistent cry of the Government of President P. W. Botha. There could be no question of talks with the ANC until it declared itself against all violence and, in the view of the Government, ceased all 'intimidation' especially in the townships.

In the course of my visits to South Africa I formed the view that the issue of violence was central to the whole debate about the future of the country. The Government claimed that violence was being employed by Black political organisations as a wrecking tactic. Black political activists claimed that violence was part of the system of South African politics and could not be fully understood except in the context of Black reaction to 'White apartheid politics'. I knew these arguments well. On my first visit to the country I met the police chief responsible for maintaining law and order in Soweto and in the townships around Johannesburg. He demonstrated an adamantine certainty about the cause of violence in the townships. I remember his words today.

'I'll tell you what's causing unrest in these townships, Mr McDonald,' he'd told me, 'it's those bloody Communists.'

I had heard the proposition before, but it was still something of a shock to hear it from a chief of police, whose position in many other circumstances might have encouraged him to place more reliance on fact than on ideological prejudice. He was convinced, and he put it to me in a very vigorous debate, that Communists were behind the growing menace of township violence. I marked that down as one of the more bizarre arguments heard in the course of my reporting international politics. What the Soweto police chief was telling me boiled down to the proposition that people who have for generations been oppressed and given an appalling deal by a system such as the South African apartheid system somehow needed the spur of an alien ideology such as Communism to tell them they were having a hard time. I could not speak for those who might have become Communists in South

Africa, but I found it difficult to imagine that everyone who opposed the government, violently or in a nonviolent way, had first become a subscriber to the ideology of Communism. Surely, I thought, it is possible to oppose apartheid on basic, principled, humanitarian positions without the need for intellectual sustenance from Marx or Lenin.

By the time a Commonwealth group of eminent persons embarked on a fact finding mission in Southern Africa in 1986, township violence had become a live issue and I had been told that it would be unwise to expect to be allowed to go back to South Africa. My reports had annoyed the South African authorities in London, and that had been passed on to Pretoria; in fact, I was summoned to the embassy in Trafalgar Square to be told so. The charges against me were wide ranging.

The Ambassador, Dennis Worral, complained that I had failed to understand and report the complexities of the problem. I had gone instead for the more sensational material, which had failed to show the changes being made in their proper light. Even worse, I had made a few damaging philosophical observations which had annoyed the authorities, including one about the danger to apartheid of a combined Black and White opposition. I had on more than one occasion stated that such a combination posed a lethal threat to the entire doctrine. The authorities had also been offended and hurt by the story I had done about latrines being moved in ahead of a forced removal of people. They even referred to the fact that I had poked good-natured fun in the course of a report I had done in London at President Reagan, who, on being questioned about South Africa, seemed to suggest that he thought the place to be a thoroughgoing, Jeffersonian democracy. Ambassador Worral was also annoyed about something I had written in one of the more popular newspapers about my visit to his country, which is worth recalling in some detail.

If Black South Africans thought the tri-cameral legislature a travesty of justice and common sense because they had been formally excluded from playing any part in the governance of their country, White South African Conservatives thought the plan had gone too far in the opposite direction. They felt it was heresy even to include the Indians and the Coloureds. They thought it was inherently flawed because it might give Black people a glimpse of the possibility that they too could one day be included, and that was anathema. They felt it was, as they told me repeatedly, 'the thin edge of the wedge'.

I had been persuaded by some White Conservative acquaintances to go to a rally one Sunday just outside Johannesburg. It was a fairly predictable event with predictable speeches until, at the end, I was invited to meet Connie Mulder, a former Minister, who was then in disgrace and who was serving out the end of his years in politics as a Conservative. Mulder and I had a fairly lively exchange of views, which he suggested might be continued over lunch. He had then, meaning absolutely no ill will and as if it were the most natural thing in the world, asked his colleagues where he might take me to lunch. What he was saying, in effect, was that there were several places near by where a Black West Indian would not be permitted to eat, even in the company of a former Minister. What I found amusing about the incident was that the South Africans in our group had grown so accustomed to this kind of dilemma that they took it entirely in their stride. The other thing which struck me was that no one in the group was embarrassed to talk about the problem and dealt with it almost as if I were not there.

My recollections of this incident and its implications, as I saw it, incensed the South African authorities, at least those at the embassy in London. I felt it was worth recounting because it seemed to me to make a point of some substance in that South African Whites never actually factored Black people into their consciousness. At airports and in other public places Blacks silently and wordlessly would appear to take bags to waiting cars and then disappear; in White South African homes Black servants did their jobs without making their presence too strongly felt. There was never any Black/White conflict, never really the possibility of too much Black/White friction. Blacks did their jobs, but they made no waves, they were not there. There was more Black/White friction in a bus queue in London or in Washington. The separation of the races had been complete.

I did not visit South Africa at the time of the visit of the Commonwealth team of eminent persons in 1986, but they were evidently struck by the level of township violence and came to the view that it was born of political frustration. The tri-cameral legislature had told Black South Africans in plain, incontrovertible terms that they had been shut out from the political process for ever; they had nothing to lose.

I saw horrifyingly graphic examples of what had come to be known as 'Black on Black' violence. In crude political terms it was expressed as a battle between the African National Congress and the Inkatha Party led by the Zulu leader Chief Mangosuthu Buthelezi. I was taken many miles into Natal province to see houses which had allegedly been burnt to the ground by Inkatha activists, and I remember the eye witness account of one victim, who was a schoolteacher. She explained that what had really appalled her was that the people who arrived to destroy her house had denied her even the dignity of disguising their identity. As we were standing in the yard of what had once been her family home, she told me, 'It would have been preferable had they shown the shame of covering up their faces. They didn't. They came to my house, they asked me to get my family out and they then fetched gallons of petrol from the van, which they poured all around our house, before setting fire to it.'

I saw a great deal of Chief Buthelezi on my visits to South Africa and he always denied with force any suggestion that his people were responsible for violence of this nature. I found it impossible to make a judgement, but there was a considerable body of cir-cumstantial evidence to suggest that the Zulus were locked in a deadly struggle with the ANC and that both sides were guilty of the most desperate acts of brutality.

The people who were given time to leave their houses before they were razed to the ground, sometimes in broad daylight, were almost the fortunate ones. Other Inkatha/ANC battles were marked in the blood of countless victims. I recall the great pain with which one of my ITN colleagues based in Johannesburg told me that he was beginning to find it difficult to contemplate the business of reporting any more township funerals. I had been to only a very few, but I knew what he meant – they were occasions of heaving emotion. The grief of those who had survived was as real as in any capital anywhere, yet it was somehow compounded and made mountainously worse by the knowledge that there would on any other afternoon one might care to name be more killings, more funerals, more defiant graveside declarations and more expressions of nationalist fervour which perhaps naively combined religious faith with political hope in looking forward to the day when all Black suffering would come to an end.

THE next time I went to South Africa preparations were being made for the release of Nelson Mandela after twenty-seven years in prison. Much to the good fortune of the South African authorities he had never lost his hold on the imagination of the world and of thinking South Africans. To entire generations of people, Black and White, he had come to be viewed as the only man who could help negotiate the path to a different South Africa.

It was wonderful to return to the country at a time of such excitement and expectation. Although South Africans had always tried to convince the world that they had borne the trials of international isolation with equanimity, they were keen to re-enter the affairs of the real world. Forced to rely on their own devices by policies which shut the door on outside influences, they had at times appeared to suggest that they could do without the patronage of the world at large, and there are elements in the Afrikaaner psychology which make that partly true. On the other hand South Africans, like most of us, need the approbation, acclaim and sympathy of others. And the release of Nelson Mandela was the key to that.

I was overjoyed to be there at that time for another reason. Despite everything I had seen in the country, I never lost the persistent belief that an accommodation among its peoples was possible. I had come to that view for a simple reason: nowhere in the country did I detect deep-seated feelings of hate between the oppressed and the oppressors. I had talked to Blacks who had been subjected to the most inhumane treatment at the hands of brutal policemen and criminal prison guards, and who managed later to emerge with well-rounded personalities to talk of compromise and the need for reconciliation. Black South Africans bore no burning dislike of their White compatriots. They hated the system, but somehow they managed to separate the two. The Blacks, as a race, were not intent on killing all Whites as a means of redressing the fundamental and degrading imbalances in society. In some circumstances Black South Africans might have been excused for harbouring feelings of murderous ill will, but they did not. Hate, such as I saw in the eyes of the protagonists in Northern Ireland or in Beirut was almost totally absent. Blacks wanted to be part of the system, to end the discrimination which had so grotesquely distorted their lives. They wanted a political voice but did not seek revenge. They were seized of the sophisticated appreciation that their country, properly ordered, could house and feed all its people. In those qualities they mirrored the views of Nelson Mandela.

We arrived in Johannesburg forty-eight hours before Mandela walked from prison a free man. We stationed ourselves in a house opposite his own in Soweto and, on the day of his release, we broadcast live for the first time directly from a South African township. Although we were well aware of the township's reputation for crowds and noisy celebrations, we had underestimated the Mandela phenomenon. My colleague, David Mannion, who had been asked by the African National Congress to assist them in dealing with the international press representatives whose numbers they had misjudged, discovered one evening the difficulties of working in a Soweto totally overwhelmed by the return of their hero. Dave, having kindly volunteered to go to the home of Archbishop Desmond Tutu, who was appearing live on one of our news broadcasts, reached the Archbishop's house through the surging crowd with some ingenuity, but getting back to our broadcast position was not as easy. The crowd outside Tutu's house had become a solid mass. Having promised me that he would get the Archbishop to our broadcast point, Dave began to force his way through, when an unexpected movement in the mass was literally swept him off his feet and he found himself, much to his subsequent concern, being carried along on a moving tide of humanity on the Archbishop's back. If, in the confusion of it all, the Archbishop realised what was happening, he did not let on. And, as is possible only at extraordinary events and in massive crowds, Dave was carried by Desmond Tutu all the way. We never let him forget it and he was ribbed unmercifully about how he had taken unchristian advantage of a man of the cloth.

Back at the trailer at the top of which we were to broadcast, we had failed to take account of another small factor – the effect on the crowd of the presence of one of their stars. The volume of noise which greeted Archbishop Tutu, when he arrived, was such that I quickly lost all hope of what we said being heard in London, satellite or no.

My fears were put to rest, however, by the timely intervention of Stewart Purvis, who possesses one of the sharpest intellects in our business. While I fussed and bothered about the noise, he summed up the situation with great calm. Watching the mêlée from which we hoped to make ourselves heard from the control room in London, he got through to me to say that I should, 'Go with the crowd and the atmosphere. Don't try to fight it or to worry too much about it. It's a great scene and will be enjoyed as such.'

Stewart was right. Somehow I got through the links which I had committed to memory and interviewed the Archbishop about the implications of the release of Nelson Mandela against the sound of the music and dancing which had by then begun to overwhelm the place. A few drops of rain appeared and so did a number of umbrellas held by helpful onlookers who refused to get out of our camera shot. I tried to get the Archbishop to address the proposition that, with so much hope riding on Mandela's release, the reality of his political return might be disappointing. The Archbishop would have none of it and declared with conviction that Mandela's release would live up to all its advance billing and was an occasion for unqualified joy. The crowd caught the sense of that and there was an enormous acclamation. The Archbishop went into a spontaneous jig, attentively pursued by the umbrella-holders, and, grabbing me by the arm, invited me to join in Soweto's historic night of rejoicing. I ended the interview and handed back to the studio in London ... just. It was a unique end to a news broadcast.

Restrained by the discipline required in anchoring the news, I managed to resist the Archbishop's persuading, but not by much. The joy of Mandela's release spread through Soweto like a raging contagion and it was impossible to remain unaffected. As we made our way down from the trailer, the heavens opened. Portentous thunderclaps drowned out the noise of the crowds who had kept us in tune with their emotions all evening and, as the rain came down in torrents, Soweto was lit up by blinding flashes of light. It would have been tempting to think of all this as a signal of divine approbation had I not been warned long before leaving London about the problems of planning outside broadcasts during the season of Johannesburg's kaleidoscopic summer storms.

That broadcast from Soweto was significant in another respect.

It was the first time in South Africa's history that a foreign television company was allowed to route a programme to its home port without first going through the Government-run South African Broadcasting Corporation.

The next event in the calendar of celebration was Mandela's return to his home in Soweto. After spending the night in Cape Town, he was making his way slowly to Johannesburg. The day of his arrival dawned bright and clear; the storms had done their cleansing work. By mid-afternoon an immense swell of people began to make its way to Soweto. Arrangements made earlier had long since slipped and no one could say for sure when Mandela would arrive. His Soweto house was modest by any standards and one feared it could easily be flattened by one surge from the gathering crowd. Helicopters swooping low over the township gave the game away. Where once they struck terror into the hearts of the residents of this place, now they were keeping a wary eye on a small procession of cars making its way along dusty streets to Mandela's address. The cars stopped and the acclaim which greeted Mandela's arrival seemed to go round and round, shaking an entire nation to its roots. It was a long time before it subsided sufficiently to allow him to speak.

Mandela was immediately impressive. He managed, despite the profound emotion of the moment, to keep his feet firmly on the ground. There were no grandiloquent phrases about freedom or destiny, no rhetorical flights of fancy about political redemption, he never once talked about the undeniable pain of his long incarceration and he refrained from any references to the evils of apartheid. Mandela had an altogether much more serious agenda. Standing next to Walter Sisulu, who had been let out of prison some time before, Mandela addressed his comments to the young. He and Sisulu had almost run their earthly course, he said, and soon it would be time for a new generation. That new generation must be prepared, for they could ill afford the luxury of living on memories of former heroes. The key to success, he told the young people, was education: 'Go back to school,' he said. It sounded more like a lecture from a concerned teacher than a message from a political leader anxious to claim the affection of his supporters. Boycotting classes had become a form of township protest and less than forty-eight hours after his release Mandela was seeking to change that. 'By going back to school,' he said, 'you can prepare yourselves for the task ahead. You may not be equipped for that, if you fail in your search for education. So, I say to you today, go back to school. Prepare yourselves for the task which lies ahead. We have so much to do.'

It took me no time at all to discover how effective Nelson Mandela's admonition had been. Late that evening I overheard an exchange between a mother and her son in the Soweto house in which we had stationed ourselves to await Mandela's return. It went something like this:

Mother to son: 'So Thomas, what are you doing tomorrow?'

Son: 'I'm not sure yet, Mum. I might go into town...'

Mother, interrupting impatiently: 'Did you hear what Dr Mandela said? Tonight you'll pack your bags and tomorrow you'll be going to school. Now no ifs and no buts. Tomorrow and everyday from now on is school. That is what Dr Mandela said and that is what you'll do. No arguments.'

There were no arguments. The following morning, when we turned up, Thomas had gone to school for the first time in months and the Soweto school boycott was effectively over. It was a powerful example of the esteem in which Mandela is held by his people and of the enlightened way in which he had decided to exercise his influence.

When next I saw him, he was walking into the tiny crowded garden of his house to begin a series of television interviews. The place still hummed with the excitement, though altogether quieter than the night of Archbishop Tutu's joyous dance before the thunderstorm. There was this time only a relatively small crowd outside the gate of the Mandela home, and four or five guards.

Inside, a genial mix of people were caught in a commotion of mild disbelief, congratulation and hope. There were some ANC supporters, close friends of the Mandelas, members of his family, a small army of officials and advisers, cameramen, journalists and still-photographers galore.

ITN had won the toss and I was about to do the first interview with the African National Congress leader since his release from prison. Mandela showed the same unrelenting realism as he had in his speech to the young people of Soweto the day before.

My main line of enquiry was about the possibility of a political accommodation between the ANC and the South African Government. This, after all, was the key, because the stated positions of the two sides were on most questions diametrically opposed. How might it be possible, for example, to reconcile the fact that the White Minority Government had set its face like steel against any possibility of one man one vote? How could the ANC ever give ground on that and survive as a credible political force?

Mandela began by telling me that it was not always possible to determine the shape negotiations would take and how they would end before talks began. All the points I had made on the difficulty of opposing positions, he said, would be solved during talks between the main political players.

I pressed him, saying that some positions could simply not be reconciled because they were, for both sides, matters of conviction and deeply held principle.

Mandela replied that, when genuine negotiations began, the participants should be prepared 'to compromise on fundamental issues'. He went on: 'That's how you succeed. In all talks, there will have to be give and take. That is how negotiations proceed, if they are to succeed. You must be prepared to compromise on fundamental issues.'

Much later we had some difficulty with that response, believing that the ANC leader had misstated his case and had actually meant to say that you *cannot* compromise on fundamental issues. But

Mr Mandela meant precisely what he said and it was the first indication of the degree to which he was committed to finding a political solution to his country's problems. No problem I could advance, he seemed to say, was intractable. He answered every point as it was put to him. He addressed the question, framed his response with great care and then stopped. He never rambled, never lost sight of the sense of the question, and moved from point to point with precision and logic. A Black man in a country which had persecuted Blacks, he nevertheless talked the universal language of the brotherhood of all men. There were no cheap shots, no crude appeal to any section of the population. Neither was this simply empty rhetoric. In his very first minutes as a free man, on his drive from prison, he had stopped his car to talk to a group of White South Africans who had been waiting at the roadside to catch a glimpse of him. He left me in no doubt that, as far as he was concerned, South Africa's was a multiracial future and the divisions of apartheid had to be healed. I must confess my admiration: it was a spellbinding performance.

Warm, engaged, but never trivial, he approached every enquiry from a lofty, broad-minded view. It proved impossible to get him to gossip, to be petty or to betray the slightest trace of personal bitterness. I tried, employing many of the tricks of my trade, to get Mr Mandela to speak about his time in prison. To be quite honest about it, I was looking for something sensational, something which would make banner headlines, but I had gone to the wrong place. Instead, he talked sensibly about the problems his imprisonment had posed for his family; they were the people who suffered, he told me, and that was almost all he would say about prison life. He had said much the same thing in his very first public engagement after his release in Cape Town. Forgetting past indignities, Mandela had fixed his gaze on the future. 'You must understand,' he went on, 'all that is in the past. We have to look ahead now. There is a great deal to be done, to bring all the peoples of this country together in unity and in harmony, to devise a system which will enfranchise all South Africans. White South Africans have to be reassured. Black South Africans have to be given their place in our society.'

Failing to get any good lines about the awfulness of twenty-seven years in prison, I embarked on another hunting expedition. Mandela's last years in prison were spent in much greater comfort than his earlier ones, one reason being that certain South African Ministers had acquired the habit of dropping in on him for conversations about politics. Commonwealth leaders, too, had been to see him, and the Christmas before his release a South African cabinet member had taken in to him a decent bottle of whisky. I wanted to hear about that.

'I talked to anyone who came to see me about the problems facing our country and how we can address them. They were all very timely, important discussions about South Africa's political future and the role we in the ANC can play.'

But in what capacity did you hold these discussions?' I wanted to know.

'Ah,' he said, seizing the point immediately, 'what you must understand is that while I was in prison, I was acting in the role only as a facilitator for discussions which will come later. I did not negotiate, because I had not been instructed to do so. As a servant of the ANC, I am only empowered to do what I'm told. I was a facilitator, not a negotiator. And, in any event, only free men can negotiate.'

I refused to give up. 'You know,' I said, launching into a question much longer than is wise in television interviews, 'I would love to have been a fly on the wall during your meeting with President P. W. Botha. Here, after all, was this dinosaur of apartheid. How did he treat you? What were his opening words? Did he offer you a drink? Did he ask if you preferred tea?'

I felt sure I was on to a winner this time. Mandela, as he was wont to do when he wanted to exercise great care, paused and smiled.

'He was very courteous.'

I waited, hoping the pause, the suspense might tempt him to say more. He did not. Again that was all. Time to try again, I told myself, you cannot give up now.

'What about your meeting much later with President De Klerk?'

'Ah, that was very different. What you should understand is this. When I went to see President Botha, it was a courtesy visit. I had been asked to go and I went. When I saw Mr De Klerk, we talked business. I had read Mr De Klerk's speeches while I was in prison and I felt he was a man I could do business with.'

That simple answer said so much about Mandela's political grasp, his perspicacity. From a locked cell the prisoner had already mentally consigned Botha to the political wilderness. He had gone to see him, but that was all. Looking far beyond the term of President Botha, he had begun to sketch the outlines of a political deal with his successor. Talleyrand himself would have envied Mandela's diplomatic skills.

These were unquestionably the discussions which had laid the groundwork for his release. Some time later President De Klerk told me much the same thing about Nelson Mandela. In terms of the international community and even with passing regard for domestic South African politics, no progress was possible with Mandela still in prison. Beyond that, though, was the fact that, as De Klerk told me, he felt Mandela was a man he could do business with.

I returned in my conversation with Nelson Mandela to his role in future talks. The high emotion surrounding his release failed to lure him away from the ever cautious answer. He told me again that he was a servant of the African National Congress and that his future role in the negotiating process would be determined by them.

The time passed all too quickly. I felt invigorated by meeting a legend, although in hard journalistic terms I got nothing sensational in an editorial sense. After a mere three days out of prison, Nelson Mandela had made the passage from Black political leader and former prisoner to South African statesman. In my conversation with him then and in several others since that day he refused to be anything else – there was too much at stake, too much hope rested on his shoulders. We journalists, corrupted by cynicism and transfixed by the possibilities of failure, even when reporting the greatest human endeavours, had gossiped endlessly about how Mandela would cope with the harsh realities of South African political life once he was released. The mystery acquired in prison can soon burn away, we argued, in the warmth and comfort of freedom. We had speculated about the yawning gap between what would be expected of him and what he could realistically deliver. I had been told that he had kept up with all the major political developments from prison by watching television and video tapes, and one of my South African colleagues had even managed to get to him some of the reports I had done in his country. But was that the kind of access, we asked ourselves, to prepare him for the struggles of being a leader again? In one respect, we concluded, in a journey through the minefield of political uncertainty, prison might have been the easy part.

For me all those anxious questions evaporated after I met Nelson Mandela. I came to the view that the South African Government was profoundly wise to release him when they did. They had done it neither out of compassion nor as a gesture to humanity, but because they had to. They did it to break a dangerous log jam in the political process, to try to begin to wipe away the dreadful stain of apartheid and to give their country hope. No matter how rocky the course of negotiations are, I remain every bit as optimistic as the day I met Nelson Mandela. When the greatest difficulties arise, Mr Mandela will be prepared to compromise on fundamental issues. The South African Government will never get a better offer. They ignore it at their peril.

Many months later I was encouraged to recall those heady days in February 1990 when Mandela walked from prison and returned in triumph to Soweto by an invitation from the Borough of Richmond, in which I live.

Richmond, which had to the best of my knowledge made no great mark on the international political stage, was about to award the freedom of the borough to Archbishop Desmond Tutu. I had no idea why it was being done and was never told whether the Archbishop had any connections with our corner of England, but I was delighted to be asked, having seen little of him and his delightful wife since Soweto.

It proved to be an unexpectedly moving occasion. The Tutus swept in to great wintercoated bear hugs and an all White choir sang what has come to be regarded as the anthem of the African National Congress. The Archbishop, very touched, made a generous speech in which he told the people of Richmond that, although they were many miles from what had been going on in South Africa, their support for the international campaign to free Nelson Mandela had made a difference. The thrust of his speech was that people should never be reluctant to make their contribution to world movements for fear of their seeming insignificant. Mighty protests, he argued, grew from a multiplicity of much smaller ones; that had been the experience in his country. He concluded with these words:

> So sometimes, in those dark days, when there seemed to be no hope for our country, you may have wondered, how can a seemingly insignificant place like Richmond help? What voices can we raise to help bring about Mandela's release and to end the fighting and the killing and to get the talking started? I have come here today to tell you that whatever little you did to help us in our long struggle, in our hour of need, you made a difference. I am here today to thank you for making a difference. The smallest voices are heard by God. Your voices, your help, however little, made a difference.

I had never before felt particular pride in the Borough of Richmond, but I did that day.

'MY apologies to Attila,' Clemenceau is reported to have said,
'but the art of arranging how men are to live is more complex even
than the art of massacring them.' Many months after Archbishop
Tutu's stirring speech in Richmond in Surrey, South Africa is
discovering the truth of what Clemenceau said. The process of
designing a post apartheid political structure, which begins to
acknowledge and to address the injustices of the past and which
is sufficiently wide to embrace for the first time the hopes and
aspirations of all its people, has been long and difficult and is as
yet, by no means complete.

But during the long process, South Africa has undergone many
significant changes. The multi-party constitutional negotiations
have made sound progress despite bitter disagreements. They have
done so well that it has been possible to set a date for the country's
first ever totally multi-racial elections. May the gods ensure that it
holds. Responsible political voices everywhere have praised that
development as the watershed in the country's history. In their
more optimistic moods, responsible political voices have dared to
whisper the word 'democracy'. It is not long since President de
Klerk came as close as he had yet done to apologising for the
untold misery apartheid has caused the vast majority of his country's people. Unveiling a new National Party flag and colours, he
said the new emblem was 'a statement that we have broken with
that which was wrong in the past, and are not afraid to say that
we are deeply sorry that our past policies were wrong.' It was by
no means an unequivocal apology, but after so many dark and
interminable years in which the perpetrators of apartheid had so
stubbornly refused even to hint that they might have destroyed the
lives and crushed the spirit of generations of their countrymen and
women, it was a start. It seemed to be an attempt to make a clean

break with a shameful past, an indication of a desire to seek a new beginning.

Any day now the Commonwealth, the United Nations and the United States will bring to an end the policy of sanctions against South Africa. The country would then be re-integrated into the corporate and business affairs of the world, outside of which it had for so long remained starved of vital development funds. I was fortunately in Washington to interview President Clinton on the day he received Mr Mandela and Mr De Klerk to discuss this very question. Both South Africans were also to be fêted by Americans for their courageous political stand.

The new political horizons are not uniformly bright. The country is still torn by violence; extremists on many sides threaten to make trouble: the Zulu based Inkatha Freedom Party, an important element of any post apartheid agreement, is yet to be fully brought into the process, and putting into place those last pieces which will complete the jigsaw of the new South Africa, will be fraught with suspense. But for the first time in nearly half a century, South Africa looks out at the world and does not feel itself a pariah. The country is rapidly shedding its fanatical introspection and is bold enough again to look beyond the laager.

I cite one example to show why this might be so.

The cold blooded killing of the Black nationalist leader, Chris Hani earlier this year, by a White, extremist right wing clique, might have destroyed South Africa and set the reform process into reverse. Hani's murder sparked genuine outrage and more than a week of angry demonstrations. Lives were lost and the unrest was widespread.

But it was contained through the efforts of Black and White South Africans. For several tense and anxious days, South Africa teetered on the edge of crippling disorder, but restraint and good sense prevailed. That they did are unmistakable signs of the new age.

I had one brief encounter with Chris Hani before his death. I had challenged him in a good natured way about his personal transition from dedicated guerrilla fighter, to fervent advocate of democracy and order. Hani laughed loudly. He slapped me on the back and responded by quoting a passage from Aimé Césaire's *Return To My Native Land.*

> For it is not true that the work of man is finished
> that we have nothing more to do
> but be parasites in the world
> that all we need do now is keep in step with the world.
> The work of man is only just beginning
> and it remains to conquer
> all the violence entrenched
> in the recesses of his passion.
> No race holds the monopoly of beauty, of intelligence, of strength
> and there is a place for us all at the rendezvous of victory.

Index